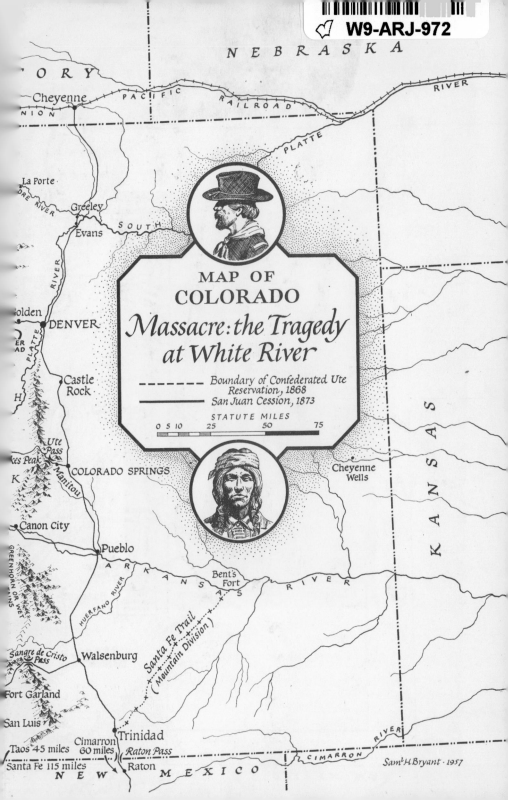

NEBRASKA

ORY

Cheyenne

PACIFIC RAILROAD RIVER

UNION

PLATTE

La Porte

DRE RIVER

Greeley

Evans

SOUTH

RIVER

Golden

DENVER

ER AD

PLATTE

Castle
Rock

H

Ute
Pass

Kes Peak

Manitou

K

COLORADO SPRINGS

Cheyenne
Wells

Canon City

Pueblo

ARKANSAS

GREENHORN OR WET MTNS

Bent's
Fort

RIVER

HUERFANO RIVER

K A N S A S

Sangre de Cristo
Pass

Walsenburg

Santa Fe Trail
(Mountain Division)

Fort Garland

San Luis

Taos 45 miles

Cimarron
60 miles

Trinidad

Raton Pass

Santa Fe 115 miles

Raton

N E W   M E X I C O

CIMARRON RIVER

Sam'l H. Bryant · 1957

MAP OF
COLORADO
Massacre: the Tragedy
at White River

- - - - - Boundary of Confederated Ute
Reservation, 1868
———— San Juan Cession, 1873

STATUTE MILES

0 5 10   25   50   75

BY MARSHALL SPRAGUE

THE BUSINESS OF GETTING WELL

MONEY MOUNTAIN

MASSACRE: THE TRAGEDY AT
WHITE RIVER

Massacre

The Tragedy at White River

Massacre

The Tragedy at White River

by
MARSHALL SPRAGUE

WITH ILLUSTRATIONS

LITTLE, BROWN AND COMPANY
BOSTON   *TORONTO*

66595

Published simultaneously in Canada
by Little, Brown & Company (Canada) Limited

PRINTED IN THE UNITED STATES OF AMERICA

To
JOE, STEVE, *and* **SHARON**
who always forgive us for being parents

Foreword

ON THE MORNING of September 29, 1879, a small band of Ute Indians went wild in the Colorado Rockies and ambushed a force of soldiers at Milk Creek. They had never killed white men before. That afternoon, they murdered their Indian Agent and all his employees on White River twenty-five miles away. Then they captured the Agent's wife, his attractive daughter and another young white girl and held them as hostages for twenty-three days, during which they performed certain rites on their persons as required by Ute custom.

All told, this small Ute band killed thirty white men and wounded forty-four more. Their punishment was the usual. They and their neighbors, the Uncompahgre Utes, who had had nothing to do with either the ambush or the massacre, were branded as criminals without trial by commissions of doubtful legality. Their treaty rights which had been guaranteed them by the United States Senate were canceled. Their rights to be American citizens as described in the Fourteenth Amendment were ignored. Title to their twelve-million-acre Colorado homeland, which they had owned exclusively since pre-Columbian times, was extinguished. They were moved at gunpoint to barren lands in Utah. By these means, the last and largest chunk of desirable Indian real estate in the nation, the Western Slope of Colorado, was thrown open to white settlement.

When I first read of the White River massacre, I judged it to be just another local melodrama in which some more Indians drew life sentences for the cardinal sin of blocking the economic progress of the United States. I changed my mind soon. The massacre wasn't local. The handful of White River Utes had been driven to extreme violence by pressures so national and so varied as to comprise almost a case history of an era.

Here in one story were all of the forces, good and bad, which built the nation and destroyed the red man's world — the insatiable land hunger of white men, their vast immigration, fantastic industrial expansion, monumentally corrupt government, Federal-State feuds, Army discontent, intellectual unrest and the yearnings of the Transcendentalists and the Fourierists for a better world. And here was the conflict of opposed philosophies which had caused all our Indian wars. The Indian revered nature and was content to abide by its laws. The white man made his own laws and worked incessantly to subordinate nature to them.

And when I got going on the story, it was the human beings caught up by the forces who interested me even more than the forces themselves.

There was never an Indian Agent remotely resembling Nathan Meeker of White River, former Greenwich Village poet, ex-Phalangist, one-time war correspondent, former New York columnist, and founder of Greeley, Colorado, the West's most successful experiment in cooperation. There was never an Indian chief with such depth of wisdom and experience as Ouray, head of the Colorado Utes, whose mind could comprehend three intricate Colorado civilizations, Ute, Spanish and American.

Major Thornburgh, commander at Milk Creek, was the perfect Army officer — handsome, suave, conscientious, humane and a fine judge of whisky, women and Irish setters. Josie Meeker at age twenty-two was a dear, warm and eager heroine, adored by all the boys at White River, red and white. General Charles Adams made an intriguing hero for his mission of mercy into the Ute wilderness, though he was not really a General and his name was not really Adams. He was a naturalized German who brought to an American problem a perspective which it needed badly — that of a man who had seen in the pogroms of Europe how racial injustice can blight a people beyond repair.

And Carl Schurz, President Hayes's Secretary of the Interior, who appointed Nathan Meeker as Ute Indian Agent in the first place — what can be said of him? Schurz was the most upright, picturesque and unbiased American of his day. Though the White River massacre ruined his public career, Schurz was not to be prevented from restoring honor to American government after a decade of political degradation.

One last thing. The Meeker story took place more than a mile high in an enchanted land of endless allure. The Colorado Rockies are not just ordinary mountains. They form the most beautiful, the most spectacular uplift in the nation, and one of the great mountain masses of the world.

MARSHALL SPRAGUE

Colorado Springs
September 1, 1956

Contents

Illustrations
(Between pages 110 and 111)

Nathan Meeker
Arvilla Delight Meeker

Horace Greeley
Ralph Meeker
Senator Henry M. Teller

Chief Ouray
Otto Mears
Felix Brunot

Ouray with his Wife, Subchiefs and White Friends
Frank Dresser
Alfred Packer

Flora Ellen Price
Johnnie and May Price

Lida Clarke
Major Thomas Tipton Thornburgh

Joe Rankin
James France
Count August Dönhoff

Rozene Meeker
Josephine Meeker
Mrs. Charles Adams and Chipeta

Main Characters

NATHAN MEEKER, who became White River Indian Agent, 1878

ARVILLA MEEKER, his wife

RALPH

ROZENE

MARY　　　} their children

JOSEPHINE

HORACE GREELEY, editor, the *New York Tribune*, Meeker's
mentor

OURAY, head chief of the Colorado Ute Indians

CHIPETA, his wife

DOUGLAS, chief of the White River Utes

JACK, a White River Ute subchief

JOHNSON, a White River medicine man

SUSAN, Johnson's wife, Ouray's sister

JANE, Mrs. Meeker's Ute housemaid, wife of Pauvitz

PERSUNE, Ute warrior who wanted to marry Josephine Meeker

COLOROW, a Comanche chief adopted by the Utes

MAJOR THOMAS T. THORNBURGH, commanding White River
Expedition

LIEUTENANT SAMUEL CHERRY, his adjutant

CAPTAIN J. SCOTT PAYNE, his subcommander

JOE RANKIN, his guide

COLONEL WESLEY MERRITT, commanding Fifth U.S. Cavalry

CAPTAIN FRANCIS DODGE, commanding Company D, Ninth U.S. Cavalry

FELIX BRUNOT, chairman, Board of Indian Commissioners, 1870–74

CARL SCHURZ, Secretary of the Interior under President Hayes

GENERAL CHARLES ADAMS, his special agent

FREDERICK W. PITKIN, Governor of Colorado

WILLIAM B. VICKERS, his private secretary

HENRY M. TELLER, Senator from Colorado

OTTO MEARS, a trader with the Ute Indians, and road builder

Massacre

The Tragedy at White River

CHAPTER I The Child of Enoch

NATHAN COOK MEEKER was born on July 12, 1817, the product
of union between a man from Newark, New Jersey, and a
woman from Northampton, Massachusetts. The place of birth
was a breezy homestead in view of Lake Erie on the Western
Reserve. The name Nathan, meaning "given" in Hebrew, was
picked for no special reason. The Cook was added because
Mr. Cook, a kind neighbor, came by that day with a gift of
fresh eggs.

Though dirt-poor, the Enoch Meekers had distinction. Their
English ancestors had emigrated to New England in the long
ago. Enoch's grandfather had had his hand shaken by George
Washington for contributing eighteen sons to the Revolution-
ary Army. Lurana Meeker was a Hulbert and a progeny of
John Eliot, the eminent divine who translated the Bible into
Algonquin and persuaded a whole tribe of Massachusetts
Indians to stay on a Reservation.

The Western Reserve was a three-million-acre strip of land
running one hundred and twenty miles along Lake Erie. Enoch
Meeker arrived there too soon. The Indians had gone but the
region had few settlers and a scant market for produce. He
sank deeply into debt and the family knew very hard times
until things improved with the opening of the Ohio and Erie
Canal in 1832. The Meeker farm was part of the tiny community of Euclid. A few miles west was another tiny community, Cleveland. Eastward were Claridon and Painesville.
On the south were Hiram and Warren.

The Enoch Meekers accepted their first child calmly. They

were modest people and they did not dream that this puling lump of gristle and brains, so casually conceived in the wilderness, was a most remarkable baby. At the age of five, Nathan began to teach himself to read and write. At twelve he was tutoring his four brothers and writing poems on love and religion, vice and social injustice and, especially, on the horrors of poverty and debt. He developed a strong aversion to manual labor, but he enjoyed following his father around the fields to tell him how he could grow better crops if he used more intelligent farming methods.

The day came when Enoch got tired of being told. There was an argument and father and son parted company. Nathan, now seventeen, headed south on foot. At Cairo, Illinois, he boarded a steamer for New Orleans. That night he tripped on a hatchway and fell twenty feet headfirst. It should have killed him. But his plug hat was stuffed with his poems. They absorbed the shock of the fall and saved his life.

He got a job as copy boy on the *New Orleans Picayune* and mailed out essays on the South which were published by the *Louisville Courier* and the *Cleveland Plain Dealer*. He wrote rapidly, often producing a thousand words in an hour. But he yearned to be a poet. In the late 1830s, he taught school at Cleveland and at Philadelphia, saving his money until he had enough to go to New York and rent a poet's attic room at 116 MacDougal Street. He haunted editors for weeks; and at last N. P. Willis of the *New York Mirror* agreed to use some of his poems.

Of special note was his "Araby's Daughter," a stark ballad on the evils of drink, printed in August, 1842. Meeker reached the height of the tragedy in Stanza Four:

> One night as I entered my comfortless dwelling,
> My infant was dead in his mother's embrace,
> Her heart in its overwrought anguish was swelling
> As tears of deep agony streamed down her face.

Naturally, the unhappy sot fled to the nearest saloon. But before he could get blotto "an angel of mercy unlocked the sealed wells of my soul." He signed the teetotaler's pledge and

> Once more am I happy, thou demon of slaughter,
> And light is the heart of my now happy wife,
> So I drink to thy death in a cup of pure water,
> No more shalt thou rule all my fortunes in life.

Meeker's social views were suggested to the *Mirror*'s readers by the last verse of his "A Working Man's Soliloquy":

> I would not change my humble life,
> My prattling babes and darling wife,
> For all the Glory, Power and State
> Of those the foolish world calls great.
> Ah, No! The home my labor buys
> (Though poor it be) I dearly prize.
> I'd rather all my toil endure
> Than live upon the hapless Poor.

After some months of MacDougal Street, Meeker concluded that the wages of poetry were starving him to death. He returned to Euclid, now a thriving market center, and went to work as a traveling salesman. His diary entry of July 12, 1843, reads: "This day I am 26 years old. I'll write a sonnet on the occasion."

By now he was a handsome man, tall, lean, eager and blue-eyed. He had a nice smile which he tried to make worldly-wise and cynical to conceal his wild romanticism, his indestructible hopefulness. Next to debt, he hated slavery the most, and then conformity, capital punishment, Daniel Webster, luxury and New England conservatism. In his quest for perfection, he studied all the lush revolts of a revolt-loving period — the celibate Shakers, the amorous Oneida Community, the fanatic Mormons, the Brook Farm transcendentalists. He favored agrarianism and hard work, temperance and eugenics, Jacksonian reform and eating carrots for better vision at night.

He had gone to New York an ardent atheist, but his ardor died when Editor Willis declined to print his epic poem "Hell." Back in Euclid he resumed an informal belief in God. As he drummed about Northern Ohio that summer, he became absorbed in the front-page articles on Charles Fourier, the French socialist, which Albert Brisbane [1] was writing for the *New York Tribune*.

Fourier believed, and Meeker agreed with him, that individualism and competition stifled human nature. This stifling included restraints on the gratification of desire, which led to misery, vice and violence. The solution was to replace government with cooperative groups called "Phalanxes," of 1600 adults each. Fourier had died in 1837 without much honor in his own country where Frenchmen seemed unaware of any undue restraint in the gratification of their desire. But Brisbane's reports showed that Fourier's scheme was sweeping the United States. Men like Nathaniel Hawthorne and Ralph Waldo Emerson applauded it. Dozens of Phalanxes existed already, and one was being formed at Braceville, an Eagle Creek settlement near Warren — which was on Meeker's beat.

In a Fourier Phalanx there were no parasites, idlers, armies or tax collectors. Members could be rich or poor, bright or dumb, handsome or ugly. But all must live together in one huge apartment house, and eat from a common kitchen. Politics and religion were private affairs. Marriage was not encouraged; but if a man insisted on being conventional he was supposed to experiment until he found a wife who gratified his desire in a big way.

Nobody was permitted to do jobs which were distasteful to them. The theory was that cooperation created a natural balance of activities. Newborn babes were put in a common nursery to be nursed and reared by women who liked the work. When these "Little Hordes" reached the age of ten they were assigned to unpleasant tasks like washing dishes and liming privies. After two years they were presumed to have paid their debt to discipline.

Raising and marketing crops were the basis of the Phalanx economy. The proceeds were divided into twelfths, five of which went to the laborers, four to the capitalists and three to "talent" — meaning office workers, doctors, teachers and such.

Meeker perceived that he fitted the "talent" category. But before joining any Phalanx he decided to organize his love life. For some months he had had his eye on a farmer's daughter, identified only as "Maria." He wrote in his diary:

> Two years ago I first saw thee. It was as though I was listening to music. Thou aren't not beautiful. Thou has large hands and art somewhat bony in body. There is little that is ethereal in thy flesh. I know not but I am trying to write myself in love with thee. Thou has said little more to me than "Good morning" and thou doest wear corsets. Yet thou washes dirty linen and dishes — redeeming grace.

And then at Claridon on his sales circuit Meeker met Miss Arvilla Delight Smith, the shy gray-eyed child of Levi Smith, a retired West Indies sea captain. Arvilla was a native of Cheshire, Connecticut, but her family had been in the Western Reserve almost as long as the Enoch Meekers. She had small hands and she was quite ethereal. Meeker's diary implies that it was love at first sight. He took the offensive at once, using Greenwich Village tactics. The diary narrates: "I walked up to her, put my arm around her waist and with great delicacy kissed her."

Arvilla was not sure that she liked being kissed by Meeker. She was a Congregationalist and did not want to marry a man who had been an atheist and who still belonged to no church. Furthermore, traveling salesmen were notorious philanderers and Meeker might be true to type. Finally, she was more than two years older than he and she feared that gossips would make much of it when the marriage license data came out in the *Cleveland Plain Dealer.*

However, Meeker did not mind joining a church for love of Arvilla. After some study, he declared for the Disciples of Christ, nicknamed Campbellites, who purified their faith by restoring primitive ritual and who seemed to Meeker to be freer of hypocrisy than most Christian sects. Arvilla was dubious about the Campbellites; but she came around to recognizing them, particularly when Meeker posted an affidavit with the Trumbull County clerk putting his birth date in 1814 instead of, correctly, 1817.[2] Arvilla was born March 5, 1815, so the official difference in their ages was about right.

They were married in April, 1844. Meeker abandoned his roving career and proposed settling in a Fourier Phalanx. Arvilla approved. Meeker applied first to a New York State group and recorded his bride's reactions: "My girl is willing to go to Community Place, tho' I see that she does not think the folks quite orthodox. But she is willing to receive the truth. She is entirely passive. When I asked her how she would like to go, she said she was glad they had soft water! Gods and little fishes! Here is this Community of men struggling to convince the world of the most important truths, and they are commended for having *soft water!*"

Since Community Place had no vacancy, the Nathan Meekers joined ninety-three other families at Trumbull Phalanx, Braceville, Ohio, which was fifty miles southeast of Euclid. The Braceville board assigned Meeker to "talent" with a vengeance. He served concurrently as Phalanx librarian, auditor, secretary, teacher, historian and poet laureate. Arvilla taught kindergarten, being a non-nurser. The first two of her five children, Ralph Lovejoy (January, 1845) and George Columbus (August, 1847) went to the common nursery.

The Trumbull Phalanx was dissolved in the fall of '47. Its demise was hastened by its damp location, mosquitoes, ague, laziness of members and bitterness caused by cliques exploiting the altruism of others. Most members left Braceville owing the Phalanx money. Meeker was an exception. For his three years of "talent" he emerged with an uncollectible credit of $56.04. And still he did not lose his enthusiastic faith in Charles Fourier as the holder of the key to heaven on earth. Of the Trumbull experience he said merely, "I learned there how much cooperation people would bear."

FOR THREE YEARS after Braceville Meeker ran stores with his brothers around Euclid until they failed. Then he opened his own store in the Disciples of Christ community of Hiram. The Campbellites were building a college there and invited Meeker to help. He had been a baptized member of the Disciples of Christ since '44 but the Hiram deacon held up his application for transfer on grounds that he had been selling whisky. This was true, though by prescription only. Meeker, furious at the deacon's action, quit the Disciples of Christ. He never joined a church again.

In Hiram, Meeker studied the Mexican War and began extensive research on the West. His special joy was the career of John Charles Frémont, whom he had worshiped at Braceville as the shining knight of Manifest Destiny. He read and reread Frémont's thrilling reports on the Rocky Mountains and he dreamed joyfully of that vast varied region where landless Americans like himself, sick to death of debt and of the jaded East, could escape from bondage and have a second chance.

A Mormon neighbor told him a great deal about the Mormon colony in Utah. Inspired by Brigham Young's success and Fourier's theory of cooperation, Meeker wrote a novel, *The Adventures of Captain Armstrong*. This ingenious sailor, who resembled Meeker strongly, was shipwrecked on a South Pacific isle. In a brief period, by the power of personality alone, he induced the naked savages to give up barbarism and adopt a Utopian civilization of modern arts and industries, stripped of all vice. The novel made no great splash when it was published in New York in 1856. But in hindsight it was significant. The Captain's plan for civilizing his Polynesians was exactly the same plan which Meeker presented to the Ute Indians a quarter-century later.

The Adventures of Captain Armstrong had an angel. Meeker was a subscriber to the *New York Tribune,* and it was natural for him to mail his manuscript to the *Tribune*'s editor for his professional opinion. The editor, Horace Greeley, liked it and found a publisher for it.

Thus began an association which became the prime influence of Meeker's life. The two men had much in common. Both were teetotalers and poor businessmen. Both could be tactless and opinionated. Both admired Jesus Christ, not because He was the Son of God but because they judged His ideas to be sound.

Greeley, six years older than Meeker, had been born even more acutely poor in New Hampshire. He too was self-educated. At the very least he deserved to be called a character. He had the pink, mild face of a contented infant. His voice was a squeak and his whiskers were limp as corn silk. His handwriting was unreadable. He wore outlandish clothes. Though his income was large, he was usually short of cash, being a soft touch for endless charities. He was a Free-soiler and a student of spiritualism. He abhorred artists, opera, Paris, the theater and Turkish baths which "destroyed the electrical coating of the body." He opposed Catholics and Germans because, he said, they drank too much beer.

In the 1830s, James Gordon Bennett offered him a half-interest in the *New York Herald.* Greeley declined, feeling that Bennett put circulation above principle. Instead, he started the *New Yorker,* which became the *Tribune* in 1841. Soon he achieved the huge national circulation which made the *Tribune* the most powerful paper in the nation. Through it Greeley was able to express for three decades what he con-

sidered to be the conscience of America. His opinion was law to
millions. His approval of "the Kansas gold fields" in 1859 trans-
formed the Pikes Peak rush into a mass demonstration of his
favorite slogan, "Go West, young man!" His opposition to
William Seward for President assured the nomination of
Lincoln. His brave act of signing Jefferson Davis's bail bond
caused an uproar which rumbles still.

Greeley's sponsorship of the new Republican Party in 1856
led Meeker to campaign around Hiram for John Charles Frémont's Presidential candidacy. Next year the financial panic
put his Hiram store under. Meeker fled from his debts for the
third time. He took his family to Dongola, a hamlet in Southern Illinois above Cairo. His Dongola store prospered. He attracted customers with free copies of Ayer's *American Almanac*
and he sold a bit of everything — oatmeal and China, crowbars
and cassimeres, white ties and letter paper. Soon he acquired
a small fruit farm, where he could read and write in peace
while Arvilla and his oldest boy Ralph ran the store. He tried
rewriting the Bible but gave up after constructing a five-foot
genealogy of Saul and Joseph. He sent articles on the Mississippi Valley to the *Cleveland Plain Dealer* and to the *New York
Tribune.*

When the Civil War began, Horace Greeley needed a reporter to cover the movements of General Grant and John
Pope below Cairo. Greeley remembered that Meeker lived in
that neighborhood, and he wired his staff man at Cairo, Albert
D. Richardson, to lure Meeker from the seclusion of his fruit
farm and assign him to the Cairo Military District.

Meeker turned out to be a first-rate war correspondent. His
vivid dispatches on General John Pope's victories at New Ma-
drid and Island No. 10 influenced Lincoln in choosing Pope
to head the Army of Virginia. The choice was bad, but General
Pope was grateful to Meeker ever after. When the war ended,
Greeley brought Meeker to New York as the *Tribune*'s Agricultural Editor. The ex-poet returned to MacDougal Street

with his family, and happy years followed. The Dongola properties brought high prices; Meeker went ahead financially for the first time in his life. His graceful literary style and apparent knowledge of farming made him the most popular of rural columnists.

His second book, *Life in the West, or Stories of the Mississippi Valley* (1866), sold well. Even the great Henry Ward Beecher, the Congregationalist preacher, praised his articles. He had arrived, in the newspaper world; and he gave Horace Greeley the credit for his arrival. His devotion to his editor became as great as his love for Arvilla. In '67 he was touched when the *Tribune* hired his boy Ralph, aged twenty-two, as a cub reporter. And yet Meeker and Greeley never became close friends. The emotional plane of their relationship was more that of the respectful employee and the august employer.

Of their mutual interests one was paramount — the growth of the West. Such growth, they believed, would save the nation from its besetting evils — the terrible bitterness and despair which followed the Civil War, rampant industrial expansion, the widespread debt in the South, the degradation of Reconstruction politics. It would ease the pressure of population in the East, fantastically increased by immigration each year after the Irish potato famine of 1847 and the German Revolution of 1848. Horace Greeley had supported the Preemption Act of 1841 (land for settlers at a dollar and twenty-five cents an acre). Thereafter, his advocacy of free land helped to pass the great Homestead Act of '62, by which anybody could acquire one hundred and sixty acres of public land for nothing.

In October, 1869, Greeley sent Meeker on his first trip beyond the Missouri to prepare a series of articles on the Rocky Mountains. At Kansas City, Meeker boarded the cars of the new Kansas Pacific Railroad, which ran 350 miles toward Denver to the Sheridan railhead near the Colorado line. A Kansas Pacific executive, General William Jackson Palmer, learned his identity and asked him into his palace Pullman — which was on promotion duty to impress seventeen Eastern tycoons with the richness of the K-P's land grant.

General Palmer, a thirty-three-year-old Philadelphian, was just the sort of cultured young dude whose elegance should have riled Meeker's plebeian instincts. When Palmer began discussing Colorado, Meeker reacted with his most insulting brand of elaborate inattention. But he soon found himself listening intently. Before the train reached Sheridan, he was listening with rapture.

CHAPTER 11   Utopia, Incorporated

It is not surprising that Meeker was moved by Palmer's rhetoric. The General was not merely a Civil War hero, a Rocky Mountain explorer and a railroad genius in charge of building the Kansas Pacific to Denver. He was also head over heels in love. What Meeker heard from him about Colorado were the musings of an empire builder who happened also to have a very pretty girl, Queen Mellen of Pittsburgh, on his mind.

Meeker already knew the epic story of Colorado Territory, but Palmer's zest and imagery gave it new grandeur. After Zebulon Pike's visit in 1806, its dramatic mountains and plains were enjoyed for half a century by the Indians and a few white trappers and traders. The Forty-niners admired it and hurried on. Then came the gold stampede of 1859, a chaotic surge of humanity to the Pikes Peak region almost as great as the California rush. These gold seekers, Palmer explained, were alien to the country, though they were fond of the climate and scenery. Unlike the trappers before them, they did not care for indigenous things. Their urgent desire was to transplant in this splendid wilderness the Eastern environment which they had been so glad to leave. That was why the trails West were crowded with bull trains importing featherbeds and kid gloves, tin bathtubs and plug hats, iron deer, melodeons and umbrella stands.

The gold rush subsided with the Civil War, and the Territorial economy had to become more self-sufficient. Many men quit the diggings and took homesteads along the streams to grow crops and meat. Small-scale irrigation helped solve the problem of the scant twelve-inch annual rainfall. Westerners went to work making their own iron deer. Now, in 1869, the one hundred and four thousand square miles of Colorado Territory had forty thousand white inhabitants, living mainly in a small mineral belt around Denver and Central City.

But, Palmer told Meeker, the mere forty thousand were just the beginning. Ahead was a decade of vast expansion, sparked by that most potent of growth factors, the development of Western railroads. The handful of whites would increase tenfold, pervading the Territory even westward up against the Ute Indian Reservation. The white hordes would bring innovations in agriculture and in manufacturing and in tourism. Improvements in smelting would create a second and larger gold rush. Native coal would come into demand, and silver would emerge as the metal of tomorrow.

Palmer added that Denver would become a glittering metropolis as soon as the Kansas Pacific arrived there from the Sheridan railhead. The General was laying tracks also for the Denver Pacific, which would connect the Kansas Pacific at Denver with the Union Pacific at Cheyenne in Wyoming Territory. Trains had been running since May on the Union Pacific from Omaha to San Francisco. And Palmer would be quitting the Kansas Pacific soon to build his own line south from Denver, past Pikes Peak to the Arkansas River, over the Sangre de Cristos, and down the Rio Grande to Santa Fe. Spurs of this Denver and Rio Grande Railroad would penetrate the lush mountain parks of the Territory at a dozen places. In a Pikes Peak canyon near the Garden of the Gods, he would build an English castle fit for Queen Mellen. And he would found Colorado Springs, a model resort city, if he could locate an organizer of colonies.

The General was not lavishing his Rocky Mountain ecstasy on Meeker alone. Those seventeen Eastern tycoons were in the palace Pullman also. Among them, Meeker met Cyrus Field, who was about to go to Europe to peddle Kansas Pacific bonds and to attend the opening of the Suez Canal. Meeker noted that Field listened to his views on the West with respect. He began to wonder if he might be qualified to organize a colony for Palmer at Pikes Peak, using his experience as a follower of Fourier and as the creator of Captain Armstrong.

But he was repelled later by the shameful goings-on at Palmer's town of Sheridan where, Meeker wrote, it seemed usual at breakfast to aim your six-gun at the head of the man next to you and remark, "Pass the butter." The Sheridan graveyard was full of men who had been hung for capital crimes like holding five aces. The tracks were lined with saloons and gambling houses. In each hotel doorway Meeker was shocked to note short-frocked hussies who wriggled their hips and crooked fingers at him.

From Sheridan, Palmer, Field and Meeker continued West in a four-horse spring wagon over the brown prairie, inspecting the rich valleys of the Arkansas and Huerfano Rivers. On the Huerfano, Meeker was enchanted to find a steam engine powering a machine which threshed wheat. Frontier life, he decided, wasn't all roulette wheels and dance-hall fiddles. They arrived at Pikes Peak safely, though Cyrus Field spent a bad night in a farmhouse when his bed slats broke.

Somewhere between the Sheridan hussies and the bed-slat incident, Meeker ceased to think of himself as the famed journalist, comfortably established with his family in suburban New York. He was fifty-two now and past his prime. And yet his wild yearning to create his own perfect world peopled by his own idea of perfect human beings was as youthfully strong as it had been when he led the passive Arvilla to Braceville in in 1844. The time had come to put the East behind him and take the rough road of Manifest Destiny.

They had reached Pikes Peak after midnight; but Meeker rose before dawn, so excited by the "awful majesty" of the mountain as seen dimly from his tent that he wrote an ode to it. The "awful majesty" turned out at sunrise to be a haystack. Pikes Peak itself was less impressive, and the poet destroyed his ode.

Palmer showed him the springs at Manitou and the Garden of the Gods and traced the boundaries of his dream Colorado Springs in Monument Valley. Then they continued north to Denver, a dusty, bustling city of five thousand, where Meeker was welcomed by William N. Byers, who had founded, in '59, Colorado's first paper, the *Rocky Mountain News*.

This Byers, an attractive, galvanic man in a constant state of creative turmoil, struck Meeker as the embodiment of the American pioneer spirit. It appeared that for a decade he had poked his curious nose into every sort of Territorial activity from railroads to irrigation to keeping Democrats out of power. Meeker was drawn to him also for his high moral principles. As unofficial censor of the Denver and Central City theaters he saw to it that his paper panned plays which might give citizens immoral ideas. Byers told Meeker that he was Colorado agent for the National Land Company, which handled the Denver Pacific's government land grants. He added that several fine tracts were available around Evans, the Denver Pacific's railhead fifty miles northeast of Denver.

Byers introduced his journalistic colleague to Governor Edward M. McCook, a brittle young politician, suavely handlebarred and pomaded, who had served until lately as United States Minister to the Sandwich Islands. Territorial Governors were Presidential appointees. Because of Colorado's small vote and remoteness, President Grant viewed the job there as far less important politically than, say, the postmastership of Steubenville, Ohio. The governorship made a nice present for a former comrade-at-arms, and Grant was glad to rescue McCook from the hula hinterland and send him to Denver — even though he had to remove the incumbent Governor, A. C. Hunt, also a Republican.

Hunt turned his office over to McCook under the impression

that he would be allowed to keep on handling annuities and rations for the Ute Indians as Superintendent of Indian Affairs. But McCook had just married a girl from Peoria, Illinois: Mary Thompson. Mary had an easy-going, curly-haired playboy of a brother, James B. Thompson, who hadn't had a job adapted to his disposition for years. So McCook forgot about Hunt, made James Thompson his private secretary, and put him in charge of the Colorado Utes. This was fine for everyone except ex-Governor Hunt. McCook remained ex-officio Superintendent of Indian Affairs and enjoyed to the full its mysterious emoluments. Thompson did the work, which wasn't much.

Governor McCook did not explain these family matters to Meeker when they crossed the South Platte to watch Thompson distribute rations to the Utes. At the warehouse, Meeker took an adverse view of the people he would come to know so well. He disliked their vigorous cosmetics, their variety of dress, the way they pampered their papooses and their inability to speak his language "though the babies cried in genuine English." He was irked because he couldn't always distinguish women from men, and he deplored the racy effect achieved by young cavaliers whose blue jeans "were stitched close to the leg leaving much of the cloth extending like the back of a fish."

It was Meeker's way to absorb knowledge in bold, quick snatches. Thus now, after a thirty-minute snatch, he gave his million *New York Tribune* readers his profound conclusions, not only on these Utes but on all red men:

> The extension of a fine nervous organization is impossible in the Indian, because he is without brain to originate and support it.

The day would come when Meeker would wonder how on earth he happened to write that sentence.

MEEKER'S TRIBUNE ASSIGNMENT called for an article on Utah's

Kingdom of Deseret, the fruitfulness of which was being demonstrated by Brigham Young's seventeen happy wives and forty-seven healthy children. However, an early November snow blocked the Union Pacific in Wyoming west of Fort Steele. Meeker turned eastward at Cheyenne which he reached on the Denver Pacific from the Evans railhead near the junction of the South Platte and Cache la Poudre Rivers.

His mind seethed with ideas for a "Union Colony of Colorado" based on Fourier cooperation as modified by his experience at Trumbull Phalanx. He arrived home chewing tobacco and dropping his "gs" like a Western pioneer and outlined for the patient Arvilla a complete Colorado program which could be offered through the *New York Tribune*.

"Temperance people of good moral character" who longed for a fuller, freer life would be asked to give one hundred and fifty-five dollars each to a fund for the purchase of a vast tract of cheap fertile farmland in the Colorado Rockies. In exchange for his one hundred and fifty-five dollars the Union Colony member could buy a lot at a nominal price in the Colony's town and up to one hundred and sixty acres of farm land near the town. All surplus lots and farmland would, of course, increase immensely in value above the Agricultural Script purchase price of ninety cents an acre. These surplus lands would be sold off as needed to finance the Colony's irrigation system, schools, cattle herd and cooperatives for washing clothes, baking bread and wholesale buying.

Arvilla heard her husband out with poignant misgivings. She recalled that she had borne the brunt of their struggle to live at Trumbull Phalanx, at Hiram, and at Dongola where her spouse withdrew to his fruit farm to be idealistic in ink while she tended the store and rode herd on the five children. She could not bear the thought of trading her suburban comforts for another shack in the wilds. She was horrified at Meeker's willingness to gamble his entire savings of ten thousand dollars or more on Union Colony.[1]

She pointed out that their second son George, aged twenty-one, was seriously tubercular and might die on the trip West. She mentioned that their eldest daughter, Rozene, twenty, was frail and mentally unstable for fear she might become an old maid. The pretty younger girls, Josephine and Mary, aged twelve and fifteen, were very popular and were getting the education in New York which had been denied the other children during their father's addiction to frontier life.

But passivity was still Arvilla's dominant trait, as it had been a quarter-century before when Meeker married her instead of the corseted Maria. In the end, she agreed to give up New York, take Josie and Mary out of school and follow the Founder to an empty tract at an unknown spot in the raw West — providing the Founder stopped chewing tobacco. Meeker did more than merely accept the proviso. He became strongly anti-nicotine thereafter.

Horace Greeley approved the Union Colony plan and wrote an enthusiastic endorsement to accompany Meeker's famous "Call" in the *New York Tribune* of December 14, 1869. The magic of Greeley's name, and the considerable prestige of Meeker's, caused "The Call" to be reprinted everywhere. It was an immediate sensation. Young Ralph Meeker, who worked on the *Tribune* real estate desk, spent a hard week answering thousands of inquiries.

The first and only New York meeting of Union Colony took place on December 23 at Cooper Union near the Bowery. The long basement room was "crowded to overflowing with gentlemen from all parts of the country." Horace Greeley presented his tall, handsome former Agricultural Editor, who told the cheering throng that the aggregate wealth of those answering "The Call" exceeded fifteen hundred thousand dollars, which was enough to buy a great deal of Colorado land at ninety cents an acre. Women wept as the Founder described one possible Edenlike location "well watered with streams and springs, dotted with pine groves and with an abundance of coal and stone." Thunderous applause met his remarks on the joys of temperance and monogamous morality, on religious tolerance and on education which would make Union Colony a cultural model for all the world.

The members elected Meeker as President and chose a Locating Committee consisting of President Meeker, a General Robert A. Cameron and somebody named Mr. Fisk of Toledo, Ohio. In February, the Locating Committee collected nine hundred dollars from Treasurer Greeley and headed for Colorado to decide where Union Colony would locate. The men enjoyed their long jaunt to Cheyenne, south to Denver and Pueblo, back to Cheyenne and west some more to Mormon country. Mr. Fisk of Toledo took no perceptible interest in Colony sites but he ate lavishly, slept often and inspected a number of Territorial saloons and dance halls. At Chicago, homeward bound, Meeker grew suspicious of him and learned by wiring Ralph Meeker in New York that Fisk was not a Colony member. When Fisk stepped from the train at Toledo he told Meeker that he had never had any idea of joining the Colony and could not understand why he was picked at Cooper Union and given a free de luxe tour of the West.

The Fisk affair was typical of the contretemps attending the birth of the most successful colony in the West. Meeker's latest adaptation of the Fourier Phalanx became the proving ground for the whole theory of Western irrigation which has — at least as much as mining or scenery or climate — made Colorado the leading mountain state by a wide margin. And yet the wonder is that Union Colony survived the duplicities, the confused leadership, the disillusionment of its first five years. That most of the members hung on shows how desperately people of that day longed to leave their unhappy Eastern environment and find in the West the Founder's dream of a "fuller, freer life."

Their longing explains, too, why completely honest men like Meeker could be less than honest in the all-purifying name of Progress. The glorious end justified the shabby means. The

Edenlike location depicted by Meeker at Cooper Union was a myth, though he wanted it to sound like Monument Valley at Pikes Peak to please General Palmer. Pleasing the General was important just then, since Meeker was seeking bargain rates for his people coming to Denver on the Kansas-Pacific. Actually, the Founder had eliminated Monument Valley weeks before as being too narrow for large-scale irrigation.

The site finally picked, to which 200 colonists flocked in the spring of 1870, had no slight resemblance to Meeker's promised land. Instead of "pine groves sheltered by majestic mountains," they found an unprotected tract on the treeless plain along the Cache la Poudre River.[2] The nearest mountain, Longs Peak, was fifty miles west and ghostly in the dust raised by the constant wind. Meeker's "abundance of stone and coal" was still more remote.

Fifty of the Colonists stared briefly in horror at this bleak setting and caught the night train from Evans bound for Cheyenne and home. The rest lingered on to be benumbed by successive waves of disenchantment. The Founder had bought only twelve thousand acres, for which he paid the outrageous price of five dollars an acre, much of it to Land Agent William Byers, for the benefit of the Denver Pacific. Before the members had left the East, Ralph Meeker had told them that his father had bought seventy thousand acres at ninety cents an acre. Much of the twelve thousand acres proved to be useless, having been acquired, Meeker confessed, sight unseen.

Byers, in the heat of his selling fervor, unloaded six hundred and forty acres of presumed land grant which the Denver Pacific didn't even own. Meeker insisted on buying up the homesteads of several old settlers, who displayed later intense bitterness toward Union Colony. One reason was their discovery that Meeker considered them to be a loose bunch morally. Another cause was a *Tribune* article by Ralph Meeker, describing them as "squatters" — which was far worse than impugning their paternity. Thereafter the old settlers referred to the Colonists as "the Saints." And they called the Founder "Father Meeker," in derision.

The biggest heartache was Meeker's irrigation fiasco. Unburdened by experience, the Founder plunged blithely into hydrodynamics, the pitfalls of which have made experts quail for millenniums. He planned four ditches to water twenty thousand acres at a total cost of twenty thousand dollars. The first three-mile ditch alone cost twenty-five thousand dollars, and the Colonists had to wait a week before the diverted river water trickled out the other end.[3]

The first ditch actually irrigated only two hundred acres. Most of the Colony's gardens which were put in below it dried up and blew away. Meeker wanted water power to grind corn, and he built a ten-thousand-dollar millrace through town. But there wasn't enough water most of the time for irrigation and water power both. When there was enough, water leaked from the millrace and flooded many cellars, the repair of which dissipated the profits from town lot sales.

The colonists applauded Meeker's choice of "Greeley" as the name of their townsite, in honor of their baby-faced treasurer, though a few were critical of the fact that the nation's greatest editor couldn't bring the Colony's books within two thousand dollars of balance. Greeley, like P. T. Barnum, the Tom Thumb man, was one of two hundred and fifty absentee members of the Colony, but he took great interest in it and he mailed the Founder frequent excerpts from his best-selling book, *What I Know about Farming.*

One thing Greeley thought he knew about farming was that the Cache la Poudre Valley around Greeley town was on the order of the Shenandoah Valley of Virginia and was therefore ideal for fruit, nut and shade trees. So Meeker bought a carload of walnuts and hickories, apples and pears, elms and maples. To increase aboreal confidence he named Greeley's north-south streets after these trees, and the Colonists planted all fourteen hundred of them while the old settlers, who had seen the fate of non-native trees that far from the mountains, watched with interest. Only three of the trees lived more than six months.

Another Horace Greeley notion was that fences were an insult to free men in Colorado's wide open spaces. Herdsmen, therefore, guarded the Colony cattle, but many escaped into town and ate such of the imported trees as had not already expired from the climate. When Greeley came from New York on his single visit to Greeley town in October, 1870, and saw that his beloved trees had been eaten, he became ardently pro-fence and approved spending twenty thousand dollars for fifty miles of smooth wire to enclose the Colony's common pasture.[4] The old settlers laughed a lot over that fence which, they said, "Father Meeker built to protect the Saints from us Heathens 'round about."

FOR ALL HIS MISTAKES, Meeker held the loyalty and affectionate admiration of his colonists. His industry was fantastic and more than once his friends put him to bed for fear he would kill himself working. They rallied around him when his boy George, soon after arriving, died of tuberculosis in Evans before a decent house could be built in Greeley for him to die in. George's burial near Greeley was construed as touching proof of the Founder's faith in the Colony's permanence.

The members saw in Meeker a selfless visionary who would sacrifice everything, including his family's well-being, if he could advance what seemed to him to be the welfare of the human race. Arvilla wept many times as her husband's ten-thousand-dollars-plus savings melted away, often on Colony expenses which he forgot to collect from Treasurer Greeley. While his marriageable daughter Rozene worried about her lack of dowry and Josie and Mary made do with faded hair ribbons and scuffed shoes, Meeker built the most expensive house in Greeley, placing it away out on the corner of Plum and Monroe Streets, half a mile from the center of town, as a measure of his belief. He was already in debt in October of 1870 when he borrowed a thousand dollars from Horace Greeley to start the *Greeley Tribune,* which could not be expected to pay him a salary for months.

During those difficult days there were enough practical farmers on hand to hold things together until the area's real potential for agriculture began to show. Meanwhile, Meeker's steady stream of articles for the *New York Tribune* were widely read, making Union Colony one of the best-publicized of all Utopia's. Because of its celebrity, the original twenty-five-dollar price of Greeley home lots rose to five hundred dollars and hung there through the worst of the Colony's growing pains.

Meeker's old horror of debt did not bother him too much, because he depended on Greeley to buy his articles and to loan him money. A Greeley loan never seemed like debt anyhow, being made with the understanding that Meeker was not to repay it until he was able. Greeley, true enough, was beginning to claim poverty and even hinted that he was relaxing his grip on *New York Tribune* stock. He wrote also of multiple ailments, but he was still only sixty-one and Meeker observed that he had enough resources and health to seek the Presidential nomination on the Liberal Republican ticket at Cincinnati in May of 1872.

This reformist revolt against President Grant's circle of corrupt Republicans was fomented by Carl Schurz, the famed journalist and Senator from Missouri. Schurz was a former German rebel who had fled his country in '48 and fought through the Civil War, some of the time as a division commander. His rise to political power in the United States resulted from his control of the German vote. His candidate for the Liberal Republican nomination was the diplomat, Charles Francis Adams, but he lost control of the Cincinnati convention and Greeley won the nomination.

Meeker went to work with a will for his patron. Through

the campaign summer, the *Greeley Tribune* reeked with Horace Greeley propaganda, which split Union Colony into bitter factions, Meeker's Liberal Republicans and General Cameron's Regulars. In September Meeker noted that his mentor's letters were getting fewer and more querulous. Greeley intimated that he knew he was not a popular Presidential candidate. His nation-wide speaking tour was becoming a nightmare to him. At its end, Mrs. Greeley fell ill. Her already exhausted husband stayed beside her without sleep until she died on October 30. Nine days later, President Grant and all his crowd were re-elected in a landslide.

It was all too much. Greeley's mind broke and he died insane in New York on November 29. Deeply bereaved, Meeker published in the *Greeley Tribune* the Associated Press story describing how thousands viewed Greeley's body lying in state in City Hall and how the service was attended by President Grant, Vice-President Colfax, Chief Justice Salmon P. Chase, and a thousand others. The funeral oration was delivered by Meeker's literary admirer, Henry Ward Beecher.

THE OLD ORDER changed in a hurry. Meeker's Christmas present was a crisp letter from the managing editor of the *New York Tribune* stating that Whitelaw Reid now owned the Horace Greeley paper. Meeker's articles from Colorado would be accepted no longer. His *Tribune* income, which had sustained him so long, was a thing of the past. A little later, when Meeker wrote to Charles Storrs, the executor of Greeley's estate, explaining that Greeley didn't really expect Meeker to repay the thousand-dollar loan, Storrs replied that Greeley had died almost broke. That changed everything. He had a duty toward Greeley's unmarried daughters, Ida and Gabrielle. Storrs advised Meeker to pay off the thousand dollars to the Greeley estate or face legal action.

Then the panic of '73 began, culminating in the failure of

the great private banking house, Jay Cooke & Co. The price of corn and everything else fell far below the cost of production. Union Colony had nothing to sell even at a loss. Most of its crops were consumed during a plague of red-thighed grass-hoppers.

Then Nathan Meeker reeled under yet another blow — shocking news from his beloved son. Ralph Meeker had been showing much promise with one good job leading to a better one. He had left the *New York Tribune* in 1870 and had spent time on *Frank Leslie's Weekly* and on something called the *Jolly Joker*. But the panic of '73 had put even Ralph on the street. He had looked for work high and low. At last, though he knew how unhappy his father would be about it, he joined the staff of the *Tribune's* arch rival, the *New York Herald*.

CHAPTER III Ralph Meeker, Crime
Buster

THE NEW YORK HERALD in the mid-1870's was still avid for circulation and for the kind of sensational news that would get it. Its founder, James Gordon Bennett, who disbelieved everything except the selfishness of man, died seven months before Meeker's romantic idealist, Horace Greeley. When Bennett's son and namesake took over the *Herald,* Whitelaw Reid of the *Tribune* thought the time had come at last to run the *Herald* out of business.

The second James Gordon Bennett had a superb background for ruining a prosperous family enterprise. His loving mother, spurned by New York high society, had brought him up in Paris with the help of private tutors. In his early twenties, his loving father put millions behind him and sprung him on New York, where his Gallic sophistication overwhelmed the relatively simple *haut monde* of Fifth Avenue. He was admitted into its sanctum sanctorum, the New York Yacht Club, and soon was running the place. In '66, he became the most famous dandy on earth when his schooner *Henrietta* won the Transatlantic run and a purse of ninety thousand dollars.

As Whitelaw Reid dreamed of triumph over the *Herald,* young Bennett moved back to Paris, bored with the rusticity of Manhattan. He began directing his New York paper from cafés on the Rue Royale. One day he summoned the wandering Welshman, Henry M. Stanley, and set in motion one of the greatest of news stories — Stanley's search for the lost explorer,

Dr. David Livingstone. The extent of the explorer's lostness was a moot point but there was nothing moot about the *Herald*'s soaring circulation by the time it was able to report, from the depths of Unyamwezi, Stanley's immortal words: "Dr. Livingstone, I presume?"

When Ralph Meeker went to work for Bennett he was a moderate Bohemian who dwelt at 40 East Seventh Street in Greenwich Village. Early in '75, he covered for the *Herald* one of the tragic Oshkosh, Wisconsin, fires. Meanwhile, Bennett in Paris was looking for another long-term Stanley-like sensation. He became intrigued by rumors of Indian Bureau frauds along the Missouri River in the Sioux country. The frauds seemed exciting, so Bennett wired his New York office to send its nearest reporter on a six-month tour of Sioux agencies. The nearest reporter was Ralph Meeker, just turned thirty. He left Oshkosh heading West instead of East and set up crime-busting headquarters at Bismarck, Dakota Territory.

Nathan Meeker's son was the antithesis of the venturesome Henry Stanley, though once at Union Colony he had surprised his father with his derring-do in trying to burn down a whisky mill which had opened inadvertently near Greeley. Ralph was Arvilla's child — gentle, kind, dreamy, patient and meek. He loved his mother very much and might have stayed in Greeley to be near her except that he couldn't stand his strident and self-centered sister Rozene. By contrast he adored his other sisters, Mary and Josephine — especially Josie, the youngest, whom he had named at birth. He was a smallish man with an oddly high forehead, blond wavy hair and pale blue eyes which had been weakened, Arvilla said, when Nathan held him too long in bright sunlight as a baby. His pockets were usually full of pills as he never knew when he might have an attack of catarrh or gastritis or toothache.

RALPH HAD BEEN MOVED to some study of Indian history because the Utes were still in Colorado. The history was upsetting. When the first Englishmen landed in North America they found a native civilization as profoundly different from their own as some fantastic social system on Mars. The Indians were not numerous — half a million perhaps — and it had been no great trick to push the Eastern tribes West by cajolery, bribery or minor warfare. In each case the wind-up took the form of a solemn treaty as between sovereign nations.

The Indians outnumbered the whites through most of the colonial period and so the whites had great respect for the solemn treaties which kept the Indians off their necks. However, between 1790 and 1849 the white population rose to twenty-one millions and the sovereignty of the various Indian tribes became a myth. But the white Americans were too busy with their own affairs to tell the Indians about the myth. It was easier and cheaper to let each tribe keep on thinking it was an independent nation.

During the 1790–1849 period, a vague sort of Indian policy was directed by the Indian Bureau under the War Department, with Congress assuming control of commercial relations in 1834. The theory for a while was that the Indians could have everything west of the Mississippi. Then the boundary was advanced to the Missouri. In '49, while the Army was preoccupied with making ex-Mexican lands safe for settlement, the Indian Bureau was transferred to the new Department of the Interior.

From that point on the Indians found themselves to be pawns in what was to them a perfectly incomprehensible game of political chess. After passage of the Homestead Act in '62, tens of thousands of settlers streamed on Indian lands. Every few months government officials made new treaties guaranteeing the Indians annual supplies and monthly rations forever, in exchange for the lands ceded. The compensation costs swelled the Indian Bureau's budget to five million dollars annually.

This huge sum was more than enough to make the Indian Bureau a key factor in political patronage involving the Interior, Treasury and War Departments and a vast body of purchasing agents, contractors, freighters, warehouse owners and distribution clerks. And the expenditure of so much money was not the sole political aspect. After the Civil War, the pampered Army had to come down to earth. Instead of saving the Union, its menial job now was to manage a pack of savages. Worst of all, it had lost its autonomy. Since the savages were under the jurisdiction of the Indian Bureau in the Interior Department, General Sherman and his staff were just a domestic police force bound to take orders from the Secretary of the Interior.

The Army didn't like to take orders and its officers used most of their energy pushing schemes to win transfer of the Indian Bureau back to the War Department. Their case had promise, since the Democrats were always happy to attack the Republican status quo. Up to 1871, they were encouraged further by the fact that the House of Representatives saw in transfer a means of wrecking Senate control of Indian affairs, which the Senate exercised through its exclusive right to make treaties. The House challenged the Senate often by refusing to appropriate funds promised in the Senate treaties. Let the Indians starve! Politics before justice! But in '71 the quarrel ended with the abolition of the treaty system. Congress dissolved the Indian nations, declared all red men to be wards of the government, and named itself their guardian and trustee. How this action squared up with their citizenship rights under the Fourteenth Amendment nobody bothered to ask.

Though Ralph Meeker was as anti-Grant as his father, he could sympathize with the President, who had braved Army scorn by opposing transfer and had formulated a noble civilian Peace Plan in '69. By this plan Indian Agents were nominated by church societies. The Indian Bureau was policed theoretically by a nonsalaried Board of Indian Commissioners composed of philanthropists of awesome integrity. The failure of the Peace Plan in the period 1869–1875 broke the President's heart. Godly agents proved to be as dishonest in many instances as the ungodly had been. Grant's patronage-hungry crowd throttled the policing Board of Indian Commissioners by count-less tricks, including denial of their office expenses. Purists attacked the Peace Plan as violating Constitutional bans on religion in government.

THROUGH THOSE SIX MONTHS OF '75, Ralph Meeker took his gastritis and catarrh by buckboard and stage up and down the Missouri River for two thousand miles. He reported that some fourteen bands of the fifty thousand Sioux were divided among twelve agencies scattered from Nebraska far northwestward to Fort Peck and Fort Belknap in Dakota Territory. He described their desperate need for food and clothing because the whites had almost destroyed their buffalo. Furthermore, the Sioux had lost their beloved hunting grounds, the Black Hills, to General Custer and the white gold-seekers, though that region only seven years before had been given to them "forever." Custer himself had started the rush in '74 by confirming the existence of Black Hills gold during a military visit.

Ralph was sickened to observe that thousands of white Americans were thriving on Sioux misery. Drunken white "squaw men" robbed Sioux women of what little they had by promising them favored treatment at the agencies. Ralph corroborated stories that rotten beef and wormy flour were the usual rations at Red Cloud, Standing Rock and Spotted Tail Agencies. At Crow Creek and Fort Buford annuity goods were 90 per cent swindles. Ralph examined picks and shovels almost as pliable as wet spaghetti. At Fort Peck he bought pocket knives in-tended for the Assiniboins from Carl Stanley, the Agent. He learned details of a tunnel running fifty feet from Stanley's warehouse to the post trader's store, through which goods as-signed to the Yankton Sioux were moved for sale to post em-ployees.

Ralph followed leads as far north as Winnipeg in Canada to

check a gigantic fraud in which ten thousand sacks of flour —
the main 1875 winter food supply for six thousand Sioux —
were shipped up the Missouri by steamer from St. Louis and
were reported ruined by fire near Fort Peck. The situation was
crucial. Very soon Fort Peck would be isolated by snow and the
Sioux would starve.

A Winnipeg firm wired the Indian Bureau that it could replace the ruined flour at the fort in time. The feat seemed impossible, and yet the shipment did arrive before snow. Ralph
discovered why. The original flour had been packed in double
sacks at St. Louis. There had been no genuine fire on the
Missouri River steamer, though the flour had been unloaded
and piled on the prairie under brush. The Winnipeg firm had
now merely rushed down ten thousand empty sacks by mule
pack, and these Canadian sacks had been substituted for the
outer sacks of the flour from St. Louis. In this way, the prin-
cipals were paid twice for their wormy flour.

The disclosure of such facts to the *Herald*'s half-million
readers forced President Grant to dismiss his Secretary of the
Interior, Columbus Delano, and the Commissioner of Indian
Affairs, the Reverend Edward P. Smith. By Christmas of '75,
Ralph was back in his Greenwich Village apartment, not quite
so dreamy and meek after his emergence in the public imagination as a steel-nerved newsman as quick on the draw as Deadwood Dick. He was worn out, his teeth needed fixing and he
yearned for peace and quiet. He was under indictment in
Dakota Territory where a Bismarck judge had ordered him
to answer libel charges.

But he was an important factor now in the battle between
President Grant's coterie and the Carl Schurz reform wing to
win control of the Republican Party. Mysterious informers
found their way often up the stairs to his bachelor quarters on
East Seventh Street. One of these informers brought him new
material on the Honorable William Worth Belknap, Grant's
Secretary of War, who possessed the longest beard in the Cabi-

net. Belknap had been charged with taking twenty-four thousand, four hundred and fifty dollars from Indian Bureau contractors as a bribe for appointing a man named Caleb P. Marsh
to be post trader at Fort Sill, Indian Territory. Belknap had
denied the charge, though expressing amazement that his
household accounts after 1870 showed the spending of vast
sums which he had not earned. Ralph's tipster learned that
Belknap's wife had taken the bribe without the Secretary's
knowledge and had induced him to approve the Marsh appointment. In the impeachment proceedings, the Republican
Senate cleared Belknap, holding that a Cabinet member, especially a Republican Cabinet member, should not be held
responsible for the peccadilloes of his wife.

In the spring of '76, Ralph's *Herald* stories caused the House
Committee on Indian Affairs reluctantly to conduct a white-
wash of the Indian Bureau which it called a "thorough investigation." Ralph was summoned to testify but was prudently
evicted from the closed hearings when he refused to reveal his
news sources. Actually, the sources were Washington newsmen
and clerks in various government departments. One of them
told him about a strange young Irishman named Samuel Parker.
From Parker or Parker's friends Ralph learned details of the
culminating scandal of the Grant Administration.

In '72, this Samuel Parker had applied to Felix Brunot,
Chairman of the Board of Indian Commissioners, for a clerk-
ship in the Board's Washington office. Parker was a distressing
sight, having smashed his nose, lost an eye and had his tongue
cut in two during a drunken brawl while serving in the Army.
Felix Brunot had a soft heart. He loved to help the underdog
and the alcoholic, and battered Parker was about as far under
as anyone he had ever seen. First, Brunot had asked Parker
to kneel with him and for some minutes had read appropriate
prayers from his Episcopalian psalter. Then, after Parker had
promised not to drink on duty, Brunot had put him on the
payroll of the Board of Indian Commissioners.

Parker had proved to be an accounting genius and a first-rate detective. His discoveries formed the basis of many of the stories which Ralph wrote for the *Herald* during 1876 exposing the sensational conspiracy called the Indian Ring. In a year-end summary of the whole affair, Ralph wrote:

> To fully understand the peculiar power possessed by the Indian Ring one should bear in mind that it is really a national political organization. It is republican in sentiment but democratic enough to give the offices and money to the opposite party when emergencies require official whitewash or special legislation.
>
> The leading members are James W. Bosler of Carlisle, Pa.; Clinton Wheeler of New York and A. H. Wilder of St. Paul. Bosler is a politician and bosom friend of Columbus Delano. Bosler is the Napoleon of the lobby. He knows how to win the good will of Congress, and make an 800-pound steer weigh 1,600 before the eyes of the Indian Bureau inspector.
>
> After careful figuring it is estimated that Bosler & Co. have robbed the government and the Indians of the following amounts since 1870: On beef, $296,693; on flour and salt, $90,272: on freights, $114,000. Their total frauds amount to more than $800,000.
>
> It may be said here that so long as the Ring sends men to Congress and furnishes money for Presidential campaigns it is probable that its members will continue to steal and to corrupt legislation.[1]

Ralph added by implication that, when Columbus Delano found himself connected with the Indian Ring by Parker, he joined forces with the War and Treasury Department officials. Everybody worked on the bibulous Parker. By threats and blandishments they silenced him — holding his Army record for drunkenness over his head and giving him a soft Treasury Department job where drinking on duty was both permitted and encouraged. A little later, the agents of James Bosler made friends with Parker, wined and dined him in relays and at last, "while almost stupefied with liquor, a bargain was made. Next week Parker sailed for Ireland where his few remaining days

were spent in delirium and remorse." Parker died of alcohol-
ism in July of '76. From his sister, Ralph received a packet of
nine letters which she said had been written by James Bosler
and his agent to Parker in Ireland indicating that Bosler had
paid him seven thousand dollars in cash and an income of five
hundred dollars a month for leaving the United States.

RALPH'S INDIAN BUREAU ARTICLES were read and digested in
Greeley by his proud father, who began taking a mild interest in Indian affairs. They were read, digested and even used
in speeches by Senator Carl Schurz of Missouri, and this pleased
Ralph very much. Schurz was himself a fine journalist, having
been editor of the *Detroit Free Press* and of the *St. Louis
Westliche Post.*

Actually, Ralph had admired the brilliant Schurz for years,
though he was too kind to let Nathan Meeker know that he
preferred Schurz's dynamic liberalism to Horace Greeley's un-
yielding idealism. Schurz was heartily and effectively pro-In-
dian. He was, Ralph felt, the first important politician to face
the fact that the Indians were not going to perish as a race,
that they could not be exterminated like coyotes and that something rational had to be done about them. Besides, public opinion was shifting in their favor. Soon Congress would find that
it could not afford to kick them around as carelessly as in the
past.

After the failure of Greeley's Presidential candidacy in '72,
Schurz had liquidated his Liberal Republican organization and
had returned to the regular Republican Party. But he was more
than ever determined to beat the Grant crowd and to master-
mind the election in '76 of his own reform candidate, Governor
Rutherford B. Hayes of Ohio.[2]

He found Ralph's *Herald* articles both a help and a hin-
drance. The Sioux agency fraud stories gave the War Department new ammunition in its old fight to get back the Indian

Bureau. Schurz had beaten the department for years, arguing that Army control meant mere imprisonment of the Indians and retelling often how the Army had agreed to haul the Cherokees to Indian Territory for ten dollars per Indian and then had collected one hundred and three dollars per Indian. He had maintained further that only civilians could solve the problem which was how to induce the Indians humanely to adopt the white man's economy. And now Schurz had cogent private reasons for opposing transfer. If Hayes became President, he was pledged to reward Schurz for lining up the German vote by making him Secretary of the Interior. Schurz wanted that powerful post with all the trimmings. The most important trimming was the Indian Bureau.

The House did pass a transfer bill, in spite of Schurz, but just then the sins of Mrs. William Belknap as reported by Ralph compromised the War Department and stalled a Senate vote on transfer up to June 25, 1876. The nation was stunned by the Little Big Horn disaster on that day in which the Sioux slaughtered General Custer and two hundred and sixty-four of his men. Thereafter, Schurz knew that transfer was no issue for the present. Too many voters interpreted Custer's defeat as proof that Army officers in general did not know as much as they thought they did about Indians.

Governor Hayes beat James G. Blaine for the Republican Presidential nomination on a breast-beating platform of honest government, tolerance to the South, hard money, conservation of resources and civil service reform. However, in the big fall campaign Hayes could not get better than a draw against Samuel J. Tilden, the Democratic candidate. Furthermore, to win the election he had to approve deals with conservative Southern Democrats which cast doubt on whether he stood for honest government after all. But he had a big ace in the hole. In March of '77, a special commission threw the contested election to Hayes. Before anybody could cry foul, President Hayes appointed as Secretary of the Interior the nation's leading reformer, Carl Schurz. That proved his sincerity to most people.

The Schurz appointment delighted Ralph Meeker. At Greeley, the Founder was not so pleased, recalling how Schurz had opposed Horace Greeley in '72. As for the attitude of Mr. James Gordon Bennett, Ralph's elegant boss, he was indifferent, now that the election story and the Indian Ring story were washed up. He cabled Ralph a few words of praise, gave him a month's vacation in Paris and ordered him on from there to cover the Russo-Turkish War.

In addition, Bennett raised Ralph's salary to a fat thirty-five dollars a week. That sum allowed him to send five dollars a week to his father in Greeley. Nathan Meeker had been needing financial help desperately for some time.

CHAPTER IV The Foundering Founder

DURING THOSE YEARS of national depression it seemed to Nathan Meeker that the whole world conspired to destroy him and his dream of a better life at Union Colony. His debts as he approached the age of sixty were ten times what they had been when he went broke in Ohio. Charles Storrs in New York hired two Greeley lawyers to badger him constantly for the thousand dollars owed by him to the Horace Greeley estate. Henry Ward Beecher's *Christian Union* held him liable for a loan of several hundred dollars which the paper had made to another colonist in 1870.

As the Greeleyites got hungrier and more desperate, they blamed the Founder for their troubles, and especially for successive grasshopper plagues and the failure of the rain to fall normally on the mountain watershed of the Cache la Poudre. A coalition of convivial members and old settlers led by General Cameron tried to ditch Meeker's whole temperance program. His establishment of a liberal Union church where all sects could meet was thrown up to him as proof that he was an atheist.

Actually, Meeker had become deeply religious in his unorthodox way. He believed in a just God within whose mind the affairs of men occurred and he felt that the personal purity of each human being was a part of that Universal Divinity. He still approved the moral teachings of the New Testament and he admired the intelligence of Jesus Christ. But he did not care for the dogma of Evangelical Christianity. He teased Arvilla about it, accusing her of being unable to admit that anyone could be tolerably respectable outside of her church. Arvilla was a devout Methodist those days and it confused and frightened her that her husband would not accept the New Testament literally. She wished he would not talk about God as though he were some not-too-respectable neighbor down the street.

To boost his failing income, Meeker went to New York and tried free-lance writing. He had less success than he had had as the *New York Mirror*'s water-loving poet in 1842. He also tried Territorial politics, seeking a seat as a Liberal Republican in the biennial assembly. General Cameron ran against him and beat him badly. To counter Meeker's anti-Grant editorials in the *Greeley Tribune,* Cameron induced a few friends to start an opposition paper, the *Colorado Sun.* The first *Sun* editor was William B. Vickers, whom Cameron had known back in Indiana. Vickers was a radical Republican and a savage promoter of prejudice. One of his peeves was Senator Charles Sumner, the liberal abolitionist who was a hero of Meeker's. Another peeve was the Colorado Ute Indians, whom he wanted to exterminate. Vickers was just the sort of person Meeker had hoped to exclude from the idealistic atmosphere of Union Colony.

While Ralph Meeker was in Dakota Territory making a name as a crime-buster, his weary father was moving toward a nervous breakdown. He lost weight. He developed a discouraged stoop which spoiled his good looks and gave a fragile cast to his tall, spare figure. His habitual expression now was a cold smile, half cynical, half pitying.

All his worst traits emerged under pressure of his frustrations. His brusqueness and tactlessness got out of hand. His Puritanism became so militant that he spent weeks trying to exclude a pool hall from Greeley and urging the populace to play chess and checkers. He spoiled the fun of the weekly lyceums which he had organized by preaching like a frenzied revivalist on the sins of drinking, smoking, gambling and being lazy. He could not argue dispassionately. He just told people.

At times he was needlessly offensive to neighboring communities. Of Cheyenne's young men he wrote:

> Detroit dandies wear earrings to keep their ears from flapping about in the high winds. In Cheyenne, the same class tie their ears over their heads.

He showed a vindictive side by keeping those he disliked out of the popular Farmers' Club. He lost friends by berating them in public for not taking up pet causes of his such as the annexation of the British Isles and Canada or vegetarianism or the abolition of profanity in children. He seemed to hunt ways to be obnoxious. Greeleyites loved trout fishing and picking wild flowers along the mountain streams to the west. Meeker campaigned against both. Fishing, he said, was cruel to trout. Picking wild flowers was childish.

The Founder could not quite decide where to stand on sex. His admiration as a youth for sexual liberty had been based more on his scientific interest in eugenics than on a belief in careless love as emotional therapy. Later he wrote that "friendship between the sexes is more useful than love since great minds have been developed thereby." His relations with Arvilla had produced five children in twelve years but at times he seemed to think that there was something a bit indecent about his virility. He puzzled his wife once by declaring that, for all her physical charms, her conversation had always stimulated him more than her body. Arvilla was not sure that this was a compliment.

From the start at Greeley, Meeker had declaimed against traveling theatrical companies, and he had moral doubts even about plays presented by the Greeley Dramatic Association. But his strongest aversion was dancing, which he described as being "in the highest degree unfavorable to mental culture." To illustrate its dangers further, he published a satirical essay, "Waltz-ing Girls of Nevada":

> A Winnemucca girl — yum, yum! — creeps closely and timidly up to her partner as if she would like to get into his vest pocket, and melts with ecstasy as the strains of "The Blue Danube" sweep through the hall. A Virginia City girl throws both her arms around her partner's neck, rolls up her eyes, and, as she floats away, is heard to murmur, "Oh, hug me, John!"

While Meeker was denouncing man's base instincts, an un-kind fate added to his perplexities the sensational trial of his old friend, Henry Ward Beecher. Since 1847, when Beecher became pastor of Plymouth Church in Brooklyn, Meeker had been uplifted by his noble personality even though he dismissed his evangelism. In a world of shifting values, Beecher was Meeker's granite point of reference, his proof that a man's spirit could be incorruptible.

Incredibly, it was one of Beecher's best friends and his col-league on the *Christian Union,* Theodore Tilton, who charged the great man with seducing Elizabeth, his pretty wife. Eliza-abeth was twenty-two years younger than Beecher. Tilton claimed that he was married to her by Beecher in 1855 and that Beecher controlled his base instincts where Elizabeth was concerned until July 3, 1870, when he was fifty-seven years old. On that fatal day he slept with Elizabeth experimentally and continued to sleep with her for quite a while afterwards.

The trial attracted as much world-wide attention as the Battle of Gettysburg and it cost Beecher one hundred thousand dollars in defense fees. It ended in a hung jury and Beecher continued at Plymouth Church as though nothing had hap-pened. But Meeker had to confess that his idol was a "lavender-scented paradox," particularly when he signed a statement admitting improper relations with Elizabeth, and then repudi-ated it.

From January to July, 1875, Meeker followed the scandal

on the Associated Press wire with helpless fascination as it un-
folded in Brooklyn City Court. To the hundreds of columns
of testimony which he published in the *Greeley Tribune,* he
added tragic side pieces about the trial's effect on Beecher's
sister, immortal author of *Uncle Tom's Cabin,* Harriet Beecher
Stowe. He printed the remarks of the suffragette, Susan B.
Anthony, who construed the trial as a warning not to under-
estimate the power of a woman. He published the joyful com-
muniqués of the free-love advocate, Victoria C. Woodhull. She
argued that if a man of Beecher's moral grandeur got around
to doing what came naturally to him, so should everyone else.

Meeker had barely recovered from the Beecher affair when
he was shaken by scandal close to home. The accused this time
was the incorrigible booster of Colorado, William N. Byers,
who had been so helpful during Meeker's Denver visit in '69
and who had sold him much Denver Pacific land for Union
Colony. Meeker had denounced Byers in '73 for promoting
wild irrigation schemes on the South Platte. But the editor
of the *Greeley Tribune* deeply admired the editor of the
pioneer *Rocky Mountain News* and regarded him as one of the
West's greatest men.

Meeker admired Byers also as the upholder of righteousness
among Denver's giddier elements. But, on April 19, 1876, a
young lady named Mrs. Hattie E. Sancomb tried to shoot
Byers in Denver with a pearl-handled pistol, stating that he
had not been exactly righteous in his relations with her and
besides he had broken her heart. Byers was too paralyzed with
fright to duck, but his wife grabbed the pistol and detained
Mrs. Sancomb until police arrived. They tossed the lady into
jail to reconsider the wisdom of attacking one of Colorado's first
citizens.

At the start of the hearings, Mrs. Sancomb was described by
a reporter as a graceful milliner from Lawrence, Kansas, "with
eyes of coal gray tint, regular features, dazzling teeth, pencilled
eyebrows, small poised head and wavy auburn hair. Her voice

was soft and her manner caressing." She said that she had been the loyal mistress of Byers for four years in a comfortable love nest at Golden and had copies of his letters to prove it. She had given up the original letters, she said, after the attempted shooting as the price of her release from jail.

In his rebuttal, Byers declared modestly that Mrs. Sancomb was insanely jealous of him and had persecuted him for two years because he had not returned her love. But she could not claim to have been a loyal mistress. She was, Byers said, free with her favors, "only recently having had connection with a man named Burns." The hearings petered out with no decision. Meeker summarized the matter in the *Greeley Tribune* of December 5, 1877: "The lesson is that the purity of the family relation should be guarded with as much care as the gold and jewels and the riches of all the world."

The Meeker family relation was of sterling purity, though the Founder had a deep interest in women and did his best to encourage female participation in Union Colony affairs. He built the big square two-story Meeker home of adobe brick, partly for its effect on Arvilla's morale. It was hard on the budget but it gave Arvilla confidence, especially when town gossips began tearing Meeker to bits for being financially irresponsible while putting on airs as a man of superior intelligence.

Debt or no debt, the Meekers boasted two bright, tasteful parlors, each with fireplace. You would have had to go to Denver to find anything as fine as the Founder's eight-foot-high cherry desk or Arvilla's marble sideboard and Palestine china and imported Italian vase in the shape of a braceleted hand. There were wall mementoes from Trumbull Phalanx and from Greenwich Village and framed letters signed by Henry Clay and Ralph Waldo Emerson. A feature of the big kitchen was a faded sampler *Wrought by Arvilla Smith, 1827, aged 12.*

It was Meeker's love for Arvilla and her love for him that carried the Founder through these several years of personal crisis. She believed in him as completely as she believed in a

literal God with a beard. Her pride in him was so great that
she could weep with happiness just thinking about it. Her most
bitter moments came when she allowed herself to become a
trifle impatient with his sublime disregard of the realities. After
a quarter-century of marriage she could still write him adoring
valentines like this:

> The love that lasts through every strife
> 'Mid all the marring scenes of life
> Is just the love for me.
> This priceless heavenly treasure
> Is what I've found in thee.
> I'll sing this love forever,
> The love of you and me.
> The love that lasts through every stage
> Of youth and beauty and old age
> Is just the love for me.
> This godlike precious treasure
> Is what I've found in thee.
> I'll sing this love forever,
> The love of you and me.
> > *Your wife*
> > A. D. S. MEEKER

Meeker reciprocated her feelings. She was the one object in
his life which he accepted almost headlong, almost but not quite
without intellectual reservations. On March 10, 1873, while he
was in New York striving to make money, he wrote to her:

> I am, of course, alone, but being alone, thoughts pile upon
> me. It seems to me it is but a short bridge to cross into a
> brighter and more beautiful land and that I have to make
> only a determined, a well-directed sharp-cut effort to reach
> the bridge. It seems to me I am standing between two worlds
> and that I see much but still obscurely of both. I want, first, to
> pay my debts, though in one sense I owe nobody on earth,
> unless it is you. Then I want to do all that I can that will do
> anybody else good. Farewell, Dear Wife.
> > Truly,
> > N. C. MEEKER

A month later, he wrote in grateful response to her encouragement:

EVER-BELOVED WIFE:

I am well and in good spirits and I think of you by night and by day and with thankfulness that I have been able to make the later years of your life happier. Apparently my affairs are unchanged but this may not be so, for all things at all times are changing, and a change of some kind will come to me soon. I do not ask, I do not wish, I do not need much for myself, unless it be to live with you always. But I would like to be in a situation to help the girls and Ralph and to establish more firmly the cause of Temperance, Morality and Religion in our Valley, that the longing and the cheerless and the faithful everywhere may be encouraged.

In October of '76, Meeker's affairs were improving a little; he wrote Arvilla from Philadelphia in a gay mood:

Suppose we should be separated, suppose we should have another wife and husband. Suppose you had servants and a carriage and money to spend as you pleased and that your new husband were handsome and polite and correct in all his habits, that he treated you most respectfully, that he were honored by the world. Still you would not have any reccollection of past experiences, the youth we had together.

On the other hand, should my new wife be handsome and rich and kind and loving and true, should she be proud of my name and take delight in me, should she welcome me as I come to her chamber with the tenderest marks of affection her eyes shining with that light no husband mistakes. Still, I could not forget the little wife of my youth, could not forget her prophetic confidence in me. I could not forget her painful labors, her kindness and condecencion.

(All his life Meeker had trouble spelling words like "recollection" and "condescension.")

He continued the letter, referring to his despairing return to Greeley from New York in August of '73:

Above all I could not forget the sparkle of those innumerable millions of diamonds as rained on me in our chamber on that summer night of my return while she alone of all the household had waited up for me. But we are not separated. We have not chosen new companions. We remain to each other still bound by the cords of the dearest love. I expect now you will think I am still courting you. Well, I am!

Meeker now threw grammar to the winds:

To cherish is the same as cultivate and what I have did was to cultivate my love for you, to admire you all I could, to be blind to some things and to make all I could of your good qualities. What you might be in comparison with other women was not to be considered. To me you was to be the only woman in the world. I was to believe, and I *did* believe, that you was created with as much beauty and as much choice qualities as any woman, and that I would cherish you for many more qualities than I saw would be developed.

Arvilla had no complaint of her Nathan as a lover. And, since she thought he was a genius, she did not expect him to be much of a father. She was merely amused at the way his long legs carried him rapidly down Monroe Street to safety in the *Greeley Tribune* office whenever his daughters threatened to bring to him their strange feminine problems. But Arvilla could be acid. Now and again she hinted that poor son George might have lived longer if his father had spent more time at Trumbull Phalanx trying to cure George's ague and less time trying to make an American success of Fourier socialism.

She held Meeker partly at fault also for the fact that black-haired Rozene had developed into a choleric spinster of twenty-seven, too selfish and complaining to hold a man. At Hiram, when Rozene was a toddler, Meeker, who was baby sitting, had let her fall into a well five feet deep while he had struggled to master the philosophy of Immanuel Kant. Her screams finally had penetrated his Kantian world of pure reason; but she was unconscious by the time he hauled her from the well, and she had remained so as the doctor tried to unwater her by rolling her over a barrel. At last Arvilla had arrived, stripped herself naked and revived Rozene by warming her against her own body in bed for three hours. Rozene's mind, Arvilla believed, was marred permanently by the near-drowning.

Mary Meeker, aged twenty-two, was Rozene's opposite — a roses-and-cream, clinging-vine type with a sweet air of needing strong male arms about her to keep her from doing something foolish. She had been almost engaged several times. At the Greeley Literary Society, people were moved to tears whenever she recited "O Mary, go and call the cattle home, and call the cattle home, and call the cattle home, across the sands o' Dee!"

Josephine Meeker at eighteen just missed having Mary's beauty. Instead, Josie had style.[1] She was tall like the Founder and her walk was proud and graceful. Her eager blue eyes gave her face a vivacious luminosity. Her waist-long hair was blond. Her voice was gentle but positive — even authoritative if she felt that way. She was, like Ralph Meeker, practical at the core. While Arvilla wept about their poverty and Meeker wrote transcendental essays on the subject, Josephine hunted up someone to teach her shorthand and got Ralph to send her one of those newfangled Yost Writing Machines with its six banks of letter-keys and two banks of numbers. She had been promised a stenographer's job soon at an awning factory in Denver.

Everyone in Greeley called her "Josie," and loved her. The children whom she taught at the Methodist Sunday School called her "Birdie Dear" and brought her fruit and pets with broken legs to fix. Her mother was a little in awe of her and called her "the Sacred One" in her prayers. (Josie called Arvilla "Goody.") Josie didn't feel at all sacred, and had her share of earthly fun on Sundays when the young people hiked up Longs Peak or rode the cars to Denver to see the sights. At Colony social affairs she irritated her father by wearing ten-button kid gloves and flowers in her hair. She rode horses astride until Meeker forbade it by edict. On her first ride in Mary's side-saddle she was thrown from the horse and had a concussion which kept her in a coma for twenty-four hours.

The slight improvement of Meeker's affairs in '76 had been

due to the steady income which he received for some months as
caretaker of the Colorado display at the Centennial Exposition
in Philadelphia. The Colorado display was a romantic version
of a mountain man's cabin with mounted bighorn sheep and
elk trophies, fat geese hanging high, big game rifles and snow-
shoes. It was immensely popular and Meeker enjoyed standing
around in buckskins looking as handsome and capable as his
own fictional hero, Captain Armstrong, and explaining frontier
life to the thrilled ladies in bustles and the sports in silk hats.
He wrote often for the *New York Sun* that summer about the
Exposition, but Editor Charles Dana wanted nothing more
from him when the Exposition closed.

Back in Greeley he faced the old money problem again. He
made it known to political friends that he would accept the
postmastership of Greeley. Nothing happened. He put his
name in for American Agriculture Commissioner at the proposed Paris Exposition of '78. But '78 was a year off. Then, on
a bleak winter day in '77, came one of Meeker's blackest moments. It was an ultimatum from Charles Storrs in New York.
The letter was the last in a long series of demands on behalf of
the Greeley estate. "We have no option," Storrs wrote, "than
to send your claim forward for collection. . . . We think you
would do well to call upon our attorneys and act in harmony
with them and, if you will make over as security for this debt
any and all properties which they could get under legal proceedings, they certainly will prefer this method and it may save
you cost and trouble to do so."

Poor businessman that he was, Meeker still was not deceived
by this threat of Storrs to seize "any and all properties which
they could get under legal proceedings." Many Greeleyites
knew the lenient oral terms of Greeley's loan to Meeker in
1870. Storrs was not likely to force their testimony into court.
And Meeker had very little property any more which could be
seized. Months earlier he had signed the *Greeley Tribune* over
to Ralph, Josie and E. J. Carver, his editorial associate. He had

put the house at Monroe and Plum in Arvilla's name, and also some nearby lots which he had taken in place of Union Colony farm land.

But the Founder was determined to pay that thousand-dollar debt, and at the earliest possible time. It had become an obsession by now, a blot on family honor that enlarged in his mind like a mental cancer. During March, Meeker rode the Denver Pacific to Denver to talk to a political friend, Bela M. Hughes, the prominent Denver attorney. His purpose was to ask Hughes about getting a Colorado Indian agency. Agents were paid only fifteen hundred dollars a year but their expenses were small. With an agency job, he ought to be able to pay off the Greeley estate in a couple of years.

CHAPTER V How to Get an Indian
Agency

MEEKER COULD NOT HAVE GONE for advice to a better man than
General Bela M. Hughes (the "General" was honorary, bestowed by his uncle, a Kentucky Governor). The genial and
imperturbable Hughes had been a promoter of Ben Holladay's
Overland Stage to Salt Lake and of the Denver Pacific Railroad.
But he was peculiarly potent as a Democrat, sharing the State's
leadership with the Golden tycoon, W. A. H. Loveland, and
Thomas M. Patterson, a Denver lawyer. Though the Colorado
Republicans warned the world daily that Hughes, Patterson
and Loveland were the worst rascals on earth, they worked with
them in matters of mutual benefit.

Hughes had admired Nathan Meeker for his long service as
a writer of anti-Grant editorials. But when Meeker came to his
Denver office and stated his desire, Hughes had to tell him that
he could ride a kite to Mars easier than he could get an Indian
agency. He analyzed the situation, reviewing how Territorial
politics had been dominated for a decade by two worshipers of
President Grant and by their Denver Republican following.
One worshiper was the richest man in the Rockies, Jerome B.
Chaffee (his daughter later married one of Grant's sons). The
other was ex-Governor John Evans. Both of these Grant worshipers had yearned to be United States Senators, which could
only occur if Colorado Territory gained enough population
and influence to be made a state. But the pro-Grant leader of
the Central City Republicans, Henry M. Teller, had yearned

to be a Senator too. He had refused to push the claims of the Territory for statehood unless he was to be rewarded with one of those two Senatorships.

While the Denver Republicans and the Central City Republicans had feuded, the despised and underrated Democrats in '74 had slipped in Thomas Patterson as Territorial delegate to Congress. This dire event had frightened the feuding Republicans so badly that they had composed their differences and had swept the new state's first elections in 1876. Teller and Chaffee had become Colorado Senators, Judge James Belford had been sent to the House, and John L. Routt had beaten Bela Hughes for Governor.

Well, Bela Hughes told Meeker, one way for a man to get an Indian Agency was through his representatives in Washington — if they were favorably disposed toward him. But no Grant Republican was apt to be favorably disposed toward the *Greeley Tribune*'s anti-Grant editor. And, in Hughes's opinion, Meeker's job-getting prospects would not be much better if he applied for an Indian agency to Secretary of the Interior Carl Schurz directly. Everyone, it seemed, had good reasons for disliking Meeker. Schurz was bound to recall that the *Greeley Tribune* had attacked him viciously during the Liberal Republican convention of '72. Furthermore, even if Schurz overlooked Meeker's past sins, he would be reluctant to grant a political favor to the father of an important *New York Herald* writer, Ralph Meeker. When Schurz had become Secretary, he had begun at once sweeping out the Indian Ring, firing Grant-approved agents and acting like a model of political purity. If Nathan Meeker got an Indian agency, the Indian Ring might proclaim that Schurz was buying Ralph's journalistic support.

Or so Hughes believed. Meeker, disheartened, returned to Greeley. But soon Hughes wrote to him expressing less pessimism. He had learned that Schurz was letting up on reform and seeking Republican harmony because he feared a Democratic victory in 1880. He was wooing Henry M. Teller, whom he had antagonized at first, realizing that the new Senator from the fast-growing State of Colorado was the political champion also of the vast Territories of Wyoming, Dakota, Montana and Idaho. When Teller joined others in asking Schurz to make Edward A. Hayt the new Commissioner of Indian Affairs, Schurz agreed, just to please Teller.

And so, since Schurz and Teller seemed to have Edward A. Hayt in common, Hughes now induced Meeker to write to Teller and to Representative Belford about an Indian agency. Teller replied quickly:

DEAR SIR:

I have your letter and have spoken to Senator Chaffee. He says you have treated him badly without cause and I am frank to say I think he is correct. I do not think you have treated him properly on the question of a grant of land to the School of Mines. But I should like to do something for you if I can. It will be difficult for me to do so without his cooperation. I think you ought to write him a personal letter.

HENRY M. TELLER

Meeker had forgotten how he had fought Jerome Chaffee's School of Mines project at Golden, hoping Greeley town would get the school land grant instead. While Meeker composed apologies to Senator Chaffee, Judge Belford's letter arrived from Washington:

DEAR SIR:

I dare say it would certainly afford me great pleasure to assist you in procuring the appointment you desire but I feel it will be impossible. No removals will be made except for cause. It occurred to me that some appointment might be got as soon as matters quiet down. Should you think of one, let me know. I will do all in my power to assist you.

JAMES B. BELFORD

These letters were not encouraging, but they were not flat dismissals either. Meanwhile, at Bela Hughes's suggestion, Meeker was gathering testimonials from friends back East, including the illustrious first citizen of New York, old Peter

Cooper, the great government geologist, F. V. Hayden, and the somewhat tarnished but still powerful Henry Ward Beecher. An old *New York Tribune* colleague, I. G. Cooper (no apparent relation to Peter Cooper) began pulling journalistic strings. On March 31, 1877, Cooper wrote Meeker:

> DEAR FRIEND:
> Believe me, yours of the 26th has stirred me deeply. Am glad you have written just as you have. I can't tell of course what may come from my efforts. But I know Carl Schurz and Whitelaw Reid are very intimate and believe that one has much influence with the other, if that influence of W. R. can be gotten, knowing as I do how hard it is to have him give it exercise. Meanwhile, our good friend Zeb White, now in Washington, and by circumstance brought nearer to Carl Schurz, may possibly be of aid to you. Have you written to him? Write freely, even as you have to me, will you not? That you have been treated shamefully where you are I need not be told. Step forward! Faint not!
> Sincerely yours,
> COOPER
> *Destroy this.*

Arvilla had mentioned Meeker's Indian Agency idea in a letter to Ralph at his Russo-Turkish war post near the Black Sea. Ralph sent a feeler to Whitelaw Reid's *Tribune* correspondent in Washington, Zeb White. On March 29, 1877, White wrote Ralph in part:

> I am informed that the Interior Department says there are no vacancies. You know things are changed under this Administration. Appointments are no longer made through political influence. If they were, and I was at liberty to use my influence, I might do a great deal. As it is, the most I can do for anybody is, after his case is presented, to say to the proper officer or to the President what I know about the applicant. That I would most gladly do in your father's case.
> Your friend,
> ZEB L. WHITE

Early in April, Bela Hughes wrote Meeker that a good post might be available soon at the White River Ute Agency in northwest Colorado. He had heard that the agent, E. H. Danforth, was not pleasing his superiors. And then, on April 16, Meeker got a significant letter from Ralph, containing data on how to approach Carl Schurz. Ralph's unnamed informant was R. W. C. (Bob) Mitchell, a young ex-newsman whom Ralph had known for years. Bob Mitchell was a friend of Nathan Meeker's friend, F. V. Hayden, and he may have gone to Greeley with Hayden in '74 to examine Meeker's mythical coalbeds. Somewhere, Bob had met and relished the graceful Josie Meeker. But it was his high regard for Ralph's integrity that induced him to run the personal risk of secretly helping Ralph's father at a time when his employer was under intense public scrutiny. For Bob Mitchell was the private secretary of Carl Schurz. Ralph wrote Meeker in part:

> DEAR FATHER:
> He [Bob Mitchell] says for you to make application to Schurz direct in simple language, giving your knowledge and experience as a matter of form and get what signatures you can from the leading people in Colorado. F. V. Hayden in Washington will present a personal application, I suppose. My friend says that when the document is ready, someone in Washington should see Secretary Schurz personally. I guess that Hayden is the best man. As you say, he will do it.
>
> Yours,
>
> RALPH

THE MEEKERS heard no more from Mitchell during '77. In the late fall, Nathan Meeker began receiving from both Colorado Senators private reports of the sort issued only to political henchmen, or to someone about to get a government job. In December, Teller sent Meeker bound volumes of the *Congressional Record* with his speeches marked. The speeches ridiculed Schurz's conservation schemes for Western lands and his suggestions for treating the Indians with abstract justice. Teller had complained to the Senate often that the Secretary of the Interior had an Easterner's unrealistic approach to Western problems.

It seemed to Meeker that Teller was informing him by way of the marked speeches that Teller, not Schurz, should be Secretary of the Interior, and might be, when this foolish Hayes crew was voted out. Therefore, if Meeker got an Indian agency, he might be wise to heed the advice of Henry M. Teller.

Through December, Meeker noted evidence that Bob Mitchell in Washington was working under cover to help him. Zeb White wrote that he had been in Carl Schurz's office one fall day and heard Mitchell recommend Meeker to the Secretary for an Indian agency.

As Meeker's hopes rose, his appetite improved and his spirit revived. Soon his imagination began to resume the extravagant soaring of his youth. Maybe the old man wasn't through yet! Maybe his fictional hero, Captain Armstrong, would become real and actually perform his civilizing miracles. Long ago Meeker had dreamed of bringing the perfect life to Trumbull Phalanx, and he had failed. He had failed not quite so badly at Hiram, and he had barely failed at Greeley.

Perhaps the Lord had planned these three failures just to test his servant's courage and to prepare him for a final brilliant success at an Indian agency. The White River Ute Agency, perhaps. With all his experience in handling sophisticated white colonists, he ought to be able to manage simple savages. He would win their love and confidence and raise them out of their misery by teaching them the wonders of modern society. He would lead them to wealth and happiness, and then he would be called by the President of the United States to perform the same miracle for the rest of the country's unhappy red men. He would be made Commissioner of Indian Affairs for life by a grateful nation, and he would go down in history as the George Washington of the American Indian.

With some misgivings, Meeker outlined the new version of his old dream to Arvilla. He was delighted to find her much less concerned about going into the Colorado wilds with him than she had been in '69 about leaving New York. She described her feelings in a letter to Ralph. Part of it read:

> When Mr. Meeker proposed getting an agency I told him he would be successful and to go ahead. He said, "why do you think so." Because, I said, everything seems a turning about somehow of what has been our misfortune to become fortunate and now it seems likely we shall in time be free from debt. Even the thought of it being so is an unspeakable comfort to me. It would be an everlasting blot on your father's name to die a penniless man because it would appear that he was nothing more than a fraud, for how could a man plan a colony if he had not the ability to take care of himself and family? This seeming neglect of family is why so many in Greeley come to look on him as they do.
>
> Affectionately,
>
> A. D. MEEKER

THE BRIGHT NEW YEAR of 1878 had hardly begun when Meeker received from Senator Teller a letter describing an interview with the Commissioner of Indian Affairs, Edward A. Hayt, whom he had assisted into office. Teller's letter, dated January 3, read:

> I went to the Commissioner of Indian Affairs and posted your claims for an agency and designated White River Agency as the one I wanted for you. Now I think I have a good show. The Commissioner said he was not at all satisfied with the agent at White River who knows nothing of irrigation or farming in the West. I am anxious you should have it because I feel you should do something that would be of benefit to our people and to the Indians. I am confident that a good honest agent in White River Agency can in a short time make great improvements in the condition of the Indians. There I believe the Indians can be taught to raise cattle and I have an idea you are the man to do it. Now

if you had the place it would pay you $1,500 a year and you would have a house to live in free, a garden and so forth. So I think you can save something. It is only 100 miles from the railroad and quite easy. If you will accept I will commence work. Let me hear soon.

HENRY M. TELLER

Ten days later, Meeker knew that he was in. He got a note, signed R. W. C. Mitchell, reading: "Just talked with Commissioner Hayt of the Indian Bureau and he said he intends giving you an agency, probably the Ute Agency." Then F. V. Hayden wrote to Meeker.

MY DEAR FRIEND:

Your name has been sent to the Senate for the White River Agency. I spoke to Mr. Chaffee about your confirmation and he said there would be no difficulty. I shall see other Senators from time to time, though I think you will soon be safe. I congratulate you much. Mr. Mitchell, a friend of your Josie's, and private secretary to Secretary Schurz, took an active part for you. I shall keep a close look-out.

Sincerely,

F. H. HAYDEN

Actual confirmation of Meeker's appointment was delayed until the Congressional Record announced it on March 18, 1878. The anxious interval of waiting had been hard on the nerves but meanwhile the Meekers had found distraction in a series of letters from son Ralph chronicling a matter which had been on his mind for some time.

When Ralph had reached New York in February after covering the Russo-Turkish War he became enamored of a Greenwich Village damsel named Miss Carmelita Circovitch. Carmelita returned some of his love, but said she could not go all the way because he had got so nearly bald in Turkey that she could see his scalp and she could not marry a baldheaded man. For a frantic week Ralph tried this and that. Then, on his day off, he hurried to see "a French doctor uptown." The French doctor examined his pate and contracted to give him a good covering of hair for fifty dollars, a reduced price, since the patient was a famous journalist.

The French doctor, Ralph wrote, was a marvel. He told Ralph that wearing hats had nothing to do with his baldness. The true reason was that his head had long been troubled with "scurf and rash in the blood" which the doctor treated by putting on "a celebrated wash from a well-known establishment in Paris. I also take little pills."

Midway through the cure, Ralph wrote that Carmelita was getting fonder of him because "soft young hair is coming all over my head. I have been troubled with itching for years in the hair and, at times, soreness. I did not suppose it amounted to anything. But it was this, and the barber's heavy brushes, that killed my hair on top of head." The dramatic climax came in mid-March. "The process is scientifically marvelous! If my hair continues to grow, I'll have some to comb soon on top as well as on the sides! Fifty dollars for the treatment hurt, but I'd rather lose $50 than have a smooth scalp."

In the next letter, Ralph said nothing about his hair but disclosed that he and Carmelita were engaged.

Nathan Meeker was busy during April preparing to go to White River — which, he found, was one hundred and eighty-five mountainous miles south of the U. P. station at Rawlins, Wyoming Territory, instead of the hundred "easy" miles mentioned by Senator Teller. He had been instructed to staff the Agency himself and he was selecting young Greeleyites for all the jobs. He wanted Josie and Mary on the payroll, too, but Ralph warned him against it. Senator Teller and Bela Hughes both sent him best wishes and advice.

The new Agent received their suggestions with grateful inattention. Already he was going on his own, picturing the White River Utes not as Indians who might present problems but as "his Utes," who awaited his coming with joy, waited for him to lead them out of barbarism and sin into a new life of spiritual purity and physical comfort.

As Arvilla explained it to Ralph, Nathan Meeker, approaching sixty-one, was looking these days like a young crusading Phalangist again. He was gaining weight. His stoop was gone. He was rereading Charles Fourier. His blue eyes sparkled with the vigor of his faith in cooperation. His swinging shoulders as he strode about were exactly like the shoulders of his hero in *The Adventures of Captain Armstrong*.

CHAPTER VI The Sky People

ON MAY 3, 1878, Meeker left Greeley for the White River Ute
Agency which served two main bands and several smaller bands,
each with its own chief. The bands had arrived separately in the
White River country for various reasons and they had no special
unity except that they acknowledged, more or less, Chief Ouray
of the Uncompahgre Utes as their tribal leader. The Uncompahgres were called the Tabeguache Utes also.

Ouray's Tabeguache ancestors were the first Utes in Colorado
though by no means the first human beings. The first illustrious pioneer was the Folsom Man, who is alleged to have
crossed Bering Strait many millenniums ago and to have moved
south along the Rockies to New Mexico.[1] Much, much later,
during Christ's time, the highly civilized Basket Makers flour-
ished along streams flowing into the Dolores River, and along
the San Juan River of southwestern Colorado, but they were
mysteriously displaced around A.D. 700 by the round-headed ancestors of the Pueblo, the Cliff Dwellers. These Indians expanded
the Basket Maker pit house into the delightful cliff dwellings
preserved in Mesa Verde National Park. After some centuries,
the Cliff Dwellers began to depart southward and reappeared
as the Pueblo Indians, who remain scarcely changed today in
the Rio Grande Valley. By A.D. 1298, the last of the
Pueblos had left Mesa Verde, partly because the climate had
turned arid and partly because they were being harried by
unattractive newcomers — filthy and miserable nomads who
lived on roots, berries, fish, grasshoppers, rats and rabbits. They
ran around naked winter and summer. The filthy and miserable

nomads were the Ute Indians, and where they came from nobody knows. They were kin to the ambitious Aztecs and spoke
a similar tongue-twisting language full of harsh consonants.[2]
While the Aztecs were conquering Mexico in the fourteenth
and fifteenth centuries, the Utes were wandering around the
Rockies trying to keep out of the way of the Athabascans (whose
singsong language sounded like Chinese). The Athabascans
had been filtering south from the Yukon country and were
settling in New Mexico and Arizona as two separate peoples,
the Navajos and the Apaches. The Athabascans were fearsome
because they possessed a new weapon, the bow and arrow.

The Utes, most of them small, dark and stocky, were a branch
of a linguistic family called the Shoshone, which included the
Snakes, Bannocks and Comanches of Wyoming and Idaho.
The Shoshone on the whole were up-and-coming but the Utes
were pitifully gauche, weak and too lacking in good sense to
come in out of the rain. They had no political structure and
they lived in small family groups scattered over a vast expanse
of Colorado mountain and Utah plateau lands which nobody
else wanted. They were oddly various. Some of them grew
straggly beards. Some were as big and as tall as Sioux Indians.
It is not certain whether they ever saw the Spanish conquista-
dores of the sixteenth century. In the early 1600s, a huddle of
Ute families in Southwest Colorado heard about the Spanish
colonists at Santa Fe and Taos and longed to visit them. However, they put off the two-hundred-mile trip east for fifty years,
fearing that the Navajos would shoot arrows into them on their
way down the Chama River to the Rio Grande.

They traveled to Santa Fe at last in 1660 and they may have
been escorted the last hundred miles by a band of friendly
Jicarilla Apaches who lived along the Chama. They found
Santa Fe to be a collection of boxlike adobe homes for a Spanish
population of five hundred. All around it, and especially northward to Taos, were Spanish haciendas and Pueblo Indian
villages. The subject Pueblo Indian population was about

seventy thousand people. There may have been a total of three thousand Spanish colonists in the whole Rio Grande valley.

The Ute tourists took a polite interest in Santa Fe homes, the Catholic church, cigarettes, onions, waltzing, peppers, blankets, the long brown gowns of the priests and the muskets of Philip IV's presidio soldiers. But what really thrilled them was the spectacle of the horse. Western history has no more fascinating story than that of these Spanish horses, brought to horseless America by men like Cortes during his conquest of the Aztecs in 1519 and by explorers like Coronado, who toured New Mexico with hundreds of them in 1540–1541.

At first sight of these fabulous creatures, the Utes were terrified. But, as they watched the colonists wrangling them, feeding them, grooming them and, above all, riding them without fatalities, their fear changed to ecstatic adoration. Before these Indians headed homeward, the thought of owning horses was all they could talk about, and it was not long before they did acquire a few gentle mounts in exchange for buckskins. By this time, they had learned how to use the Athabascan bow and they were killing enough deer to establish a buckskin economy.

No less authorities on equines than Frank Gilbert Roe and J. Frank Dobie have written that the Colorado Utes were among the first, if not the very first, North American horse Indians. Roe has stressed that most Indians who took on horses were not intrinsically altered by them. But in contrast to most, the imaginations of the Utes were fired by horses to such a pitch as to completely change their tribal personality. From the start, they revered horses out of gratitude for being freed from horseless millenniums of misery and inferiority. They put them in the same beloved class of personal property as wives, children and dogs. As their joy in life replaced their fear of it, they lost their hangdog psychology and became a happy, musical, curious, poetic people, full of dancing and mischief.[3]

They never could conceive of such sacrilege as eating a horse, though some other tribes were able to ride them and eat them too, and some just ate them. Inspired by their horse-love, the Utes mastered horsemanship as quickly as motor-loving Americans mastered motor cars. In a few generations, they became superb riders, equaled only by their cousins, the Comanches, who left Wyoming gradually after 1680 and moved to eastern New Mexico so that they could raid Spanish ranches for horses.

It was wonderful how well it worked out for the Utes. Decade by decade, the use of horses passed from Ute family to Ute family, northwesterly along their Rocky Mountain corridor, across the magnificent divides of Western Colorado and over the Uncompahgre-Tabeguache Plateau into Utah. In the process, they made a discovery: the high valleys which nobody else had wanted contained grasses of very high protein content. Using these grasses for forage, they developed a pinto pony fourteen hands high — wiry, self-supporting, sure-footed, requiring no care, and so strong as to wear out two Rio Grande horses.

The divine creature vastly extended the Utes' geographical range. It allowed them to hunt more fruitfully in their own country and to trespass on the hunting grounds of old enemies like the Navajos in the south. It allowed them to accumulate buckskin in commercial quantities and to transport it for sale in Santa Fe and in Taos. And soon they ceased to be nomads and practiced instead a vertical migration. They spent their winters at permanent camps in secluded mountain valleys under seven thousand feet of altitude, where snowfall was light and where grass was thick for the horses. In summer, they followed deer up the streams to alpine meadows.

As their food supply increased, they were able to live in much larger groups. Families combined into clans and clans into bands of a hundred people or more. The art of politics was born. Heads of families assembled and chose chiefs and sub-chiefs of the bands. Promising youngsters were made captains to carry out policies formulated by the elders. Ambitious chiefs plotted to set up someday as head chief of the whole Ute tribe.

All the while, the Utes continued to acquire breeding stock because they needed horses much faster than they could raise them. Increasingly, they became middlemen, buying horses from the Spanish colonists, wrangling them through their mountains and selling them to the Snakes and Bannocks of Wyoming and Idaho, who passed them along in turn to the Crows, Blackfeet, Sioux and Cheyennes in the north and to the Nez Percés and Flatheads in the northwest.

In this way, the Utes made the pleasant transition from passive, starving, dirty proletarians to plump, clean, aggressive capitalists with time to bathe or go trout fishing just for fun. But Spanish horses were expensive, and the buckskin supply was limited. So the Utes went into the slave business. They captured Navajo women and children and traded them to Santa Fe and Taos families for horses. They captured Paiute children, also, from beyond Salt Lake — and even occasional Pueblo Indians and half-breed Spanish from around Abiquiu. The colonists trained the slave girls to be housemaids. The slave boys became vaqueros and sheepmen and piñon-wood gatherers. The Spaniards treated them well because they hoped to make good Catholics of them. When the slave children grew up, the colonists usually set them free. If the Utes had no Navajo slave children on hand, they sold to the Spaniards their own children, instructing them to rejoin the tribe later.

All these changes occurred to the Utes in three or four generations. And then Ute horsemen expanded boldly east from their home mountains, over the Continental Divide, across the parks of Colorado and into the Great Plains. Here they ran into mounted bands of Algonquian Indians — Cheyennes and Arapahoes — who had been pressed out of the Dakotas by the Sioux and who meant to exclude all others from their hunting lands between the Arkansas and Platte Rivers. They met also their Comanche cousins, south of the Arkansas, and a buffer band or two of Jicarilla Apaches who held the Comanches east of the Front Range of the Rockies. By now, the Utes and Jicarillas were relatives as well as friends, having intermarried a great deal.

The Utes were awed by the wealth of the Plains Indians, which derived from the buffalo as supplier of inexhaustible food; hides for robes, clothes, moccasins and warm, palatial tepees; and bones for tools and ornament. All their property seemed superior to the Utes', but the Utes learned soon not to fear them. As products of a sterner environment, the Utes had been taught from childhood to bring down the wariest small game and to outmaneuver unseen foes. They could handle a bow faster and see better than most plainsmen, who didn't need to hit anything smaller than the stupid, ponderous buffalo and whose eyesight had only to meet the easy requirements of open country.

With their fast, sturdy ponies, the small, mobile Ute bands roamed at will over the Plains far east of Pikes Peak to Kansas, and southeast to Texas. If a Plains band was unwise enough to chase the Utes into one of their mountain parks west of the Front Range, the Utes lured them into ambush and often whipped them. And still, the Utes had great admiration for their well-to-do Plains enemies, and imitated them. Before the eighteenth century ended, they had given up the last trace of the Stone Age, bug-eating culture of their Shoshone ancestors. The new Ute economy merged their buckskin-slave-horse business with the lavish buffalo materialism of the Plains. The merger promised a nice livelihood matching the grandeur of their own land which they regarded now as stretching from Pikes Peak west for six hundred miles to Great Salt Lake; from Taos on the Spanish frontier north to Green River country of Wyoming.

Ute-Spanish relations in the Spanish colonial era were mostly

good, creating a Ute tradition of friendship with white men
which would last up to 1879, despite the most disreputable
white efforts to destroy it. Soon after their love-at-first-sight
meeting with Spanish horses, the Utes in 1675 pledged peace at
Santa Fe with Antonio Otermin, the Spanish Governor of New
Mexico. They honored the pledge five years later by refusing
to join the Pueblo Indians in their bloody revolt which sus-
pended Spanish rule of the Rio Grande Valley until 1692.
When De Vargas reconquered New Mexico, he made a tactful
visit to the Utes' San Luis Valley just north of Taos. Here he
gave presents to Ute leaders and invited them to resume the
horse and slave trade with the returned colonists.

De Vargas went north beyond the Spanish frontier only a
hundred miles, but no white man had passed so far into the
utter unknown and his trip was a hint of what the Utes had
coming. In 1706, Juan Ulibarri made a jaunt of three hundred
and twenty-five miles into the Plains by way of Taos, Raton
Pass and the Front Range, skirting lands along the Greenhorn
Mountains which the Utes and Jicarilla Apaches held in common. While moving down the Arkansas River, Ulibarri saw to
the northwest the blue beauty of Pikes Peak exactly a century
before Zebulon Pike saw it. In 1719, Governor Valverde re-
traced Ulibarri's route, chasing imaginary Frenchmen. Next
year Pedro de Villasur crossed Raton Pass after the French
again, and moved incredibly far northeast across the Plains. He
met Pawnees instead of French and was killed by them in
remote Nebraska.

And then began that cataclysmic period of world history
which destroyed both French and Spanish empires in the West,
raised England to first power and created that superb product
of idealism and ruthless energy, the United States of America.
Though the Utes were remote from the nerve centers of the
new imperialism, they felt its pressure even before the United
States became a fact. Thereafter, step by step, they watched the

events which brought to this small tribe, at least for quite a while, a standard of Indian living which was plush beyond their fondest dreams.

The Ute Golden Age was to derive from Ute control of commerce along the Colorado-Utah part of the Spanish Trail, perhaps the most romantic, and surely the longest and crookedest, of Western trade routes. The Spanish Trail, for pack animals exclusively, had its origins in 1761 and 1765 when white men proved at last the reality of the Rockies by entering them at one of their most spectacular points. The leader of the small party was Juan María Rivera, who liked exploring but was moved mainly by greed for gold and silver.

This first of Colorado prospectors rode beyond Abiquiu through the delicious sage up the Chama, crossed the Continental Divide near Horse Lake, and joined the current westering path of the Denver and Rio Grande narrow-gauge railroad. The party touched at present Lumberton, Dulce, Arboles and Ignacio and went on to Mancos, just north of the prehistoric Mesa Verde settlements of the Basket Makers and Cliff Dwellers. In the orange-streaked La Plata Mountains, Rivera anticipated history by finding some pay silver. In 1765, he followed Ute trails beyond Mancos to the Dolores River, where his role as a Spanish Trail pathfinder ended. He had to detour east out of the Dolores' high, stony banks to the Uncompahgre, and he rode down that genial stream to the grassy glade where the big Gunnison poured in. Here he carved a cross and his initials in a cottonwood and called it a day. His initials marked the future site of Chief Ouray's first headquarters for the Colorado Utes.

A month after the first American Fourth of July in 1776, another white party said good-by to the known world at Abiquiu and headed up the Spanish-Trail-to-be. Two of the party wore long brown gowns — the Zuñi pueblo missionary, Sylvestre Velez de Escalante, and the New Mexico mission officer, Francisco Atanasio Dominguez. The guide was Miera y Pacheco and there were seven other civilians, one of whom spoke Ute, though probably not much. The alleged aim of the trip was more startling than it would be today if two soft-voiced clerics and eight wacky civilians pointed their rocket at the moon, waved gaily at friends and relations and lit the fuse.

They were going, they said, to find a Spanish military route from Santa Fe to the mission at Monterey, California, which was being bothered by snooping Englishmen and Russians. A southern route to Los Angeles had been marked lately along the Gila River of Arizona and across the Mohave Desert. But the Gila River Apaches were a murderous breed, quite different from the Jicarilla Apaches who hung around Santa Fe and Taos with the Utes. On the southern route, forage was uncertain and, if the Gila River Apaches didn't get you, the Mohave Desert would.

The Long Gowns started out gay and stayed that way. Their joy increased as the landscape grew wilder and more forbidding and their chances of survival diminished. They prayed and sang and kept a dairy and told the red willows and the big blue jays that God was protecting them. They struggled northwest over the bleak Dolores River plateau until their beef herd foundered (near present Bedrock). Here, like Rivera, they had to leave the Dolores — and the future Spanish Trail — and cross east to the San Miguel near Tabeguache Creek. They were lost but didn't mind. God would provide. They rode serenely up the San Miguel, which pointed them southeastward toward Santa Fe — except that majestic mountain masses blocked the way. The masses were the soaring San Juans, among the highest and most impassable peaks in North America.

After sixty miles of motion in the wrong direction, the Escalante party shifted northeast, clambered over Dallas Divide and emerged on the Uncompahgre near the spot which Ouray would choose in 1875 for the new Los Pinos Ute Agency. At the fertile Gunnison juncture, the priests found Rivera's cross and tried to interest the local Utes in prayer. These natives were not pleased to find white men again in their Uncompahgre-

Gunnison paradise. They declined to pray and urged the priests to go home before they got hurt.

Graciously, Escalante turned down the advice, having met some Utah Utes who would help them along toward Monterey, California. The priests distributed around some crucifixes and set out with their Indian guides. Ahead loomed Grand Mesa, the largest flattop mountain on earth. The Utes called it Thigunawat, or Home of Departed Spirits, but that did not keep them from hunting up there. They were not a deeply religious tribe. Grand Mesa divided the Gunnison River drainage from that of Grand River (later called the Colorado). The two rivers met forty miles northwest of the Uncompahgre-Gunnison junction and then curved westerly into Utah.

It was clear to the priests that the shortest way to Utah was westerly along Gunnison and Grand Rivers. The Utah Utes had other notions. They took a grassy, well-watered trail up the North Fork of the Gunnison which they liked to use in driving horses from Santa Fe to the northern tribes. From North Fork, this trail followed up Leroux Creek and looped around the east side of Grand Mesa to Grand River along Buzzard, Kimball and Wallace Creeks. It ran through spruce-cedar forests, meadows sumptuously flowered, and past little azure lakes. It was as roundabout as possible but inexpressibly beautiful and the Fathers loved it.

The white men and Utes forded Grand River at present Una and took the broad dusty route over Roan Plateau to White River by way of Roan and Douglas Creeks. From White River they continued northwest and west to Utah. At Utah Lake, the Fathers decided serenely to forget about California since nobody knew where it was and winter was coming. The Escalante party returned on January 2, 1777, to Santa Fe through northern Arizona, having pioneered another piece of the Spanish Trail from Utah Lake south through the Sevier River valley. They used a Ute slave-raiding passage over the canyoned Colorado — to be known thereafter as "the Crossing of the Fathers."

It was a truly miraculous safari. The ten Spaniards had ridden unarmed fifteen hundred inconceivably arduous miles, and had seen fifty thousand square miles of Ute domain which had not existed on any map previously. They had had no trouble at all. When they gave thanks to God for their safe arrival at Santa Fe, the priests were as gay and full of bounce as they had been when they had left civilization one hundred and fifty-eight days before.

Their trip made the Spanish Trail inevitable. In a year or two, Spanish traders out of Abiquiu persevered down the Dolores River and on, to Utah Lake, crossing the Colorado River near present Moab, and the Green River near the present town of Green River, Utah. Later, all sorts of adventurers including Ute horse thieves pushed the Spanish Trail southwest until it reached Los Angeles by way of the Sevier and Virgin Rivers, Mohave Desert and Cajon Pass. And so it was Santa Fe to Los Angeles, through friendly Ute country, with only one desert stretch without water and forage.

A variation of the Spanish Trail developed in the late 1700s from Ute buffalo routes out of the Colorado mountains to the Great Plains. It was called the North Fork and it ran north from Santa Fe and Taos along the Rio Grande and beyond it to the upper San Luis Valley. Here it crossed the Continental Divide at Cochetopa Pass ("Pass of the Buffalo") and followed the Gunnison and Colorado Rivers west until it met the regular Spanish Trail near the mouth of the Dolores River in Utah.[4]

Meanwhile, modern Ute politics were foreshadowed in 1778 when Juan Bautista de Anza reached Santa Fe as Governor and found the Comanches under Chief Greenhorn (Cuerno Verde) raiding haciendas for horses. The Utes yearned to join the Comanches before they stole all the horses. Anza summoned a Ute Chief, Mano Mocha (Maimed Hand), gave him a fine uniform, a general's commission and a gold medal engraved with Charles III's profile. Also he named him head of all the Colorado Utes. General Mano Mocha got the idea. He was right there at Anza's side with two hundred fighting Utes, the next year, when Anza's army chased Greenhorn up San Luis Valley, over Poncha Pass, down the Arkansas and south along the Front Range. Anza and Mano Mocha trapped Greenhorn near present Walsenburg and killed him and thirty-eight of his warriors.

Perhaps Anza informed General Mano Mocha that the Ute Nation belonged to Spain. If so, the Ute chief would not have understood. He was head of the Utes and had not authorized any transfer of Ute land. He would have understood no better in 1801 if told that Napoleon had bought from Spain South Park, Middle Park and North Park — four million acres of prime Ute hunting grounds between (roughly) the Front Range and the Continental Divide.

Two years later these superb chunks of Ute property became American, as part of the Louisiana Purchase. Lieutenant Zebulon Pike came West in 1806 to look them over with a powerful force numbering all of twenty-three men. The Santa Fe Governor sent one hundred dragoons and five hundred mounted militia flying east to stop Pike, but they had an attack of nerves in Southern Nebraska and fled home. So General Mano Mocha was asked to put his Utes on Pike in case the Americans trespassed on Spanish soil south of the Arkansas.

The Utes shadowed well. Pike didn't see them as he visited Pikes Peak and the Royal Gorge. They remained invisible as the Americans ascended Currant Creek to South Park and crossed Trout Creek Pass into the Upper Arkansas valley, which was bound on the west by a dozen fourteen-thousand-foot peaks of the Continental Divide. But the Utes saw the Americans, especially as they returned down the Arkansas and moved south from Royal Gorge into New Spain down Wet Mountain Valley, over Mosca Pass to the Sand Dunes and into San Luis Valley.

The January crossing of Mosca Pass nearly finished both Utes and Americans. The Utes hurried to Santa Fe with the news and returned up the Rio Grande with a hundred Spanish soldiers. On February 26, 1807, the soldiers found the trespassing Americans in a cottonwood stockade on the Conejos River. The Stars and Stripes floated above it. Pike said that he hadn't meant to trespass but just got lost. The Spaniards took them all to Santa Fe and on to Chihuahua for questioning. They were released four months later.

RIVERA, ESCALANTE, THE SPANISH TRAIL, ZEBULON PIKE — all bits of destiny pressing in on the Colorado Utes. Pike's trip stimulated American interest in Santa Fe as a trade outlet for New Orleans and St. Louis. Mexican independence came in 1821 and the Santa Fe Trail was crowded with freighters. Travelers perceived that the Spanish Trail was merely a continuation of the Santa Fe Trail. From St. Louis to Santa Fe to Los Angeles! White civilization had spanned the continent! And American trappers heard about Taos and its idyllic life of fandangos, amorous girls and corn whisky. Dozens of them became Taos expatriates and soon were commuting on the Spanish Trail through friendly Ute country to Wyoming-Idaho-Utah beaver grounds. Or to California, where stealing horses was as easy as picking peaches.

After 1821, the populations of St. Louis and Santa Fe zoomed. Among St. Louis Frenchmen who had made fortunes in a limited Missouri River fur trade were the Auguste P. Chouteau family. They dreamed of new empires based on trade with Rocky Mountain Indians. They had contacts in Santa Fe and were friends of the Joseph Robidoux family, also of St. Louis.

The Chouteaus talked to the Robidoux. As a result, Antoine Robidoux, aged twenty-six, went to Santa Fe, turned Mexican, married a captain's daughter and opened a shop on the plaza. In the mid-1820s, the Uncompahgre Utes allowed Antoine to start a trading post near the west bank of the Gunnison River. The spot was four miles below the Gunnison-Uncompahgre junction where Juan María Rivera had carved his cross and initials in 1765. Antoine was the first, and the last, white man to own a post on Colorado Ute land.

Came the fall of 1833. Nathan Meeker was sixteen years old then, and having father trouble on the Lake Erie homestead. Antoine Robidoux was building a second Ute post near the forks of the Uinta River and White Rocks Creek in northeastern Utah. A competitor appeared at once — a small, bandy-legged, sandy-haired youngster with a pack train of sale goods from Taos. He called himself Kit Carson.

On November 13, 1833, from midnight to dawn, Antoine Robidoux, Kit Carson and everybody else in the Rockies who happened to be awake were scared half to death by what astronomers called the most brilliant meteoric shower in history. They named it "the Leonids" and it consisted of some two hundred thousand shooting stars, possibly from outer space, which seemed to ray out from the constellation Leo. Ouray was born in that year of the Leonids, perhaps in that month. But it was merely a coincidence that blazing meteors introduced an Indian child who would become a personality almost as unusual as this visitation from outer space.

CHAPTER VII Young Ute on the Make

OURAY WASN'T QUITE his original name. His parents called him "Oo-ay" because as a baby he was always agreeably saying "Yes" in Ute. Later, white men wrote it "Ulay" and finally "Ouray" (pronounced You-ray). That made it just a name without meaning, like Jones.[1] His father, Salvador, was an Uncompahgre. His mother was a Taos girl, a Jicarilla Apache. Both of their boys were born in Taos. The first was Quenche and then Ouray, in 1833, the Year of Shooting Stars. But Salvador did not like living around Taos. After a decade or so, Nevava, the new chief of the Uncompahgres, induced him to return home. He had a job for Salvador. Antoine Robidoux had been overreaching himself in matters of profit and prices, and Nevava had destroyed his trading post and had driven him from the mountains. With Antoine gone, Nevava needed Salvador's urban experience. Salvador and his wife repaired to the Western Slope where a daughter, Susan, was born in 1845. They left the two boys near Taos with a Spanish hacienda couple who treated them like members of the family and took them to Mass regularly.[2]

Quenche and Ouray earned their keep herding sheep, hauling piñon wood for fireplaces and packing on mules for shipment casks of a popular fermented wheat liquor called "Taos lightning." Taos, now over two centuries old, was still a dusty, dirty, frontier village — the last Mexican stop on trade routes east to the States, north to Fort Laramie and west to Utah and California. It contained five hundred marvelously scrambled people — Spanish aristocrats, Mexican herdsmen, American trappers and a dozen kinds of Indians, free and slave. Ouray grew up watching its careless life — the fandangos and gambling, the religious parades and bloody brawls, the casual love sold by señoritas to any trapper or trader who could offer some small token of esteem — a cigar, a pair of dice, a rosary. He was there in 1843 when his future friend, Kit Carson, the Taos mountain man, married the Spanish belle, Josefa Jaramillo.

In 1846, the teen-aged Ouray observed the power and energy of General Kearny's American soldiers as they swept over Raton Pass and captured Santa Fe in less than a week. Next year he lived through one of the most ghastly episodes of the West — the revolt of fifteen hundred Pueblo Indians and Mexicans against the conquering Americans. Charles Bent, the first American Governor of New Mexico, was murdered, scalped and decapitated in the presence of his wife and children. Then four hundred and eighty American soldiers and volunteers fought from Santa Fe to Taos through snow and bitter cold and surrounded the rebel leaders in the ancient adobe church at Taos Pueblo. They besieged it hour after hour with cannon, axes and ladders, and broke it apart at last on February 4, 1847. They killed fifty-one of the fifty-four inside, making a total rebel dead of one hundred and fifty. Only seven American soldiers were killed.

Any date now would serve to mark the start of the acute Colorado phase of what Bernard De Voto has called "America's riotous expansion." On January 24, 1848, for instance, James Wilson Marshall found placer gold in California and began history's greatest gold rush. On February 2, 1848, the Mexican peace treaty was signed and all Colorado Ute lands became American. On September 9, 1850, Chief Nevava, Salvador and twenty-six other Utes met at Abiquiu and made their first treaty with the United States, acknowledging the sovereignty of the United States government in Washington.[3]

In that same month, President Fillmore appointed Brigham Young as Governor of Utah Territory. This virile visionary and his Latter-day Saints had been in Salt Lake Valley since

'47. As Governor, Young acted also as Superintendent of Indian Affairs and began his unique Indian policy by which he kept his promises and treated Indians like human beings.

Even so, he had troubles, especially with Chief Walkara, who controlled several Ute clans in fertile valleys south of Salt Lake and Utah Lake. Five years of intermittent war ensued until Walkara died in 1855. The war was intermittent because Walkara rustled many horses along the Spanish Trail from the California ranches to Utah Lake. Brigham Young found it sensible to declare a truce whenever Walkara returned from a horse raid, so that the Mormons could buy the stolen animals at bargain prices. During one of these truces, Young baptized Walkara and made him an elder in the Mormon Church.[4]

The Northern Utah Ute clans, under Chiefs Sowiette and Tabby, resisted the Mormon invasion only briefly. Then they accepted Young's plan for them to consolidate as the Uintah Utes (population five hundred) in the Uinta River region between Salt Lake and the White River country of Colorado. Their eastward shift reduced the hunting terrain of the Yampa Utes of northeastern Utah and forced them further and further east, up White River into the Colorado territory which was the preserve of a small, shy Ute band known as the Grand River Utes. The shift was a factor in the formation and psychology of the several bands which would be known later as the White River Utes.

The hillbilly Grand Rivers numbered 200, the Yampas 500. The total for all six Colorado Ute bands was about 3,500. Membership in a band was not hard-and-fast. Some Utes belonged to two or three bands by intermarriage. The Muache Utes (population 500) lived around Taos and near Lucien Maxwell's new rowdy settlement of Cimarron just across the Sangre de Cristos from Taos. The 300 Capote Utes were Navajo-like, raising sheep and growing corn above Abiquiu and over Horse Lake Pass along the Navajo River. The quiet Weeminuche Utes (500) roamed west of the Capotes along the Southern and

Western Slopes of the San Juan Mountains. Chief Nevava's Uncompahgres held the big Gunnison heartland. They were 1500 strong, and therefore dominant.

SOON AFTER THE SIGNING of that first 1850 Ute treaty at Abiquiu, young Ouray said good-by to his Spanish foster parents and his brother Quenche and followed Salvador's trail back home — up San Luis Valley, over Cochetopa Pass and down the Gunnison to the Uncompahgre. Salvador had died lately and Ouray wanted to join his mother and his sister, Susan. His inheritance was a dozen ponies — the natural increase from a brood mare which Salvador had set aside for his son at birth.

Ouray went about learning mountain Ute ways with a will. He had much to learn, after ten years of Taos. His father's medicine man performed belated rites of puberty by rubbing the blood of a mountain lion on him so that he would have the attributes of that crafty creature. Next, he was obliged to sleep with a girl — the prettiest he could find. Ute beauty meant small hands and feet, an alluring figure, jet-black hair falling to the shoulders, a shy smile and dimples.

Getting this girl involved making an eleven-inch wood flute with whistle mouthpiece and six sound-holes, and learning to play it soft and low and full of throbbing desire. The boy had to hide behind a serviceberry or currant or gooseberry bush when he played the flute so that his melody came romantically from nowhere as the girl fetched water or bathed in the stream. He pitched the flute to match his own voice and he invented tunes, and also lyrics, like "Shining Water is Wearing My Belt." Or he might compose a riddle. He would play the tune and then sing the words. His rhythm varied with his mood — waltz time, polka, march. Riddles were always good technique. Girls stayed awake all night trying to solve them.

If the girl was intrigued by her flutist, she tracked him to his serviceberry and tossed a rock at him, which was an invitation to come to her tepee for the night. He was supposed to be quiet about it, because otherwise the parents would break up the tryst, not because they objected to the seduction of their daughter but because it was crude to be noisy about such things.

Ouray noted that his people had romantic notions about menstruation. A menstruating girl had to stay far away from the village in her "blood tepee" to which she rode on a worn-out old pony because she might make a young pony sick. She could not eat meat or fish because it would spoil the hunting and fishing of her parents. She was not supposed to make love then because her condition would harm her lover, cutting his wind, inducing fever, chills and backache. Naturally any boy worth his salt did his best to get to her in her blood tepee to show his bravery and devotion. Who cared about chills and backache? All for love!

Ute boys like Ouray were taught that sleeping with girls — quite a few girls — before settling down was a matter of common sense and morality. The Utes believed in sexual freedom at that period of life when desire is greatest. Under this system of emotional experience without overtones of fear and shame, sex problems were rare on the Uncompahgre. Two special factors made the system work. Unmarried girls seldom got pregnant because Ute women were relatively infertile and because some rudimentary birth control was practiced. Second, nobody criticized a girl if she did get pregnant. She bore her child proudly and publicly. If her parents couldn't adopt him, the whole band did, and spoiled him even more outrageously than they spoiled regular babies.

Ouray enjoyed the constant social dances and the one sacred ritual — the four-day Bear Dance in March. It was performed in an evergreen enclosure by men and women in opposed lines to the rhythm of a drum and *morache,* or notched stick. The *morache*-player rubbed another stick along the notches and the sound passed into the ground and reached all bears hibernating in caves on Ute lands. The bears were weak, discouraged and emaciated after their long sleep. The *morache* music eliminated their torpor because it told them that the Utes loved them and were sending them strength.

Though the Bear Dance began solemnly, it turned happy after a few days when the dancers knew that the bears were feeling better. Romance took over. Ouray and a girl were paired at the 1852 Bear Dance and got married soon after it ended. The process was easy. First, the suitor got the consent of the girl's parents. Then he donned his best buckskins, killed a deer and hung the carcass by the stream below the girl's tepee. The girl, all wide-eyed and innocent, sauntered from the tepee and led her pinto pony to water. She just happened to be wearing her best party dress of dazzling white buckskin fringed with long whangs and embroidered with beads and quills. She wore brass earrings and the parting of her glossy hair was painted red. She spotted the deer with girlish squeals of utter astonishment, moved it on the pony's back to her tepee, dressed it and prepared a stew, seasoned with the ambrosial herbs which distinguished Ute cuisine. The boy arrived, removed his skinning knife and pistol and ate the stew while the girl undressed and waited for him on her buffalo robe. From then on everything was legal.

A boy was born to Ouray and his wife in 1857, but the marriage did not last. Ouray never explained what happened. Perhaps his wife died. Perhaps he caught her sleeping with another man, in which case he may have cut off her nose and exiled her to another band. It is more likely that they parted by mutual consent because Ouray fell desperately in love with an Uncompahgre maiden of exceptional beauty and charm. Her name was Chipeta. Her parents were undistinguished, but Chipeta would live to find herself a heroine in the legendry of the whites — a sort of Colorado equivalent of Pocahontas.

Ouray married Chipeta in 1859. She was a sweet child of sixteen and she turned out to be an ideal Ute wife — loving, tireless, admiring and healthy. From dawn to dark she tanned Ouray's doeskins and elkskins, made his baskets and clay pipes, sewed his clothes and moccasins, prepared dried meat for travel, cooked, hauled wood, carried water, patched his elk-hide tepee, carved wood cups and kept her temper. Her diligence permitted Ouray to enjoy male prerogatives of gambling all night, rising late and spending what remained of the day in leisurely hunting, trout fishing, gathering tepee poles and telling tall tales.

Summertime was an idyll. June, July, August — Deer Moon, Hot Moon, Trout Moon. Those were the bright crisp sagy days when Ouray and Chipeta and their friends and wives and children and parents and grandparents toured their country with their big horse herd, travois, dogs and goats. They crossed and recrossed their shining land — three hundred and fifty miles from south to north, four hundred miles from east to west, and much more west if they visited the Uintah Utes for a tea dance or a horse race. Their vertical range began a mile above sea level around the edges of their land and ran to timberline at eleven thousand, five hundred feet in the central highlands. It was all trail country, not trackless point-to-point as on the Plains. Only Utes like Ouray knew this labyrinthian, interlocking system in full. Its intricacy protected them from invasion. The main trails were easy to follow — the Cochetopa Pass–Gunnison road to Salt Lake, the trail to White River up Roan Creek, the Plains gaps like Ute Pass at Pikes Peak and Mosca Pass out of San Luis Valley.

But such trite passages bored Ouray. He loved rambling around Grand Mesa. Or through the Elk Mountains by way of Gunnison and East Rivers past Washington Gulch, over the evergreen divide to Crystal River with Treasure Mountain on his left and, on his right, the cathedral uplift of Maroon Bells, and Snowmass and Capitol Peak as he rode down through the aspens to Roaring Fork and the Grand. Just as lovely was the southern trail leading north above Pagosa Springs to the Con-

tinental Divide at Weeminuche Pass, and the rich pasture of
Antelope Park along the high Rio Grande. From thence the
trail passed up Cebolla Creek, over Slumgullion to Lake San
Cristobal, down the Lake Fork of the Gunnison, and so on
home to the Uncompahgre. Grizzly bears were common around
Lake San Cristobal, and summer thunderstorms — Wagnerian
spectacles which fired the peaks, stirred the soul, broke the
eardrums and filled the body with crackling electricity. Just
when people thought they could take no more, the storm
would pass leaving the mountains serene and the spectators
bemused.

Kit Carson and other white acquaintances from Taos could
have told Ouray about comparative geography, stressing the
unsurpassed grandeur of his Ute country. Its magnificent ag-
glomeration of fourteen-thousand-foot peaks made it the largest
and highest pyramid of land in North America. In its secret
heights were the sources of some of the nation's greatest rivers
— the Rio Grande, San Juan and Dolores; the Gunnison and
Grand joining the Green in Utah to form the terrible Colorado,
an inexorable grindstone cutting the world in two; the rushing,
high-rippling White and gentle Bear (Yampa); the cottonwood-
lined Arkansas and sky-mirroring South Platte carrying the
melted snows of a thousand alpine meadows to the Plains from
the Continental Divide and South Park. The North Platte ran
north toward Fort Laramie, draining North Park. The Cache
la Poudre (Josie Meeker's picnic-and-wild-flower stream) tumbled from the Medicine Bows to meet the South Platte at Union
Colony where Mr. Meeker would toil to realize a vision of how
he thought life should be for himself and for all reasonable
men.

Meeker's would be one of so many American visions for the
West! Their dynamism would make them like creeks tributary
to the river of Manifest Destiny, their total aspiration pressing
with terrible force against the land of the Colorado Utes. There
were thirty-two million acres of that land! It was a vast private

game preserve, matchless for size and abundance in the nation. And owned by a mere thirty-five hundred Indians.

ONCE A YEAR, Ouray joined a group of young warrior friends, maybe twenty lodges in all, and raided far east on the Plains for buffalo. The trips involved incredibly hard and continuous riding. There were skirmishes with Cheyennes and Arapahoes and Comanches. Nothing entertained Ouray more. He was fully grown now, five-feet seven inches tall, barrel-chested, mostly muscle and surprisingly fast on his feet for a heavy Indian. His training under Chief Nevava and War Chief Benito had made him into a fine horseman, a crack pistol shot, a calm, able man with a knife. He loved to fight — for ambition's sake as much as for the sport and danger of it. He fought Utes as readily as Comanches if he felt it would advance his tribal standing. He killed more than one member of his own band to enforce discipline for Chief Nevava.

Some Utes resented him for his implacable will to rise, his egotism, his scheming. And still they trusted him. They knew that he was more than just smart and tough. He was contemplative and perceptive and honest. He was wiser than they were because of his background which had given him an education unexampled, perhaps, among Western red men. He was perfectly at home in many worlds. He lived the daily life of two kinds of Indians, Ute and Apache. He could see the totally different points of view of two kinds of white men with whom he had grown up in Taos — Spanish and American. He spoke four languages fluently. In brief, he represented in his own person that merging of white and red civilizations, that resolution of bitterly opposed white and red economies which time would prove to be the only answer to the Indian problem.

Above all, Ouray loved his people and was proud of them. They were good people. Though they had violent tempers, they couldn't stay mad long. They had advanced far from their root-digging days and still they did not take themselves too seriously, except for their love of their children, their ponies and their dogs. They were equally enamored of goats. Their religion was an effortless and warm-hearted pantheism, an outpouring of gratitude to the Great Spirit for giving them their beloved land and their benign climate. The land provided their munificent hunting and fishing and the scenery which brought them joy all their lives. To them the only great sin was desecration of this hunting land — desecration by plowing, for instance.

Besides loving them, Ouray became more and more convinced that he had a duty, to guard them from their own naïveté and from worse dangers gathering about them. One danger was encroachment. Settlers were invading the San Luis Valley from New Mexico and founding towns like Conejos and San Luis. They were encouraged to settle by the establishment of the United States Army post, Fort Massachusetts (later Fort Garland), only one hundred miles southeast of Cochetopa Pass.

A subtler danger was false witness. The whites were saying, for instance, without a shred of evidence, that Old Bill Williams, the famous guide, was killed by thieving Utes rather than by his Mexican packers during his attempt in 1849 to recover baggage from the hills south of Cochetopa Pass.[5] The baggage had been abandoned by Frémont's tragic expedition, in which one hundred and twenty mules and eleven men froze to death. While denouncing the Utes publicly, the whites joked privately about Old Bill's cannibalistic bent as implied by Kit Carson's remark: "In starving times no man who knew him ever walked in front of Bill Williams."

In 1854, Kit Carson became Indian Agent for the Muache Utes in the Taos area. Ouray got to know Kit well a bit later, when Kit opened a sort of subagency for the Uncompahgre Utes at Conejos. Now and then Kit mentioned to Ouray his feeling that the Uncompahgres ought to seek a treaty with Washington, confirming their title to the Gunnison country and specifying boundaries. In 1860, when Ouray was twenty-seven, he went to

Nevava with Kit's suggestion. But Nevava was getting old and pigheaded. He would not hear of treaties. The Utes, he declared, owned the Colorado Rockies and that was that. They would not demean themselves by asking Washington for what was theirs already.

But Nevava did instruct Ouray to take a fresh look at the Pikes Peak gold rush, which began feebly in '58 and caught fire in '59 with epic discoveries above Denver. Ouray took the familiar trail over Cochetopa, Poncha and Trout Creek Passes into South Park, down Ute Pass to Colorado City and on to Denver and Central City. What he saw shattered him. Something like 100,000 whites were scrambling insanely over the mountains and along placer streams at the north end of South Park and the Upper Arkansas Valley. Already these gold-crazy people were firing at Ute families trying to hunt on lands which they supposed to be theirs. Any day some Utes might fire back and there would be trouble.

Ouray rode back down the Gunnison to the Uncompahgre and told Nevava what he had seen. He urged that Nevava go at once to Kit Carson at Conejos and discuss an Uncompahgre Ute treaty before these wild prospectors got a notion that there was gold on the Gunnison and started swarming like locusts over Cochetopa Pass. Once again, Nevava was intransigent. Let the white men come, he said. Let them bring their soldiers and cannon from Fort Garland and Fort Union. The Utes had plenty of guns and bows and arrows. They would stop the soldiers at Cochetopa. If they ran out of bullets and arrows, they could throw rocks and repel the United States Army.

Ouray had liked and admired his father's old friend, Nevava. He hated to do what he knew he had to do. He called Nevava's councilmen, explained the crisis, got their permission to act, and stripped the old man of all but nominal power. Then he hurried to Conejos to see Kit Carson on treaty business.

CHAPTER VIII Treaty Trouble

IT WAS A FINE THING for Ouray to have Kit Carson for a friend
at this critical time in his life. Kit, that elusive introvert, knew
as much about the developing West as any man alive. As a Frémont partisan and Taos Indian Agent, he had learned some of
the twists of American politics and the errant whimsies of Congress. He noticed a thousand white ways of robbing Indians
twenty years before Ralph Meeker's Sioux articles shocked the
nation. He worried about the coming Civil War and about the
ruthlessness of Manifest Destiny of which he himself was a
symbol as the hero of Frémont's reports — the same reports
which had inspired Nathan Meeker during the 1840s back in
Ohio.

Of all Indians, Kit loved the Utes best and he admired the
forthright manner in which Ouray had risen to high Ute estate.
That was why he took the trouble to coach him in treaty strategy
before he resigned as Taos Indian Agent, in June of '61, to re-
enlist in the Union Army. Also he had a hand in the appointment of his old friend, Lafayette Head, as Indian Agent for
the Uncompahgres at Conejos. This Head, a colorful hedonist
with a sensational beard, was fondly known among the five
thousand San Luis Valley settlers as "Uncle Lafe." He had fled
from his native Illinois to escape local wrath for marrying a
child of twelve and he fought the Mexican War in the cantinas
of Santa Fe. When his child bride died, he married a corpulent,
moneyed and tempestuous Spanish widow, a Castilian version
of Lewis Carroll's pepperish Duchess. The newlyweds settled
in a big adobe house at Conejos in 1854 and made a feudal do-

main of the Upper Rio Grande Valley, replete with cattle, horses, goats, sheep, casks of Kentucky bourbon and Spanish brandy and a retinue of pretty Navajo slave girls.

Uncle Lafe saw a good thing for himself if Ouray got an Uncompahgre reservation with annuities and rations to be distributed at Conejos. The Utes had practically lost South Park, Middle Park and San Luis Valley because of Nevava's failure to have boundaries confirmed by the United States Senate before the Pikes Peak gold rush began. But nearly all of the Western Slope of Colorado was still theirs. One of Head's early acts as Indian Agent was to hire Ouray as his interpreter at five hundred dollars a year — a fabulous sum for a period when a cash income of two dollars a month was enough to make an Indian a wealthy man.

Head and Ouray rode to Denver in '62 to see John Evans, President Lincoln's choice as Governor of Colorado Territory and ex officio Superintendent of Indian Affairs. In his impassive way, Ouray offered Evans the friendship of all the Colorado Utes if he secured a treaty giving Ouray's band possession of its Uncompahgre-Gunnison heartland forever, plus annuities, rations and five Virginia stallions. Governor Evans accepted the offer with pleasure. He instructed Sam Elbert, his secretary and future son-in-law, to prepare the treaty, which was approved by the Uncompahgres and ratified by the Senate.[1]

The treaty brought Ouray nothing but misery. In May, Agent Head took him and seven subchiefs on the usual trip to Washington to overwhelm them with the power of the United States government. All the way to St. Joe on the stage from Denver, the Utes were petrified with fear of an Arapahoe attack. They were deathly sick on a Mississippi ferry. They were merely bored at the Capital when shown an Army camp containing more soldiers than there were Indians in the whole West. They were peeved about low Eastern prices for knives and kettles as compared with the high prices charged in Conejos.

Returning West, Uncle Lafe brought along his sixteen-year-old nephew, Finis Downing. Finis got the measles. The Utes thought he had smallpox and asked Head to shoot and bury him before they all caught it. Head declined. Reaching Denver, the Utes lost their money to card sharpers. Head had an ox train of presents to distribute at Conejos. As the wagons rumbled south out of Denver, an ox went wild, dumped the presents and demolished a drugstore. The one happy event occurred at Sangre de Cristo Pass above Fort Garland. Ouray, who always enjoyed youngsters, took Finis Downing hunting to the Huerfano River headwaters near Mosca Pass. There, on the north slope of snow-capped Blanco Peak, the boy shot a fine black-tailed deer. Uncle Lafe mounted the head, planning to have somebody deliver it that fall to Abraham Lincoln. The "somebody" turned out to be John George Nicolay, President Lincoln's private secretary who happened to be passing through the region.

Ouray hoped that his treaty would inspire the other Ute bands to seek treaties. But the Muaches had a new Ute agency near a saloon at Cimarron. They liked the saloon, and they liked roaming the New Mexican plains for buffalo. They didn't want a reservation. Neither did the Weeminuche and Capote Utes, who got their presents at Abiquiu.

One day Ouray's sixteen-year-old sister Susan married the handsome Yampa Ute head medicine man, to be known as Johnson. This was partly tribal politics. When Ouray usurped Nevava's power, the old chief had gone north in a huff across Grand River and over Roan Plateau to join relatives among the Yampas and to head a new grouping of bands, the White River Utes. So Ouray had encouraged the Susan-Johnson romance, hoping Susan could bring Nevava around to his way of thinking from her place of honor as one of Johnson's wives. But Nevava remained anti-treaty and anti-Ouray.

Susan, who would win fame as the brave defender of Arvilla and Josie Meeker, got practice in heroism while hunting in '63 with Johnson and his small band. They were chasing Arapahoe rustlers along the Cache la Poudre toward future Union Colony. Somehow, the rustlers captured Susan. Johnson reported the capture to United States troops guarding the Overland Trail at La Porte. The troops found Susan a mile north of where Nathan Meeker would build his fine house in Greeley. They galloped up in a photo finish as Susan scornfully watched the Arapahoes lighting the pyre to burn her alive. They were angry because a settler named J. N. Holloway had refused to buy her for an old hat and a looking glass. The troops routed the Arapahoes and took Susan to Governor Evans and on to Simeon Whitely whom Evans had set up in Middle Park as Indian Agent for the White Rivers. Whitely had Susan escorted to her band by way of the Gore Pass trail.

You can't tell. The rescue of Susan by the soldiers may have been the white act of kindness which kept the Utes at peace after the Sand Creek Massacre near Fort Lyon on November 29, 1864. This awful affair consisted of a dawn attack by Colorado volunteers on a peaceful camp of sleeping Cheyennes and Arapahoes under Black Kettle and Left Hand who thought that they were under the protection of the United States Government. In September, Black Kettle had sought peace from Governor Evans in Denver but the Governor had refused to negotiate. He had reasoned that the Plains Indians had to be punished first for having committed shocking atrocities while resisting seizure of their lands.

The attitude of Governor Evans toward Indians was colored by his political and material ambitions. He had had a distinguished career back East in medicine, business, politics and education and he came to Colorado expecting statehood soon which would advance him from Governor to the United States Senate. Meanwhile, he meant to promote railroads and to speculate in land. The shocking atrocities of the Plains Indians were triply shocking to him because they scared settlers away. Without population growth, he couldn't become a Senator and he couldn't build railroads either.

The Sand Creek Massacre was planned in Evans's absence by a political henchman under his authority, Colonel John M. Chivington, a former high official of the Methodist Church. Chivington led his one-hundred-day volunteers by night to Sand Creek and let fly with grapeshot and carbines at the six hundred sleeping Indians. As the families poured from their tepees in terror and bewilderment, the intrepid whites shot them down like jack rabbits. By noon, hundreds lay dead and some of the soldiers began hacking off parts of women and children for souvenirs.

Evans and Chivington felt that the Sand Creek Massacre would settle the Indian problem forever. Instead it set the West aflame, wrecked countless lives and made any solution of the problem impossible until Indian bitterness started to subside a quarter-century later. At first, the two officials were praised for setting up the principle that the Sand Creek Indians deserved killing because some of them may have been related to Indians actually guilty of atrocities. Later, when public opinion went against them, they found it hard to understand how anyone could object to violent capital punishment without trial for people unquestionably guilty by association.

By 1867, THE PLAINS INDIANS AND THE ARMY were temporarily tired of war and there was a lull for treaty revision. Chief Ouray wanted a new treaty too. The government was one hundred thousand dollars in arrears on Uncompahgre Ute annuities. The sugar which had been sent to Conejos was the black drippings of a Louisiana sugarhouse, mixed with dirt. The rice was wormy, the hardware defective. Governor Evans had forwarded only two of the agreed five stallions. One of the two was afflicted with infantilism of the generative organ.

Chief Nevava died on White River about now, and his death tended to increase Ouray's power. The wispy-whiskered Yampa Ute, Douglas, won Nevava's place as White River chief over

Jack, a pushing young man from Utah. But Douglas barely won, with the moral support of Ouray and of Susan's medicine-man husband, Johnson.

With Douglas in his pocket and an ivory-handled revolver in his belt, Ouray was able to bring the other Colorado bands somewhat under his leadership. He used threats and he paid each bribes out of his interpreter's income to induce the Muaches, Capotes and Weeminuches dubiously to accept his long-range program. He had developed this program over the years. It was the invention of an extraordinary mind which we have described as having resolved, for itself at least, the seemingly unresolvable differences between white and red ways of life. Ouray planned first to secure one reservation for all the Colorado Ute bands. Then he would modify the Ute hunting economy to fit the growing white market for tanned buckskin and other Ute specialties. By degrees, the Utes would cease roaming and would augment their reduced hunting income in their restricted territory by some stock raising, by shrewder trading and by insisting that their Indian agents protect them from fraud in annuity matters.

Ouray's second treaty trip East, in January of '68, was plush, as befitted his greater importance. He and assorted Ute chiefs rode the Denver stage to Cheyenne and boarded the new Union Pacific cars to Omaha, ferried the Missouri and went on by rail through Chicago to Washington. They stayed two months at the Washington House and ran up a bill of $2,592.37, much of it for Turkish baths. They met President Johnson, General Grant, John Charles Frémont and scads of other celebrities. They got medals galore and so much candy and cigarettes that they had to buy six suitcases to lug them home. They returned by way of Boston, Springfield, Massachusetts, and Niagara Falls. At Springfield Armory, each Ute was given a new rifle.

The party of ten included the blustering Muache chief, Kaneache; the young White River subchiefs, Jack and Sowerwick; and the late Nevava's mercurial nephew, Piah, who

termed himself an Uncompahgre one week and a White River
the next. The white delegation was headed by the Territorial
Governor himself, A. C. Hunt. Kit Carson was a gaunt member
— an act of love for the Utes because poor Kit was in great pain
and clearly dying (he did die in May). Also along was the
effervescent frontiersman, Daniel C. Oakes, whose wildly imagi-
native Pikes Peak guidebook had abetted the phony gold rush
of '58 and caused Oakes to be buried in effigy with his scur-
rilous epitaph writ in axle grease. Oakes had replaced Simeon
Whitely as Middle Park agent for the White Rivers. The interpreter, Uriah Martin Curtis, aged thirty, was an unparalleled
phenomenon, a white man who spoke perfect Ute. He had run
away from his Missouri home as a teen-ager to live with the
Muaches because he loved them.

Turkish baths, candy, medals and celebrities didn't soften up
Ouray at the Washington treaty table. He made a few blunt
speeches about the black sugar drippings, the wormy rice, the
imperfectly-equipped stallion and the Sand Creek Massacre.
When a Senator tried bullying him with old slanders on Ute
misdeeds, Ouray rose with Websterian aplomb, examined the
Senator from stem to stern with big brown contemplative eyes
— and called a recess. In the corridor, he assembled newsmen
and made a statement to the world. "The agreement an Indian makes to a United States treaty," he said, "is like the agreement a buffalo makes with his hunters when pierced with arrows. All he can do is lie down and give in." There was no more
bullying.

The Ute Treaty of 1868 was Ouray's masterpiece. It was regarded at the time as the most generous bestowal of rights ever
granted by the United States Senate to a minority group. It gave
the Colorado Utes forever sixteen million acres of mostly Western Slope land (forty-five hundred acres for each Ute man,
woman, and child).[2] It was precisely that vast, high, deliciously
watered, forested and bemeadowed region which every true

American sportsman today is determined to see ere death ends his earthly elk hunting and trout fishing.

Before the 1868 treaty could be implemented, General Grant became President. He removed A. C. Hunt as Governor of Colorado Territory to make a place for his dapper young Civil War friend, General Edward M. McCook. That was Ouray's hard luck, as we will note later. Worse luck still came the next year when prospectors found gold in the towering San Juans close by the headwaters of Ouray's own Uncompahgre River. The supply town of Del Norte was founded in San Luis Valley near where the Rio Grande River emerges from the high Rockies. Hundreds of whites packed in a hundred miles to the diggings west from Del Norte up the Rio Grande past Antelope Park to Stony Pass above timberline and down Cunningham Gulch to Baker Park (today's Silverton). By the spring of '73, that unbelievably difficult and dangerous mountain trail was jammed with thousands of whites hauling mining equipment and materials to build permanent towns.

The San Juans belonged to the Utes, indisputably. By the Treaty of 1868, white trespass on the Ute Reservation was illegal, indisputably. It would seem that Ouray needed only to send an angry message to President Grant who would rise in wrath at this flaunting of Federal law and would order Fort Garland troops rushed to Del Norte to close the Baker Park trail. Ouray did send the angry message, and other angry messages to Governor McCook, to Interior Secretary Columbus Delano and to Felix Brunot, chairman of the Board of Indian Commissioners. Troops did start for Del Norte; but then the usual howl went up in Congress about soldiers firing on taxpayers. President Grant recalled the troops.

The recall was just as Ouray expected. He had seen the truth from the beginning. The San Juan gold rush was no fly-by-night affair. It was the start of one of Colorado's greatest industries, covering an eighty-mile mountain square — four million acres. Here, with magical speed, grew a brand-new political faction powerful enough to impress the Chaffee-Evans Denver crowd and the Henry Teller Central City crowd. In years to come it would produce two hundred million dollars in mineral wealth, and would create such spectacular fortunes as that of Tom Walsh, who used some of his San Juan gold to buy his daughter, Evalyn Walsh, the world's most coveted jewel — the Hope diamond.

The miners who composed the rush were nothing local. They were inextricably a part of the whole nervous system of the American people. Appeals to the President, to Congress, to the Supreme Court, to the United States Army to protect the sacred rights of one small Indian tribe were futile. The flocking miners had sacred rights too, based on the earliest American traditions. The government could no more control their right to improve their condition than it could control their sneezing. Ouray believed that there were no exceptions. In the United States, Manifest Destiny always won in any contest with abstract justice.

What to do? He could lead the Utes in hopeless resistance and lose his life as a martyr and romantic hero while the other Utes were rounded up and hauled to Oklahoma Indian Territory to die of homesickness and disease. That was the easy way. Or he could struggle on as a statesman, striving to retain as much of the 1868 Reservation as possible, striving to hold the shaken confidence of his temperamental bands and to keep them on good behavior until his long-range economic plan began to show results. That was the hard way.

OURAY CHOSE THE HARD WAY. In the spring of '72, Congress named a three-man Commission to negotiate the San Juan cession. The Commission was headed by Governor McCook, whom Ouray distrusted intensely. The others were General John McDonald and John D. Lang. They arrived from Denver at the new Ute Agency just over Cochetopa Pass in late August. For psychological effect, McCook brought a squad of Fort Garland soldiers, Governor Arny of New Mexico and Felix Brunot, the kindly Chairman of the Board of Indian Commissioners, whom we last saw hiring the alcoholic Samuel Parker to uncover fraud at the Sioux Agencies.

Felix Brunot, at fifty-three, represented the finest flowering of American gentility. He had amassed a large fortune as a partner in the Pittsburgh steel firm of Singer, Hartmann and Company. He lived in perfect nuptial harmony with a stately wife (née Mary Hogg) and twenty or thirty servants in a many-pillared mansion above the Monongahela. He had built hospitals, and founded libraries with the help of Andrew Carnegie, and was deeply involved in the affairs of the Episcopal Church. His wife Mary wrote poems and for years taught a Sunday School for Negro children.

Brunot had declined a Civil War generalship, choosing instead to spend his time and money caring for the wounded and supplying coffins for the dead at Shiloh, Gaines Mill and Savage Station. He spent some time with wounded prisoners at Libby Prison. When sedatives were scarce, he tried to soothe the men by singing "Just As I Am." After his parole, he organized the Pittsburgh Sanitary Fair and raised three hundred and twenty thousand dollars for wounded soldiers. He became interested in Indians as a founder of the American Church Missionary Society. In '69 he accepted with headlong idealism President Grant's offer to make him Chairman of the Board of Indian Commissioners. This nonsalaried board would exercise joint supervision with the Secretary of the Interior over government money appropriated for the operation of the Indian Bureau.

He went to work inspired by dreams of keeping politics out of Indian affairs and making the government stick by its promises. He did an immense amount of traveling, visiting most of the Western tribes and smelling out revolting masses of corruption. By 1872, he found his voluntary Board hamstrung by the cynical machinations of the Secretary of the Interior and the

Commissioner of the Indian Bureau. His recommendations were ignored, his charges against grafting contractors were pigeonholed, and he knew that he had dreamed in vain.

He spent four days of acute pain at the '72 Ute conference. McCook's shabby tactics nauseated him, though he enjoyed the failure of the Governor's crude attempts to awe the Utes. The McCook Commission seemed tawdry and commonplace compared to Ouray's thousand resplendent warriors with their six thousand horses, their painted and bestreamered canvas tipis, their gay, vermillioned squaws, their sturdy children. Brunot fell in love with Ouray's wife, Chipeta, in her doeskin dress as white as cotton, every seam thick with fringes and decorated with marvelous beadwork and porcupine-quill embroidery. She giggled when McCook gave Ouray a shiny Germantown carriage and whispered to Brunot that she guessed it would do to keep her goats in.

Ouray's subchiefs were regal in Washington medals and long knives, six-shooters and expensive Navajo blankets. Chief Piah strutted about in a gorgeous headdress of golden eagle feathers. Major A. J. Alexander, the Fort Garland officer, talked with Chief Jack, of the White River Utes, and confided to Brunot later that Jack's military knowledge was broader than his own. As a result of Ouray's prodding, the commissioners had to announce glumly that President Grant had forwarded nine thousand, nine hundred and eighty-two dollars' worth of presents but that, unfortunately, they had been lost in transit. They had to apologize also for the fact that the United States government, in seeking to encourage a Ute sheep-raising industry, had sent Chief Ouray a total of twelve ewes and one thousand, nine hundred and eighty-eight castrated rams. They admitted that the Treaty of 1868 had promised each Ute family "one gentle American cow, as distinguished from the Mexican or Texas breed," and they could not explain how it happened that the Texas longhorns actually delivered were so wild and dangerous that no corral could hold them and they vanished into the Rocky

Mountain wilderness. To Brunot, the general level of treaty-talk was depressing. Some samples:

GOVERNOR MCCOOK: You Utes won't work.

CHIEF OURAY: We work as hard as you do. Did you ever try skinning a buffalo?

COMMISSIONER LANG (*reverently*): We are all children of the Great Spirit. Anybody who says I'm in the pay of some railroad company is lying.

CHIEF SAPOVANERO: If you white men are so honest why don't you live up to your promises?

GENERAL JOHN MCDONALD (*rising and putting on hat*): We came to buy part of your land. There's an election in November. The Democrats may win and put bad men in Congress. They may stop your annuities and rations. You'd better cede the San Juans to us now. Then the sale will be binding on the new Congress.

CHIEF SHAVANO: We won't sell.

GOVERNOR MCCOOK: Why won't you make your children go to school? Look at the Sioux! They are learning to read and write already!

CHIEF OURAY: The Army conquered the Sioux. You can order them around. But we Utes have never disturbed you whites. So you must wait until we come to your ways of doing things.

CHIEF MAICHICK of the Muaches (*a trifle tight*): All I want to do is hunt buffalo. Cimarron is my country. I never saw Government before. I do not think there is anything to prevent me making my living where I can if I do it quietly and do not disturb anyone.

BRUNOT: Wouldn't you like good teachers so that your children could compete with white children?

CHIEF PIAH: I think a lot of my boys. I'd hate to have them at school away from me and their mother. They'd be crying all the time.

CHIEF MAICHICK (*brushing away a tear*): All I want to do is hunt buffalo.

Nothing could be accomplished. But Brunot tarried until the Congressional Commissioners and their deflated military

window dressing had retreated, in not very good order. Then
he had some talks with Chief Ouray. He talked also with the
new Uncompahgre Ute Indian Agent, General Charles Adams,
and with the Agency's official trader, Otto Mears. Adams and
Mears urged Brunot to return in a year with authority to offer
generous terms for the San Juan cession. They believed that
Ouray might listen to terms then, provided Governor McCook
was not present. Or any other Coloradan.

The Pittsburgh steel magnate did return in one year. He
found that Ouray had examined the San Juan mountains carefully and had determined limits which would cause the Utes
a minimum loss of pony pasturage and deer range. And so it
happened that on September 13, 1873, a Congressional Commission of One, the Honorable Felix R. Brunot, concluded with
Chief Ouray and three hundred and fifteen other Utes near
Cochetopa Pass an amendment to the Treaty of 1868.

Out of the sixteen million acres of the original Ute Reservation, the amendment ceded to the United States four million
acres of San Juan mineral lands.[3]

This "Brunot Treaty" gave the Utes hunting privileges on
the ceded land and twenty-five thousand dollars a year, additional to the sums listed in the Treaty of 1868. It gave Ouray a
salary of one thousand dollars a year for ten years, for services
to be rendered in helping his people to achieve an economy
adapted to their smaller reservation.

Happy settlement and peace! In his joy, the pious Brunot induced the more or less pagan Ouray, the Catholic Adams and
the Hebrew Mears to kneel with him in a rousing Episcopalian
prayer of thanks to Almighty God. And, in October, he influenced Congress to appropriate fifteen thousand dollars so that
Ouray and eight subchiefs could come East and marvel once
more at the wonders of white civilization.

For Ouray, the marvels were losing luster. But he did enjoy
his visit to Niblo's Garden in New York where he witnessed a
thrilling performance of that sensational ballet-show, *The*

Black Crook. It was a fair introduction to still blacker crooked-ness which Ouray, Agent Adams and Otto Mears were soon to encounter back home.

CHAPTER IX

Man Bites Man

How OTTO MEARS happened to be kneeling in prayer with Felix
Brunot, Chief Ouray and General Charles Adams out there in
the Colorado wilds is a cosmic mystery, like drawing a cold hand
royal flush.

This one-hundred-pound bundle of flamboyant mercantilism
was on his way to becoming one of the greatest men in Rocky
Mountain history. The angels wept at his birth in 1840 to a
starving couple on the bleak steppes of Russia. They kept weeping when he was orphaned two years later, and when he survived eight more hungry years with a poor uncle, and when (at
the age of ten) he battled the rats during a six-month voyage
alone in a stinking steerage to join another poor uncle in San
Francisco. The second uncle did not show up at the dock, but a
boat friend fed Otto until he learned enough English to hawk
papers. Next, our dynamic mite hustled in the mining camps,
joined the First California Volunteers on their Civil War
march to Santa Fe; he helped Kit Carson in the Navajo campaign, and wound up in '65 with a store at Conejos and an
interest in Lafayette Head's grist mill.

Greed had no part in Mears's passion for expanding capital-
ism. He was a long time making money, but he didn't care. He
treated his brains like so much popcorn. He loved to turn on
the heat and watch one idea lead to another until his mind was
exploding all over the place. In '67, the Head-Mears grist mill
outgrew local output of wheat. Mears moved eighty miles up
San Luis Valley with some of Uncle Lafe's Mexican relatives,
laid out a wheat farm and founded the town of Saguache below

Cochetopa Pass. Soon he was floating in surplus wheat. He got rid of it at the booming Granite and California Gulch mining camps after building the first of his epical toll roads — a fifty-mile stretch from his Saguache wheat fields north over Poncha Pass to the Upper Arkansas Valley.

All the while, Otto discussed Ute economics with Ouray and studied Uncle Lafe's Conejos Indian Agency. Head had lost interest in the Agency even before Ouray went to Washington in 1868 for treaty revision. So Mears took it to Saguache with Head's clerk, William S. Godfoy, in charge. Mears became official Indian trader, and for some months surprised both himself and the Uncompahgre Utes by stimulating business and making more money for everybody.

Then the blow. The 1868 Ute treaty required eventual closing of the two New Mexico Ute Agencies, Cimarron and Abiquiu. To please powerful Santa Fe politicians, Ouray had to agree to a treaty stipulation that the new Southern Ute Agency be built on Los Pinos River, "the third river west of the 107th meridian" (the meridian, of course, was the east boundary of the Ute Reservation; the first and second rivers west of it were the San Juan and the Piedra). The valley of Los Pinos River was barely in southwestern Colorado and was accessible commercially only from Santa Fe, via Abiquiu and the Old Spanish Trail.

While Mears worried about the presumed loss of his developing Ute trade at Saguache, General McCook arrived in Denver as the new Governor of Colorado Territory. He deplored the handing-over of so much Southern Ute business to New Mexicans. One month later, in July of '69, he appointed his old Army friend, Lieutenant C. T. Speer, as first Indian Agent at the proposed Agency on Los Pinos River and sent him forth to locate and build it. Speer and his crew journeyed to Saguache, conferred with Otto Mears, and rode up Cochetopa Pass on their way to Weeminuche Pass, beyond which Los Pinos River was said to exist, some one hundred and seventy-five miles from

Saguache. After fifty miles of travel on the well-worn Saguache–
Gunnison River–Salt Lake wagon road, Speer veered left off
Cochetopa Creek and moved six miles southwest along a small
unnamed stream.

Here, in·a high sage-and-aspen vale ten hours from Saguache,
Speer declared the unnamed stream to be "Los Pinos Creek."
He designated the spot as "Los Pinos Agency," which could be
construed as roughly fulfilling Article Four of the Ute Treaty
of 1868. By the ensuing spring, Speer had supervised the erec-
tion of six administration buildings, a school and a sawmill —
and had informed the Indian Bureau in Washington that "Los
Pinos Agency is perfectly situated for agricultural pursuits."
Then he bowed out of office gracefully, leaving behind a sheaf
of vouchers for salaries paid and supplies bought without
authority, and a large bill for Guckenheimer whisky obtained
at Mears's Saguache store.

While Speer located Los Pinos Agency to the satisfaction of
McCook and Mears in the southern part of the Ute Reservation, the second Ute Agency was built on White River in the
north. On McCook's order, it was located by that pioneer Pikes
Peak argonaut, Daniel C. Oakes. He reached Rawlins, Wyoming, on the Union Pacific cars from Cheyenne and rattled
south one hundred and eighty-five miles to White River by
buckboard. He measured the distance by tying a red rag to a
wheel spoke and counting the turns. Oakes's interpreter was
Uriah Curtis, to whom McCook gave the contract for delivering
treaty cattle to White River Chief Douglas. His guide was red-
headed Jim Baker, the old mountain man. Jim had a sort of
ranch and toll bridge near Denver, where he enjoyed marital
bliss with two Snake wives named Monkey and Beans (they
were sisters).

McCook sent seven Army officers in succession as Indian
Agents to White River. All of them quit when they found themselves consigned to a Siberia one hundred and eighty-five miles
from the nearest white habitation, which was Rawlins, Wyo-

ming. Then McCook sent Charles Adams, whose recent arrival in Denver, Colorado, and whose later role as hero of the Meeker massacre, were twists of fate as capricious as Mears's appearance in Conejos from the steppes of Russia.

Charles Adams's real name was Carl Schwanbeck, born in 1844 at Anklam, Pomerania. His father was a German cabinet maker. Carl was a fine Greek and Latin scholar at college, but he got mixed up in a proletarian student riot against King William and had to flee to the United States, as Carl Schurz had fled earlier for similar liberalism. Schwanbeck lived briefly in Boston, was wounded in the lungs while serving through the Civil War with the Sixth Massachusetts, spent time scouting with the regular Army in New Mexico and turned up in Denver to rest his weak lungs just as McCook assumed his post as Governor.

Carl Schwanbeck asked McCook for a job handling German immigrants who were pouring into Colorado Territory. McCook could barely afford to pay his wife's curly-haired brother, James B. Thompson, as his private secretary and as Deputy Superintendent of Indian Affairs. But he did note Schwanbeck's stunning physique, his great shoulders, his six-foot-plus frame, his bland, broad face with its blue-eyed look of stolid fearlessness. Such sanguine topography stirred two thoughts in the Governor. First, he was afraid of the Ute Indians who had a way of barging into his office and yelling at him: he could use a bodyguard. Second, his wife Mary (nee Thompson) had invited her widowed sister Margaret, and Margaret's noisy brat Willie Phelps, out from Peoria for a visit. It looked as if McCook might be stuck with Margaret and Willie for the rest of his life: he could use a husband for Margaret and a keeper for Willie.

Resourceful is the word for McCook. He began asking Schwanbeck to Sunday dinner, and soon Carl was hooked by Margaret, a tiny creature with the imperious disposition of a Pekingese. She made him change his name to Charles Adams.

Then McCook put him in charge of enough State Militia to
rate the title of General Adams. Finally, the Governor wangled
another salary out of President Grant, so that Brother-in-law
Thompson could attend to Indian affairs solely and Brother-in-
Law-by-Marriage Adams could step in as his private secretary
(and bodyguard).

The legend is that Adams was reading the *Rocky Mountain
News* on his first day in the Governor's office at the top of a
flight of stairs. McCook was out. The door opened and in barged
Colorow, a biscuit-begging nuisance who weighed nearly three
hundred pounds. Colorow waved his pistol at Adams and announced, "McCook's a liar!" Adams kept on reading. Colorow
added, "McCook's a damned liar!" Adams turned a page. A
third Colorow blast: "McCook's a God-damned liar!" The stalwart Teuton rose, strolled toward the big Indian, grabbed his
collar with one hand and his pistol with the other and threw
him out the door and down the stairs.

After some months of bodyguarding, General Adams went
reluctantly to White River as Indian Agent. His luck was poor.
The winter of 1870–1871 was a terror. Daniel Oakes had placed
the Agency at the upper end of a broad valley where White
River flowed from a canyon around a rock (still known as
Adams' Point). The icy wind was even more incessant than
usual. Rations ran low. When Adams tried to get flour at
Hahn's Peak only two sacks were available. At Christmas time,
one of the White River subchiefs, Sowerwick, shot himself in
the leg. Adams was an amateur doctor and could recognize
blood poisoning. He moved the dying Sowerwick to his own
bedroom and won his eternal gratitude by saving his life during two months of nursing.

In periods of thirty-below weather, pregnant Ute squaws became panicky. Three of them came to Adams and required him
to deliver their babes as midwife in the warmth of the Agency
office. He had a January guest from Germany, Baron von
Hagen, who went after elk with a Swiss chamois hunter in Milk

Creek basin. The chamois hunter shot the Baron accidentally and he died before Adams could transport him to a surgeon at Fort Steele two hundred miles away.

Adams was distressed further that winter because he could not nail these White River people down to learning anything. They had no tribal cohesion. Though they were curious about farming and other white wonders, they were more interested in bickering among themselves, especially the rival bands of Head Chief Douglas and Chief Jack. Adams grew quite fond of Douglas and he got special pleasure out of meeting Chief Ouray and Chipeta, who rode over Roan Plateau from Ouray's winter village on the Uncompahgre for a diplomatic visit of some weeks. Adams spoke good Spanish and he noticed that, in that language, Ouray revealed himself to be as classic a philosopher as any of the great Greeks whom Adams had studied in Germany. The Pomeranian expatriate and the Ute leader became friends. Both of them were ardent sportsmen. Both saw all races as pretty much alike by instinct and aspiration. Higher civilizations, they agreed, derived not so much from superior intelligence as from the pressures of environment — pressures like those which Ouray hoped desperately to contain until his Utes came around to a less prodigal use of their land.

Returning from the White River wilds, General Adams took his strident little Margaret and Willie to a homestead on Monument Creek, a bit north of General Palmer's Colorado Springs. For a year he tried raising cattle with no success. In the spring of '72, as Adams prepared to return to Denver, Ouray rode up to his cabin wearing his formal frock coat, white collar and black tie. Behind him in order of rank rode Sapovanero, War Chief Shavano, old Chief Guero and Captain Billy, Ouray's boydguard.

Mrs. General — that was Margaret's title for herself these days — served coffee as the emissaries sat on the floor in a circle and smoked. Then, with smiling pomp, Ouray announced that General Adams must take over as Los Pinos Indian Agent. The

incumbent, a Boston Unitarian named Reverend Jabez Never-
sink Trask, had got the Agency books in a mess — and had
just resigned after some young Utes had ridden him playfully
on a rail. The Reverend, Ouray added, was a good man, but
queer as a porcupine. His enormous green goggles and buck-
thorn stick had frightened the children. During his regime he
had waddled around glowering at everybody in his navy blue
swallow-tail with brass buttons, his skin-tight pants flaring
funnel-shaped at the ankles, his ancient broad-brimmed Puri-
tan hat. They were glad to see the last of him and now they all
wanted Adams.

The big man hesitated. But Mrs. General did not wait. Joyfully, she accepted the place for her husband. Los Pinos, she
exclaimed, was the perfect spot for a growing boy like Willie.
A month later, Governor McCook rushed Adams's application
through his mentor, General Grant, and the Indian Bureau.
With his usual finesse, the Governor remembered to change
Adams's religion on the application, from Catholic to Unitarian. The Utes were under the political protection of the latter
sect in 1872.

THEY GOT ALONG WELL — the towering, slightly pompous
Adams, the fly-weight Mears, the quiet and imposing Ouray,
the dimpling Chipeta, the pipingly regal Mrs. General. Aesthet-
ically they loved Los Pinos Agency though at almost ten thousand feet it was less suited than the Sahara Desert for the
"agricultural pursuits" reported by Lieutenant Speer (even
potatoes wouldn't grow within twenty miles of it). The sawmill rusted for want of lumber, and the school stood empty,
lacking cooperative children. To keep the Ute cattle alive in
winter, Adams set up a government cow camp on the Gunnison
River 36 miles down the wagon road, near where Gunnison
town is now; and he sent a cowboy there, James P. Kelley. He
put on the payroll two congenial compatriots: Herman Lueders

as Agency bookkeeper, Herman Lauter as clerk. When Cimarron Agency seemed about to close, he made its agent, Stephen A. Dole, his deputy. He built a summer home at Los Pinos for Ouray and Chipeta, and promised them a second home soon at their Ute Village in the fertile Uncompahgre Valley, where they enjoyed the relatively mild climate from October until the snow left the high mountains in April.

Adams, Mears and Ouray conspired for easy profits. They collected a neat fee when George Baggs asked to drive his big cattle herd from his drought-stricken ranch in New Mexico over Cochetopa and through the Ute Reservation to new pasture on the Little Snake north of White River. The Poncha Pass toll road merely sharpened Otto's expansionist fervor. In '72, he decided that the San Juan gold rush was real. He went to work with ferocious zeal to outflank the upstart supply town, Del Norte. As founder and editor of the *Saguache Chronicle*, he could warn the world that the Rio Grande pack trail through Del Norte to Baker Park was deadly dangerous. The only safe way was through Saguache and over Cochetopa. Having said so much, he had to provide the safe way. He started building a toll road west from Los Pinos to the Lake Fork of the Gunnison, and southward up that stream toward Cinnamon Pass and Baker Park beyond it. He got as far as Lake San Cristobal before snow stopped him in late '73.

During that 1873–1874 winter, Otto perfected the master plan which would result finally in some 400 miles of Mears toll roads and spur railroads through the San Juan mineral belt. For financial leverage at that early stage, he had the Los Pinos mail contract and his position as official Ute trader. At first he dreamed of exploiting egress to the San Juan mines from the East only. But something occurred which showed him that masses of miners might be drawn from the West too — Salt Lake City, even San Francisco.

In late March, Ouray sent his runner Lovo from his Uncompahgre village east up the Cochetopa Pass road to Los Pinos, with an odd tale for General Adams. In mid-January, twenty-one white men had arrived at the village, and had paid the usual fines for trespassing on the Ute Reservation. Ouray was not pleased to see them. He was sick of being obliged continually to make excuses for the whites to his people. Nevertheless, he treated them kindly and advised them to stay there with him and eat his elk until winter broke. The whites were mostly the common, rough sort of mining good fellows, aged sixteen to seventy. Three were Irish, two German, one French, four Pennsylvanians, one a Scots doctor, and so on. They had been prospecting fruitlessly around Salt Lake and had come together in Provo, where they read of rumored new gold strikes in Summit County, Colorado.

They didn't know where Summit County was exactly, but they found a sort of guide who did — thirty-one-year-old Alfred Packer, a dark, brooding one-hundred-and-ninety-pound man just off the Provo chain gang. Packer was broke, but all the others still had money. They agreed to feed him for guiding them from Provo along the Salt Lake–Cochetopa Pass road to Saguache and north to Breckenridge in Summit County via Mears's Poncha Pass toll road, Trout Creek Pass into South Park, Fairplay and Hoosier Pass.

Though Packer had never passed that way before, the whole route was well known by '73. And still this projected hike of five hundred miles in the dead of winter over the thickest and highest mountains in North America was worse than rash. That twenty-one normal-seeming men could attempt it dramatized the insane urgency of the American gold-rush era. Baker Park, only three hundred and seventy-five miles from Provo, would have been a somewhat more reasonable objective. But the Provo party was not interested in the known, the proven San Juan mines. Much better to chase the will-o'-the-wisp, reach the new Summit County Eldorado ahead of the spring rush and get in on the ground floor.

Reporting for Ouray, Lovo told General Adams that the

white miners grew restless in late January at Ouray's village. Eleven of them, Packer included, decided to risk blizzards and start on foot for Saguache, one hundred and forty miles eastward. But Packer and five others withdrew when Packer had a spat with a husky Ohioan, O. D. Loutsenhizer. The Loutsenhizer group, Lovo continued, left the Uncompahgre on February 2 with rations for seven days and reached the Gunnison River Ute cow camp, seventy miles east, a fortnight later. They were skin and bones from hunger and cold, and delirious. All through March, cowboy James P. Kelley nursed them at the cow camp to keep them from dying. On February 9, Packer and his five partisans followed Loutsenhizer's trail up Dry Fork of Cedar Creek toward the cow camp. These six had rations for seven days too. They were last seen plodding along the road through a snowstorm near the top of the Gunnison–Uncompahgre divide.

When Lovo passed the Ute cow camp in late March on his way to see Adams at Los Pinos, he discovered that the Packer party had not checked in. There was no visible game at those altitudes during the deep snow of winter. More than forty-five days had passed since the six, with their seven-day rations, had left Chief Ouray. They could not live, Lovo declared, thirty-eight days without eating. Lovo told Adams in conclusion that Packer and his five friends must have perished from starvation.

After hearing Lovo, Adams hung out a night lamp at Los Pinos to guide in wandering miners and left for Denver with Mrs. General to order supplies. They returned to Saguache about May 1 to find the little mud town in a high fever of speculation. Otto Mears was having a fit for fear the rival Del Norte might get wind of a scandal which would bring shame to Saguache. Mears brought Adams and his wife up to date on current events. The Loutsenhizer party of five had made it, finally, to Los Pinos from the Gunnison cow camp, though so pitifully emaciated still that Herman Lauter put them to bed again. Then Chief Ouray and Chipeta arrived at Los Pinos.

They reported that the ten prospectors who had taken Ouray's advice and had spent the winter on the Uncompahgre would be coming along soon. So fifteen of the original twenty-one Provo men were accounted for. Only the Packer party of six was missing.

Adams learned from Mears that Ouray and several Agency employees saw a big white man walk up to the Los Pinos office on April 16 carrying a coffeepot of hot coals, a Winchester rifle and a skinning knife. It was Alfred Packer. He was unshaven, dour and two front teeth were missing. Otherwise he looked perfectly fit, as mountain men look in summer when game is plentiful.

His tale was too simple. He said that he and his five companions must have forked off from the Gunnison too soon, thereby missing the cow camp. They had hiked south up Lake Fork, thinking it was Cochetopa Creek. They knew that they were lost when they reached Lake San Cristobal, which didn't belong on the itinerary. While Packer was temporarily snow-blind and footsore, the other five deserted him. Packer expressed vast surprise that they had not appeared at the Agency. He said he had been living on rosebuds and roots for two months. An employee asked him what he'd like to eat. Packer said he wasn't hungry but he'd take a shot of whisky. Ouray shook his hand in greeting, casually patting his arm at the same time, as weight-guessers do at county fairs. Packer realized what Ouray had in mind and backed off from him abruptly.

Soon Packer left Los Pinos, went on down to Saguache and got a job tending bar in Larry Dolan's saloon. He told Mears he was broke and wanted to make enough so that he could get along to Breckenridge. He lost thirty-seven dollars one night in a game of freeze-out and paid up from a stuffed wallet. He paid Mears seventy dollars cash for a horse and bridle. Otto's beady black eyes saw plenty of money left in Packer's wallet, plus a Wells-Fargo draft. Other Provo men turned up in town and heard the desertion yarn. They said it was all lies. Packer had

The glow of youth stayed with NATHAN MEEKER all his days. Even as he neared sixty his handsome face was scarcely lined; his figure was tall, lean and vigorous.

ough ARVILLA DELIGHT MEEKER was en provoked and baffled by her husnd's peculiar ways, she loved him ply all her life. Nathan Meeker was proudest possession.

Meeker's mentor, HORACE GREELEY, deserved to be called at least a "character." His voice was a squeak and his whiskers were limp as corn silk.

Collections, Library of Congress
(Bogardus & Bendann Bros., New York)

RALPH MEEKER had to meet crises all his life. One of the worst came while he was covering the Russo-Turkish War. On his return to Greenwich Village, his fiancée threatened to break their engagement because he was going bald.

Photo courtesy of Cyclopedia of
American Biography

Senator HENRY M. TELLER, who got Meeker his Indian Agent job, came to Central City, Colorado, from New York State in 1861 while Central was still a raw gold camp full of girls in red stockings, gamblers and drunks.

Library, State Historical
Society of Colorado

By 1873, at forty, CHIEF OURAY was in firm control of the Colorado Utes. This extraordinary man was perfectly at home in many worlds. He represented in his own person that merging of white and red civilizations which time would prove to be the only solution to the Indian problem.

Original Jackson negative
State Historical Society of Colorado

OTTO MEARS, the irrepressible mite who would become the Rockies' tycoon and transportation king of the San Juans, attributed his success to laying off whisky, taking a cold bath after every meal, and managing to fill an inside straight with surprising regularity.

Fred M. Mazzulla negative

FELIX BRUNOT, chairman of the Board of Indian Commissioners in 1873, represented the finest flowering of American gentility. Chief Ouray loved him for his genuine desire to do justice to the Utes.

Kindness of Carnegie Library, Pittsburgh

After the conclusion of the "Brunot Treaty" of 1873, Ouray, his subchiefs and their white friends were brought to Washington to marvel at the alleged achievements of white civilization. *Front row, left to right:* Guero, Chipeta, Ouray, Piah. *Second row:* Uriah M. Curtis, Major J. B. Thompson, General Charles Adams, Otto Mears. *Back row:* Washington, Susan, Johnson, Jack and John.

Meeker's 1879 spring crop of Agency employees was more like a kindergarten. FRANK DRESSER, a shy, curly-haired lad hardly out of knee pants, was so homesick that he wrote his mother in Greeley every night.

As amateur detectives, Ouray, Charles Adams and Otto Mears were too much for ALFRED PACKER, who had to confess that he had spent the winter of 1873-1874 eating five of his friends southwest of the Los Pinos Agency.

Pioneer Museum Photo,
Colorado Springs

Though FLORA ELLEN PRICE was
the mother of two children, she
was only sixteen years old and as
innocent as they were.

At the White River Agency
JOHNNIE and MAY PRICE were
pets of all the Utes, who tried to
buy them at high prices.

"Tip" Thornburgh's wedding to LIDA CLARKE was attended by masses of brass — all West Pointers, of course. Lida's train of white gros-grain silk was eight feet long. Her satin dress was short-sleeved, and there were orange blossoms in her hair.

Family photo loaned by Mrs. Harold Furlong (Mary Casement)

In the spring of 1878, General George Crooke appointed MAJOR THOMAS TIPTON THORNBURGH commander at Fort Steele. Thornburgh's appearance hadn't changed much, except for the addition of mutton-chop whiskers, since this West Point cadet photo was taken in '67.

Family photo loaned by Mrs. Harold Furlong

In Rawlins, JOE RANKIN seemed like just
an ordinary cracker-barrel citizen as a livery stable owner and keeper of the peace
among the chippies of Lower Row. But
as Thornburgh's guide at Milk Creek, his
heroic quality emerged.

Frank J. Meyers negative

*Photo, courtesy of James France's
heirs, Rawlins, Wyo.*

Young Mr. JAMES FRANCE, first citizen
of Rawlins, was not much bigger than
a large bug. He made up for it by
growing giant whiskers to his waist.

ount AUGUST DÖNHOFF regarded his Ute
lventure as the outstanding event by far
 his colorful career as a top-ranking Ger-
an diplomat. This unique photo was
ken when the Count was seventy.

*Photo loaned by Countess Marian Dönhoff,
Hamburg, Germany*

At the age of thirty, ROZENE MEEKER'S mind was displaying aberrations which suggested that her brain had been damaged when she nearly drowned in a well as a child.

Meeker Memorial Museum Photo

F. W. Cragin Collection, Pioneer Museum

Among thronging crowds in Denver, JOSEPHINE MEEKER posed for photographs in a warm suit she had made from an annuity blanket during her twenty-three days of captivity. She told reporters often that the Utes had respected her person, but many wondered if she spoke the truth.

Pioneer Museum, Colorado Springs

Old acquaintance was never forgotten by Mrs. CHARLES ADAMS and CHIPETA. They loved to sit hand in hand discussing the past, and to shiver delightedly while recalling their acquaintanceship at Los Pinos Agency with Packer the Man-Eater. This photo was taken at the Adams's Manitou home in 1912 during a Colorado Springs festival at which Chipeta was an honored guest.

left the Uncompahgre in February without money, Winchester rifle or skinning knife. All he had then was a hatchet. The articles he had now belonged to the five missing men.

General Adams fancied himself quite an amateur detective, and he planned to gather more damning data before shaking Packer down. But Mrs. General had acquired literary ambitions of late. She saw a fine detective story here for *Harper's,* and she went after it forthrightly the very next morning. Her own account (*Harper's* didn't buy it) read in part:

> There was no hotel in Saguache but our good friend Otto Mears kept open house for travelers with royal hospitality. In the Mears dining room, I saw a big, burly, sullen fellow leaning against a window. His expression was sulky, angry. I asked other diners why he was angry. "He is mad," they said, "because he had to wait for his breakfast. He is in a hurry to get out of the country."
>
> It was the custom at Mears' for ladies to eat first at the table. I said, "Oh, let him sit down with me. He wants his breakfast."
>
> The big man sat beside me. I said, "So you are Packer, are you? How thankful you must feel to get back to civilization!"
>
> He nodded.
>
> "But where do you suppose the rest of your party can be?"
>
> Strange look!
>
> "How do I know? I didn't desert them. They deserted me!"
>
> "They may be starving! It is worse than murder to abandon them! Why don't you go back and search for them?"
>
> "I'm sick. I have no money, no grub, no clothes."
>
> "Then you will be a murderer!"
>
> Packer turned pale! His trembling hands played with bread crumbs!
>
> At last he said, "Will General Adams send men along to help me find them?"
>
> "Yes."
>
> "I'll go then."

On May 3, General and Mrs. Adams, Otto Mears and others rode to Los Pinos with Packer in custody. At Major Downer's mail shelter just short of Cochetopa Pass they met the recu-

perating Loutsenhizer party of five. Of this scene, Mrs. General
wrote:

> The second division of the expedition! Even now, after
> weeks of rest and food at the cow camp and at Los Pinos they
> were a terrible looking sight! They reminded me of prisoners
> who came out of Libby and Andersonville — gaunt, thin,
> weak! Their eyes were fixed and strange! But Packer was fat!
> General Adams asked Packer to unhitch the horses from our
> covered wagon. While he was occupied, one of the Loutsen-
> hizer men told my husband there must have been foul play!
> He said that he and other Provo men would come to the
> Agency to help see that justice was done! [1]

During that week, Adams and the Provo men punched
Packer's story full of holes. But he had a new one ready and
he presented it on August 8 to a conclave of Agency employees,
several Provo men, Otto Mears and Chief Ouray. Otto was more
fearful than ever of imminent scandal. Ouray had been certain
since April 16 why Packer was so fat. It sickened him just to
think of trying to explain it to his Utes.

This time, Packer swore, he was telling the solemn truth, so
help me. He had eaten a few friends, of course, or parts of them.
But there was no law against eating people, if no crime were
committed. They'd run out of grub soon after leaving the Uncompahgre. On February 19 poor old Israel Swan, aged seventy,
had died of starvation. The five survivors ate him, lean and
tough though he was. On February 25, Wilson Bell of Michigan
killed James Humphrey of Philadelphia. Humphrey's flesh kept
the four others in meat until about March 3 when the German
butcher, Frank Miller, died accidentally. That had been a good
thing. They were hungry again, and besides Miller had rheumatism and delayed them.

The three remaining men made out on Miller until about
March 17. Then Wilson Bell, the rotter, shot and killed sixteen-
year-old George Noon. Packer had to give Bell credit for sharing
young George with him. The two ate George in a fortnight,

meanwhile reaching Lake San Cristobal. At lunchtime on April second, Bell got that bright look in his eyes. He swung at Packer with the butt end of his rifle, missed, and the stock broke on a tree. Packer and Bell fought. Packer lost two teeth and killed Bell with his hatchet in self-defense. Soon, the snow was gone and Packer followed the tracks of Otto Mears's embryo toll road to Los Pinos. He carried along enough of Wilson Bell to last him through, roasting him as needed with coals from the coffeepot.

To back up the new confession, Packer led the Provo men west to the Lake Fork to find what was left of Bell and the broken gunstock. But he wouldn't go from there on south to Lake San Cristobal. He said it would be useless. Everything looked different to him now. Nothing was found. Back at Los Pinos, he demanded his release so that he could clear out. General Adams refused, though Otto Mears told him piteously more than once that it didn't do his community any good to have a cannibal hanging around. Adams turned Packer over to Sheriff Amos Wall, a Mears man, for safekeeping in the log jail Mears had built and donated to Saguache County.

Otto was right. Packer was bad news for Saguache. All that summer of '74, tourists rode up from Del Norte to have a look at the Man-Eater and at the peculiar town where, according to the Del Norte Board of Trade, he was an honored resident. The influx burgeoned in August when Packer's second confession blew up. The remains of all five missing men were found at one spot — near Lake San Cristobal around a single campfire. Each, obviously, had been murdered with Packer's hatchet as he slept, stripped of valuables and systematically eaten. Mears was frantically worried. Discovery of this gruesome evidence meant a long horrid trial at Saguache . . . and nation-wide notoriety for Mearstown.

Well, what do you know? One dark night in September Packer escaped from the Mears-Wall jail and vanished from Colorado Territory. Otto was properly astounded — and immensely relieved. And, as things turned out, Packer's fortuitous escape did save Saguache Town and Saguache County from further connection with the case. Before Packer was recaptured, Hinsdale County had been created out of the west part of Saguache County, with Lake City as the Hinsdale County seat. Thus the scene of Packer's alleged crime was in Saguache County no longer.

The recapture was a long time coming, and beyond our chronology. In March 1883 Frenchy Cabazon, one of the original twenty-one Provo miners, stopped for the night at John Brown's ranch in Wyoming. As he drifted off to sleep he heard a familiar voice talking in the next room — Packer's. Frenchy met Packer next day and was not recognized by him. The Man-Eater had changed his name to John Swartze, and had replaced the missing two teeth with false teeth. On Frenchy's tip, he was arrested by Wyoming authorities and bound over to the Sheriff of Hinsdale County after General Adams journeyed to Cheyenne and identified him.

In his first trial at Lake City, Packer was found guilty of murder. Judge M. B. Gerry of Lake City District Court pronounced the death sentence. But the sentence was reversed and Packer was tried again in 1886 for mere manslaughter at the new town of Gunnison. This time he was sent to Canon City for forty years. In 1900, Polly Pry, a popular sob sister for the *Denver Post,* stirred up such sympathy for him that he was paroled by Governor Charles S. Thomas, who resigned as Governor the next day.

Packer lived on peacefully near Denver — raising chickens, tending babies, prospecting, odd-jobbing and finding good homes for stray cats. He died in 1907 at nearby Littleton, where he is buried.

Nobody can ever know exactly what happened at that secluded camp above Lake San Cristobal beyond the fact that Packer ate quite a few people. But unquestionably this interesting achievement changed the tenor of his life and made a happy man out of a dour and disagreeable one. In his later years he enjoyed the affectionate esteem of his community and of thousands of strangers who were proud to shake the hand of a bona fide cannibal.

Perhaps a little attention is what we all need, no matter how we get it.[2]

CHAPTER X

Uneasy Chief

THERE WAS A PARALLEL through most of the 1870s between Nathan Meeker's struggle to make his Union Colony people do what he thought they ought to do and Ouray's struggle to keep the Colorado Utes in hand so that they wouldn't lose any more of their homeland. The Weeminuche Utes and the Capotes under Chief Ignacio behaved well in southwestern Colorado on the fringe of the San Juan cession. The groups who kept Ouray awake nights were those at White River in the north and the Muaches in the southeast, operating out of Cimarron and Taos.

The White River leaders, Chief Douglas and Chief Jack, were feeling expansive, and for good reason. In 1869, the Union Pacific Railroad was completed across southern Wyoming. U. P. officials began a heavy campaign of land promotion in Eastern newspapers. Settlers by the hundreds poured into the U.P. shanty town of Rawlins, one hundred and eighty-five miles north of White River Agency, and fanned southward to take fertile homesteads on the Little Snake, which twisted along the Colorado-Wyoming border.

In those same eventful years, placer gold drew swarms of miners to Bug Town and Poverty Bar below Hahn's Peak. The diggings were just beyond the Continental Divide, perhaps fifty miles north of the Ute Reservation. Some miners got to Hahn's Peak from Rawlins. Others arrived from Denver and Central City by crossing Middle Park and ascending Gore Pass to Bear River which ran north and then west near Hahn's Peak.

It was Manifest Destiny again, closing in on the Utes from two new directions, and the White River bands found prosperity in the pressure. They had been the unregarded poor relations of the other Colorado Utes and they had inferiority complexes. Now they could make hay. They were expert hunters of deer, elk, and antelope which were fair substitutes for the disappearing buffalo of Wyoming and North Park. Douglas and Jack developed a good market for their buckskin and elk hide among homesteaders and miners.

They found a still larger game market when J. S. Littlefield succeeded General Adams as White River Indian Agent in '71 and stayed on until '74. Littlefield was too ambitious to be satisfied with his Agent's salary of one hundred and twenty-five dollars a month. He doubled it and tripled it by serving as commission man for the White River groups. Several times a year his Indian Bureau wagons arrived at the U. P. freight station in Rawlins with five or six tons of elk and deer hide, antlers and bones, which he auctioned to Omaha and Chicago buyers.

With their hide profits, the White River Utes were able to increase their pony herds and improve quality to a point rivaling even the herds of Ouray's Uncompahgre band. They assumed the airs and arrogance and self-confidence of the newly rich. Several traders set up log cabin stores on Little Snake and Bear River and competed for their business by flattering them and petting them. They sold them fine bridles and saddles, iron pots and knives, up-to-date Winchester rifles, Colt revolvers and fixed ammunition.

The Ute group noticed that the new white populations along the Union Pacific road and around Denver caused deer and elk and bighorn sheep to move out of the congestion and to head for the high wilds on the White River sector of the Ute Reservation. They began to conserve this increased Reservation game by hunting elsewhere — in North Park, in the Bear and Little Snake valleys, in the Seminoes and Sierra Madres of southern

Wyoming. They figured that such conservation would postpone indefinitely the need to start taking the white man's road as proposed by Ouray. When settlers objected to their hunting off the Reservation, Douglas and Jack told them that the settlers' valleys really belonged to the White River Utes. The settlers, they said, had gotten in through Ouray's perfidy at the treaty table.

Meanwhile, far to the southeast, the Muache Utes pursued their own peculiar anti-Ouray pattern, which requires some review because of its bearing later on White River affairs. Even in the 1850s, Ouray had been aware that his tribe's problem children were these five hundred Muaches. Their leader then was red-shirted Chief Blanco of the jutting forehead. A subchief was the swash-buckling Kaneache. Another henchman was Washington, a small, bow-legged Muache with bloodshot, crossed eyes. A fourth was Colorow, the huge, slovenly Indian given to beetling and pontifical oratory. Colorow was not a Ute at all, except by adoption. His father was a Comanche, his mother a Jicarilla Apache.

These Muaches roamed widely and spent much time in Mexican dives at Taos and Cimarron, drinking, gambling, quarreling and studiously acquiring the white man's worst habits. When Kit Carson became their Taos Agent in 1854, they were angry because he could not deliver rations which had been promised by the previous agent. Soon after, a Mexican vaquero killed a Muache for his buckskin jacket, fixing their mood nicely for Christmas Eve when Chief Blanco and fifty friends went to old Fort Pueblo on the Arkansas and asked for corn.

The drunken party of Mexican monte players, who had had an all-night session in the fort, refused the corn. The Muaches stormed in, murdered a dozen Mexicans, stole corn and livestock and rode west with hostages, including Chipeta Miera, a Mexican girl. Chipeta was sad, having just seen her husband disemboweled. The Muaches paused at a spring. Chipeta drank there and washed her tear-stained face. A Muache, angry at her for being sad in such charming company, shot an arrow through her back. Chipeta fell, clutching the arrowhead which emerged from her breast. Muache children gathered about and stoned her the rest of the way to death. Or so goes the Mexican account.[1]

Punishment came the following March. Colonel Thomas Fauntleroy and five hundred men guided by Kit Carson found Muaches massed in San Luis Valley near Cochetopa Pass trail. The Indians were bombarded, chased over Poncha Pass and harried east and south toward Texas until they made peace in July. Then they resumed their roving and haunting of the Taos dives.

Chief Ouray had to remind the Muaches constantly that their behavior reflected on all Utes, since the whites didn't know one band from another. He lectured them on the evils of drink, gambling and brawling, and urged them to try to make out with fewer wives. He asked them to join his Uncompahgre band — and had the suggestion put into the Ute Treaty of 1863. No action. The Muaches declined to be reformed, especially by Ouray, who had insulted their own Chief Kaneache. This Kaneache was a theatrical character who owned several Army uniforms and a mule employed solely to tote his liquor. He had prevented Chief Blanco from pulling a gun on Kit Carson once, and rose to Muache chief after Kit hired him as scout in his Navajo campaign of '63–'64 and in the Texas Battle of Adobe Walls against the Comanches in '64.

Thereafter, Kaneache became a barroom pet of Army officers at Fort Union in New Mexico below Cimarron. Their admiration inspired him in '67 to see if there was any punch behind Ouray's claim to be head of the Ute Nation. One bright day, Kaneache donned his best blue Army coat, tall silk hat and Washington medal and announced that the Colorado Utes had a new boss named Kaneache. Then he led his Muaches on an alcoholic bust through the Mexican settlements over Raton Pass in Wet Mountain Valley and along Huerfano River.

Hearing of the bust, Ouray sent runners to warn settlers and notified the ailing General Kit Carson at Fort Garland to hold his troops in garrison. Ouray's men would handle the Muaches. His fleet force under his deceptively gentle war chief, Shavano, hurried over Mosca Pass and clashed briefly with Kaneache's warriors. Kaneache was captured and landed next day in Ouray's camp near Fort Garland with a bad hangover and minus silk hat, Army coat, medal, pants and breechclout. He apologized to Ouray, got his clothes back and was allowed to return to Cimarron.

To UNDERSTAND HOW the Muaches happened to become so-phisticated, theatergoing, part-time residents of the great metropolis of Denver, we must return to General Edward M. McCook, who replaced A. H. Hunt as Governor of Colorado Territory on June 12, 1869, making no secret of his intention to earn easy money fast. Denver's rosy future was apparent to the dapper inventor of Los Pinos Creek whose ingenuity had created a Ute job for his brother-in-law, James B. Thompson, and produced a husband, General Charles Adams, for his sister-in-law, Margaret Thompson. McCook sold his influence at good prices to many Denver tycoons, pushing irrigation, railroads, mines, smelters, real estate and banks.

His best scheme derived from a careful reading of Ouray's Ute Treaty of 1868. As ex-officio Superintendent of Indian Affairs, McCook controlled all Ute treaty funds and Agency expenses — something like two hundred thousand dollars a year all told. The more he thought of that big Ute windfall, the more he felt that ways must be discovered to make it more lucrative to the Queen City of the Rockies, the soon-to-be capital of the State of Colorado. He was assured by Blake

Street saloonkeepers, gamblers and gunsmiths in particular that they would be tangibly grateful to him if he attracted numerous Utes to town to buy whisky and guns and geegaws, to drop cash at the monte tables, and attend the variety shows.

There were good moral, as well as financial reasons, why Denver deserved its own Ute Indian Agency. Indians, McCook asserted, should live near cities like Denver and Boston so that they could become civilized quickly. But that pesky Chief Ouray was a stumbling block, with his argument that Agencies, even in small towns like Cimarron, were poison for his people. Worse still, Ouray was pushing a sound plan for a Ute economy far from cities which threatened to let the Utes live as free men in a white world. McCook, like countless other whites, was shocked at the very thought of an unexploitable, self-sufficient, competing Indian.

It was brother-in-law James B. Thompson who solved McCook's problem. He got wind of the anti-Ouray sentiment among the Muache and White River Utes and sent word out from the Governor's office to Kaneache and Washington, to Colorow and Nevava's Ouray-hating nephew, Piah, that no Ute had to live on Ouray's Reservation if he didn't want to, regardless of Ouray's Treaty of 1868. Instead he could register with Indian Agent Thompson as a "Denver Ute" and get his supplies and annuities at the government warehouse just across the South Platte from the saloons and gun shops on Blake Street.

The weird Denver Ute Agency lasted through McCook's two weird regimes as Territorial Governor. The august Colorado Republican leaders had been perfectly aware that McCook was at least a slick operator if not a downright crook even before President Grant removed him reluctantly in '73 for Ute Indian beef contract frauds. But the Republican leaders were practical as well as august and they supported McCook because he helped their business ventures and got patronage for Colorado Territory from the President and other Washington officials. They

were not at all unhappy in '74 when Grant forgave McCook his
sins and reinstated him as Governor and they even dropped a
tear or two a year later when he had to quit politics for good.
The cause was an uprising among the rank and file who had
sent Thomas Patterson, a Democrat, to Congress as Territorial
delegate in protest against McCook's continued peculations.

McCook's Denver Utes circulated about in small clannish
groups of ten or twenty lodges each. Some of them roamed the
Front Range foothills between Colorado Springs and Denver.
Others hunted in Middle Park, patronized the mining camp
theaters and parked for weeks at a time at Agent Thompson's
Denver warehouse on their way east to the Republican River
where a few buffalo survived. Their relations with Chief
Douglas and Jack grew more and more cordial, with dislike of
Ouray as a focal point for good relations.

They rode up Gore Pass and down the Bear often, or into
North Park, to join White River hunting parties. By 1876,
Chief Kaneache, Colorow, Washington and others regarded
themselves no longer as Muaches from Cimarron but as members of the White River band.

Undeniably, these anti-Ouray, anti-treaty rugged individual-
ists added much color to the regional scene during the six-year
career of Thompson's Denver Ute Agency. Ranching house-
wives came to feel slighted if the huge-stomached Colorow
didn't bluster into their kitchens occasionally with three or
four squaws demanding biscuits, sugar lumps and bean soup.
Colorow's squaws were imaginatively arrayed, sometimes wearing bare hoops outside their skirts and white nightcaps on their
heads. Two of them wore flour sacks bearing brand names and
the flour slogans, HARD TO BEAT and ROUGH AND READY. Once
at California Gulch Colorow was induced to drink a tincupful
of Epsom salts for indigestion and went gunning for his in-
ducer next morning "looking like a busted umbrella."

Chief Piah, a small, dark Ute with a small boy's mischievous
face, dined when in Denver at Charpiot's Restaurant with white

friends like Judge James B. Belford, Colorado's first Congress-man. Piah liked to discuss state matters with Governor Mc-Cook, who urged him one day to stop loafing and try plowing, raising crops and building houses. According to McCook, Piah replied, "Me great warrior. Warriors no plow. Me go to Wash-ington and see John Grant. He no work. He no plow. He no build the White House. Me see John Grant's squaw Nellie. She told me she no work either. Tell you what you do, McCook. Ask John Grant to come here. He a warrior like me. We fight Arapahoes and kill plenty braves and catch plenty squaws. Then squaws work and me and John Grant have bully time."

Agent Thompson became fond of his meal-ticket charges, guarding them from swindlers and sending them to Dr. W. H. Williams when they were sick. His big office in the Tappan Block at Tenth and Holladay Streets served as a Ute clubroom, handsomely decorated by club members with great elk and bighorn sheep heads, buffalo robes and an admirable dried Sioux scalp. Space was reserved where archers could show their skill, shooting arrows through an inch-thick book at thirty feet.

None of these Utes were true alcoholics, though Piah and Kaneache seemed to qualify at times. One night, Kaneache weaved into the *Rocky Mountain Herald* newsroom while the editor, "Professor" O. J. Goldrick, was in the pressroom. Gold-rick — Denver's Irish fashion plate — had just bought a beauti-ful silk hat. A reporter praised Kaneache's Army uniform — but criticized his old plug hat, replacing it with Goldrick's brand-new silk number. In the hatband, the reporter stuck a large red label stating, "Superior Cocktail Bitters."

Kaneache lurched off happily down Larimer Street and was a sensation in the hat during calls at several saloons, at the American House, and at an undertaking establishment where he tried to sign up for a course in embalming. There Agent Thompson and the Denver constabulary, called out by the in-censed "Professor," descended on him and rescued Goldrick's

beloved hat. Thompson hauled Kaneache off to the Thirteenth
Street bull pen where he sobered him up on a diet of bread and
water.

Thompson conducted several Spring Bear Dances in Denver,
at which Kaneache was the efficient floor manager. But in '73,
the Agent feared municipal ire and banned an elaborate Scalp
Dance Circus organized by his interpreter, Uriah Curtis, the
Muaches' adopted white Ute. However, this scandalous event
was allowed to occur on Denver's outskirts the following summer, and the performance was attacked in the *Rocky Mountain News* by Editor William Byers, who was himself being
attacked just then for scandalous deportment with Mrs. Hattie
Sancomb, the graceful milliner with the dazzling teeth. Byers
wrote in part:

> The Utes, with the pious Piah at their head, held a scalp
> dance last evening near Sloan's Lake over three bloody Chey-
> enne topknots which dangled from three poles. . . . It was dis-
> gusting to notice among the spectators lots of ladies prominent
> in church and society circles straining for a sight of the reek-
> ing scalps, which they scanned as eagerly as if they had been
> new bonnets.

THERE IS NOTHING MORE DEMEANING than the spectacle of people stepping from their own environment into another environment which they don't understand. Ouray was distressed most
by this aspect of the Denver Utes. In aping the whites with plug
hats and hoop skirts and noisy drunkenness, they lowered the
dignity of all his race. Their acts seemed to corroborate what
many whites wished to believe — that Indians were not really
human and therefore had no human rights. He was glad when
James Thompson had to close the Denver Agency in December
of '75. Most of the Denver Utes transferred to White River
Agency and teamed up with Chief Jack, which meant no improvement in Ouray's relations with them. But he was glad to
have them out of Denver even so.

Elsewhere, Ouray's troubles had been multiplying. In '72, while he was giving his oath in Episcopalian language to Felix Brunot that no Ute had ever harmed a white man, two remote Utes had to embarrass him by murdering the Navajo Indian Agent. In '73, Chipeta's brother, Sapovanero, tried to kill him at the Los Pinos blacksmith shop in protest against the "Brunot Treaty." Ouray broke Sapovanero's wrist, threw him in the irrigation ditch and was preparing to cut out his heart when Chipeta intervened. Often he had to spike rumors that his Utes were shooting noble San Juan miners and raping their wives. Sometimes Fort Garland soldiers got halfway to the Uncompahgre before Ouray could show that the miners had staged these "Ute massacres" to scare away new prospectors. Some miners loved to hunt for "slow elk" which was Otto Mears's term for strayed Ute cattle bearing the USID brand (United States Interior Department). The initials, Mears said, stood for "You Steal — I Divide."

The surveyors were a problem — Land Office surveyors, Hayden surveyors, Army surveyors, assorted railroad surveyors and plain poachers pretending to be surveyors. They were forever tangling with hotheaded young Utes who didn't like to be cussed up and down and threatened with pistols on their own land.

The Land Office men were a double calamity. Many of their lines were way off, causing endless misunderstandings between Utes and settlers. In '74, Ouray charged publicly that the Reservation's eastern boundary was placed wrong by them to benefit landgrabbers, including former Governor Evans, former Governor A. C. Hunt and Governor Sam Elbert. Land Office Surveyor J. W. Miller ran a north boundary near White River which was seventeen and a half miles short of treaty terms. A bit south of Ouray's Uncompahgre village was Uncompahgre Park, a lovely vale four miles square. Ouray had retained it specifically for the Utes in Article One of the "Brunot Treaty." Now Miller surveyed it wrong, excluding it from the Reservation. In rushed settlers from the San Juan mining camps.

When Carl Schurz had a company of soldiers sent from Fort Garland to move them off, Teller got everyone in Congress weeping for the poor settlers who had entered Uncompahgre Park in good faith and now were about to be torn from the land of their fore — well, anyhow, the land. So Schurz relented and recalled the soldiers to keep peace with Teller, and gave the settlers six months to move — which was, of course, long enough to consolidate their position. In his Uncompahgre Park speeches, Teller perfected his anti-Ute technique. One paragraph would consist of an enraged demand that Ouray's Uncompahgre Utes become farmers. In the next, he would advocate taking Uncompahgre Park from the Utes because it was farm land and therefore the Utes didn't need it.

A bitter blow to Ouray was the resignation of General Adams as Los Pinos Agent. During the Packer notoriety, some Boston Unitarians had looked up the General's history and discovered how Governor McCook had concealed Adams's Catholic leanings. Catholics were not supposed to hold Agency jobs in country reserved for the Unitarians by President Grant. Felix Brunot had to see to it that the Commissioner of the Indian Bureau replaced Adams with someone who believed in a Unitarian God. Before Adams left Los Pinos, he obtained funds to move that Agency from its dizzy site on top of the world near Cochetopa Pass to a grassy spot at six thousand feet of altitude on the Uncompahgre River three miles upstream from Ouray's winter village. Its name at the new site remained Los Pinos Agency.

Ouray favored the move because it helped him test out the novel provisions for individual land allotment in the Treaty of 1868. On the west bank of the Uncompahgre, nine miles downstream from the new Agency, he laid out a one-hundred-and-sixty-acre farm. He didn't really want a farm, even to please Senator Teller. He would have liked to continue living in barbaric splendor on his one-thousand-dollar-a-year salary as Ute chief and be free to hunt or to race his horses whenever he wished. But he had resolved to show the Utes by example that living in a house was pleasanter than living in a canvas tepee, that raising sheep was as honorable as chasing elk, and that there was a peculiar satisfaction in owning land and having money in the First National Bank of Denver even though it was hard to explain why.

While his friends laughed at him, Ouray acquired a flock of sheep, fenced in eighty acres of hay and truck garden plots and built barns, warehouses, a root cellar and — silliest of all from the spacious Ute viewpoint — a privy. The government gave him a thirty-by-forty-foot adobe house. Chipeta furnished it with hideous comforts from Denver — spangled carpets and squeaky brass beds, golden oak tables and stifling overstuffed chairs, fragile dishes, writhing carved kerosene lamps and window shades to guard a modesty which Chipeta did not possess. Chipeta despised the inconvenience and pretension of white domestic arrangements but she went on doggedly washing endless dishes, polishing silver teapots, making beds, doing laundry on Mondays and cooking indoors over a hot iron stove. She was as determined as Ouray to show that Indians could cope with the white landscape. But she refused to use the rocking chair which Mrs. General Adams presented to her. Rocking, she said, made her sick to her stomach.

Rough going. For their pains and self-sacrifice, Ouray and Chipeta were told by Ute friends and Ute enemies that they were dishonoring their forefathers and flaunting tradition. White men were more critical still. Though Senator Teller couldn't think of any significant comment, other anti-Utes declared that the perfidious Ouray had sold out his people for a thousand-dollar-a-year salary and one hundred and sixty acres of land. And the "greedy redskin" had the nerve to set up a farm! He ought to be hustled on a rail back into the Elk Mountains and not be taking food out of white men's mouths by trying to earn a white man's living!

During the summer of 1876, in the midst of the immense

excitement attending Colorado's admission to the Union as a state, Ouray became aware that something was wrong with his marvelous physique. He was only forty-three but he was experiencing periods of weariness and depression, of failing stamina and agility. Next year he made several visits to Dr. Lewis in Canon City. Lewis found albumen in his urine and diagnosed his symptoms as chronic nephritis. Thereafter he had more frequent spells of backache, vomiting and a puffy face.

His mental health deteriorated too, as his hope faded that he could save his people from the tragic fate of other tribes. Twenty years of futility! General Adams kept him posted on white plots in Denver and Washington to steal the Reservation, now that Colorado had the power of statehood. Senator Chaffee put through a bill for study on how to consolidate the Ute Agencies at White River — signifying drastic land reduction. The Utes had few friends now — only a handful of traders and settlers. Even Otto Mears was pulling anti-Ute strings — little Otto, whom Ouray had helped on his way to San Juan wealth and power by making him official Ute trader.

And now Secretary Schurz was sending Nathan Meeker to White River as Indian Agent. Ouray knew a lot about Meeker. He had seen Greeley grow, and he knew that its founder was not the usual small-time huckster sent out by the Indian Bureau to pay some petty political debt. Meeker had force and initiative. He had contacts reaching into the Cabinet of President Hayes. And he had been hand-picked by Senator Teller, the most powerful politician in the Rockies. Teller was like Chaffee and Evans and Byers and the rest of the Denver crowd. He was committed, politically and temperamentally, to removing the Utes from Colorado — somehow, anyhow; nevertheless, regardless, notwithstanding.

As Nathan Meeker left Greeley for White River in the spring of '78, Ouray's courage began to fail, like his health and spirit. He was not afraid for himself, though he realized that he was the ultimate foe of all these anti-Ute whites. What he feared was an immediate Ute explosion which would abrogate treaties automatically.

Put a man like Meeker at a place like White River, at a time like this — and anything could happen.

CHAPTER XI

South of Rawlins

THE MORNING OF MAY 3, 1878, was on the chilly side at the Greeley depot, but Nathan Meeker paid it no mind. His handsome face, his mild blue eyes and his lean, straight figure did not seem like those of a sexagenarian on whom time was closing in. He behaved like a young man again and he felt that the world was his oyster. His shabby overcoat let the wind through; but his glowing hope, and the gay scarf Josie had knitted for him, kept him warm.

He kissed the girls all around and stepped briskly on the Cheyenne train. He was too full of himself and the boundless promise of his future to see the worry in Arvilla's gray eyes, to notice how small and fragile and old she had become. Josie, the practical one, smiled cheerfully, hiding her fears and her regrets. She loved her job and her friends at the awning factory in Denver, but she and Arvilla had agreed to join Meeker at the Ute Agency in July. Mary Meeker kissed her father good-by sweetly. Rozene's kiss was a petulant peck. Meeker had decided that Rozene and Mary could help him pay off that one-thousand-dollar debt to the Horace Greeley estate by operating a boardinghouse at the Meeker mansion while the other three were at White River. Rozene did not care to be a landlady. The first boarder had been chosen, a Montanan named F. S. Lusk. The foul smoke of his stogies made her head ache, and he was much too unrefined for romance.

Meeker did not plan to stay in the White River wilderness long. Two years at most would suffice to pay his debts, teach the Utes the joys of productive labor and establish his reputation as an Indian expert. He had remembered Ralph's plea not to put too much family on the payroll. He hired only Josie as teacher and physician at sixty-five dollars a month. Arvilla would earn a bit as postmistress but that was a Post Office, not an Indian Bureau, job (Bela Hughes, his Democratic friend, had got it from David Key, President Hayes's Democratic Postmaster General). Winfield Scott Fullerton, Mary's fiancé, would come to work for him in July. Since Mary's romance was secret, nobody would know that Meeker had hired his future son-in-law. Josie would run a boardinghouse at White River on the side, feeding all comers at $2.50 a week. Her business would prosper because Meeker was going to engage Greeley bachelors mainly for his Agency staff.

This first trip was exploratory. Meeker wanted to see how things had been left at the Agency by his Unitarian predecessor, the Reverend E. H. Danforth, and he would pay off Danforth's men. He had with him a good friend of the old days, William H. Post, aged forty-six. Post and Ralph Meeker had led the attempt to burn down the whisky mill near Greeley in '71. Post had been Union Colony Secretary for a year and then had returned to his stationery store at Yonkers, New York. When Meeker asked him to come to White River as Agency clerk, he was glad to leave Yonkers because he was having wife trouble. And Yonkers was — Yonkers.

At Cheyenne, the two men changed from Denver Pacific to Union Pacific cars and clattered West all night, through Laramie and the United States Army post of Fort Steele to Rawlins, an ugly huddle of board shacks and warehouses in the Red Desert. Everything, Meeker observed with lighthearted disdain, was wrong with the place. It was like Sheridan, Kansas, in '69 — saloons, gambling houses, buxom hussies and a six-gun at your head at breakfast to remind you to pass the butter. It was the seat of Carbon County and it served a woolly and lawless region stretching north to Fort Washakie and the Snake Reservation, west to Fort Bridger, east to the Medicine Bow Range and south one hundred and eighty-five miles to White River. A principal butte was Maggie's Nipple, honoring the distinguished frontage of Mrs. George Baggs, whose husband got Ouray's permission in '73 to cross the Ute Reservation to the Little Snake with his herd.

Meeker and Post explored the town thoroughly. They watched Chinese miners eating noodles with chopsticks on street corners, Union Pacific tie crews gossiping outside James France's store, cowboys in the Alhambra Billiard Hall, their mounts hitched to the long rack outside. In Foote's Saloon, the cross-eyed bartender, Little Van, presented them proudly to the outlaw, Butch Cassidy, and to the horse thief, Johnny Red Shirt, and to the Baltimore physician, Doc Ricketts, who seemed to prefer morphine on Front Street to respectability on Chesapeake Bay.

They met all three Rankin brothers, civic leaders who required that the frail sisters conduct themselves with dignity on Lower Row. Sheriff Jim Rankin's fame was confined in '78 to Carbon County. Soon he would be widely known for arresting Big Nose George Parrott, the eminent train robber. Jailer Bob Rankin would be famous, too, because Big Nose George knocked him out cold with his leg irons. After the hanging, enterprising Rawlinsites tanned Big Nose George's hide and made purses out of it for the tourist trade.

At Joe Rankin's livery stable, the visitors found the Agency's four-mule team and the driver, a slight young Englishman, Joe Collom, who said he crossed the Atlantic on the Great Eastern and was ranching now near the Ute Reservation. Joe Rankin told Meeker that he and Post would be the first people into White River since fall. Joe, a stout, quiet, Pennsylvanian of thirty-four, had been a soldier, an oil roustabout north of Pittsburgh, a freighter in the Sioux country, a gold miner at Deadwood, Central City and Hahn's Peak. He had come to Rawlins in '72 and helped mine the native red pigment which was used to paint the Brooklyn Bridge. He was a freighter, outfitter,

White River mail carrier *and* a founder of the Scottish Rites Masons. To Meeker he seemed a solid citizen.

Meeker crossed Front Street and introduced himself to Mr. James France, first citizen of Rawlins. France, like Otto Mears, was not much bigger than a large bug. He made up for it by growing giant whiskers to his knees. When working, France tucked the whiskers in his shirt. But meeting the new White River Indian Agent was a social event so he displayed the whiskers at full mast. He explained that he had officiated at the birth of Rawlins in '68 and opened the first store — which became the unofficial bank also. France grubstaked Hahn's Peak miners and cashed Fort Steele and Ute Agency vouchers. He supplied consignment goods to traders along the Little Snake and Bear Rivers. He held Interior Department contracts for hauling Ute supplies to White River at three dollars and a half per hundred pounds. His activities involved an annual gross in goods and services of half a million dollars.

France told Meeker a tale of woe. The White River Utes were sullen and restive for fifty reasons, all bad for the business of James France. Twenty-five thousand pounds of Ute flour and Ute oats and a year's Ute annuity supplies lay spoiling at Rawlins (since September '76), because a contractor had skipped without paying the Union Pacific freight bill. Commissioner Hayt's Indian Bureau hadn't sent any rations or annuities in '77 because, France said, Hayt was too busy: (1) running his Second National Bank of Jersey City; (2) gathering Republican votes from Polish immigrants in Hoboken; (3) clearing title to mining claims on Indian lands in Arizona for his son; (4) making speeches urging Ute removal to Indian Territory. The Indian Bureau owed the Utes one hundred and twelve thousand dollars cash for San Juan Cession and other lands.

Without rations, France continued, Douglas's band and Jack's band had damned near starved last winter. To keep alive, they scoured Wyoming, Bear Valley and Little Snake Valley for game. A few settlers objected to their wandering and heated the wires to Washington with fake claims for damages alleged to have been caused by Ute arson and shooting of slow elk. They filed claims also against the Ute annuity account for their rotted-out sheds and cabins and for ancient or diseased stock which they destroyed themselves.

France droned on and on. He had heard that William Byers wasn't regaling Chief Piah at Charpiot's Restaurant in Denver any more. The Utes had served his purposes and were just a nuisance to Byers, now that a good road crossed Berthoud Pass to his Middle Park ranch which surrounded the healing pool called Hot Sulphur Springs. The pool was a huge saucer in solid rock with the water pouring down from six feet above. Tourists didn't want to go bathing at Hot Sulphur with a lot of dirty redskins. So Byers had forbidden Piah and Colorow and the other former Denver Utes to sooth their rheumatism in their ancient spa. Furthermore, Byers apparently persuaded General Pope to guard Middle Park in summer with soldiers. The mere thought of these Middle Park soldiers, France added, sent the White River bands into tantrums. Soldiers reminded them of chains, of hanging, of being dragged to Indian Territory, of the Sand Creek Massacre and of white men hacking off parts of Indian women and children to decorate their parlors.

Everything was out of kilter, France asserted, at White River Agency itself. When the Reverend Danforth replaced J. S. Littlefield as Agent in '74, he made little progress teaching his Utes to farm and to live in houses. Uriah Curtis of the unfortunate Scalp Dance Circus was Danforth's interpreter. The Army had asked Curtis to recruit Utes to fight Sitting Bull and his Sioux, so Curtis went around telling the Indians that farming was woman's work. Danforth's most promising Ute farmers threw their hoes in White River and lit out for Fort Fetterman. Danforth was sore as the devil, and got into a two-hour brawl over the matter with the big medicine man, Johnson. The brawl ended in a draw. Then, when Carl Schurz came in as Secretary of the Interior later, he wrote Danforth and gave him hell for brawling with Johnson and for permitting his Utes to leave the Reservation to join General Crook. That was a hot one. Danforth resigned his job by return mail.

The Ute warriors had returned from the Sioux country full of whisky and venereal disease. Chief Douglas had opposed their going after conferring with Chief Ouray on the Uncompahgre. Chief Jack had favored it, and became one of General Crook's pet scouts; when Jack got back to White River he was a celebrity, having been written up as an Army hero in the Eastern newspapers.

This Jack, France declared, was a man to watch. He seemed to have some Mexican blood, and possibly some Apache. He had come up from nothing. In the 1850s he was among a batch of children put up for sale at Salt Lake City by the famed Ute chief and Mormon elder, Walkara, when Brigham Young legalized slavery in Deseret. Walkara usually castrated boy slaves because he sold them to Navajo chiefs who didn't trust complete males in their female hogans. But Jack was bought by a Salt Lake City family named Norton. Mr. Norton didn't see any point in castrating him. Mr. Norton trusted his wives, or just didn't give a damn.

The Nortons raised Jack, taught him English and got him a job driving a Salt Lake City ice wagon. Six months on the ice wagon convinced Jack that white men lived a crazy life. He joined the Uintah Utes, married a Yampa Ute belle named Tatseegah, and went to White River to live under Chief Nevava. When Nevava died and Douglas became White River Chief in '68, Jack was important enough already to go to Washington with Ouray and other Ute leaders.

Jack had informed France recently that he was thirty-eight years old and that he regarded himself as actual head of the White River Utes because Douglas was over sixty and as tired and as sick as Chief Ouray. He insisted that Ouray's peace plan was no good. The only way to get along with white people was to make trouble the way Red Cloud, Sitting Bull and Crazy

Horse and their Sioux had done. And his policy was popular. Only twenty White River lodges were loyal to Douglas now. A hundred-odd supported Jack. The small Denver Ute bands — Colorow's, Kaneache's, Washington's, Piah's — shifted allegiance from month to month.

Meeker heard France out, closely attentive and smiling faintly. The smile broadened at the end when France urged Meeker to catch the first train toward Greeley if he valued his hide; the White River Agency was dynamite and was going to blow up soon. Meeker, France insisted, could accomplish nothing there. Douglas and Jack were prejudiced against him. They had asked for Uriah Curtis as their Agent, and they knew that Senator Teller had refused to press Curtis's application because Curtis was pratically a Ute himself and wouldn't bear down on them. Obviously, Teller believed that Nathan Meeker would bear down.

Well, Meeker told himself happily, "bearing down" was hardly the phrase to describe his plan of action. By persuasion, by love, by faith and by experience, Captain Armstrong was going to lead these unhappy people out of the darkness and misery of their archaic existence into the sunlight and comfort of modern technocracy. In the wilds of Colorado, the cooperative principles of Charles Fourier, in which the new Agent still believed with all his heart and soul, were going to bloom at last.

Two MORNINGS LATER — May 6 — Meeker, Post and Joe Collom rolled southwest out of Rawlins in the four-mule Agency wagon. It was one of those incomparable upland days. Meeker bubbled over with delight at its freshness, its cool fragrance, the limpid quality of the light, the divine optimism of the blue Wyoming sky. In his picnic mood, James France's warnings seemed to him even more frivolous than the night before. "These pioneers," Meeker told Post, "always exaggerate everything. It compensates them for the boredom of pioneer life."

Everywhere Meeker looked there was splendor. To the east and southeast were the purple forests of the Sierra Madre, dominated by Bridger Peak in Wyoming and Hahn's Peak in Colorado. Distantly ahead was the tumbling grandeur of Colorado's Western Slope, the blue unfolding of range after range. Meeker found beauty and interest even in this rising sage-and-alkali stretch of the Red Desert — scampering antelope, flopping magpies, the explosive whir of sage hens. He watched enchanted as two coyotes three yards apart harried a jackrabbit back and forth between them until the jack collapsed from weariness in its own little whirlpool of dust. He would write an editorial about it. How many poor devils in the overcrowded East were like that rabbit, harried to dusty death by debts and other evils of a stagnant economy?

Joe Collom explained that two roads led from Rawlins to the Colorado–Wyoming border. The shorter road ran due south through the Sierra Madre foothills, over the low Continental Divide at Bridger Pass, ending on the Little Snake at Charlie Perkins's store. It was too steep for the Agency wagon. He was taking them the long treeless way, seventy-five miles. They crossed the Divide almost without knowing it and descended Alamosa Gulch to Sulphur Springs, where they camped for the night in the low sage. Sulphur Springs had been one of Ben Holladay's stops in the 1860s, when his Overland stage ran from Denver to Salt Lake. Its twin attractions were a bunkhouse saloon and the graves of eight white men killed by Indians or alcohol, nobody knew which.

They reached the Little Snake at George Baggs's ranch next afternoon by way of Muddy Creek. The Little Snake Valley was a grassy Garden of Eden, and George's ranch was a show place not only because of Maggie Baggs's celebrated frontage but because of its fine log buildings and the high poles from which deer meat dangled to be kept fresh. Meeker was charmed by the Little Snake, a twisting blue ribbon through the tangle of greening cottonwoods and reddening willows. Green-winged teal, orange orioles and gorgeous yellow tanagers flashed about the mile-wide valley. The bench sage was five feet high, luxuriant contrast to the water-starved stuff on the Red Desert.

George Baggs, a big cowman, gave Meeker the regional lore. The Little Snake had been homesteaded soon after Bibleback Brown and Bill Slater started the Hahn's Peak gold rush in '69. Noah Reader, a Missouri tailor, was the first resident. He bought the fine tanned buckskin of the White River Utes and created a style of fringed pants and jackets which became fashionable in the area. That evening, Baggs took Meeker and Post a few miles upstream to see old Jim Baker who had fled in '73 from Denver's fleshpots. While Jim told about guiding the Captain Marcy party across the Ute Reservation in '57 and locating White River Agency with D. C. Oakes in '73, his Snake squaws, Monkey and Beans, lovingly combed his long red locks.

From Baker's, Baggs led his visitors to Charlie Perkins's. Charlie's store had everything from violin strings to dynamite. An adjacent hotel was run by half-breed Snake girls who, Meeker decided, performed other services besides making beds. In the log saloon, Meeker met Perkins himself and judged him to be a wily drunkard, half diplomat, half bandit. Charlie said that he was getting rich by trading Winchesters and ammunition to Jack and Douglas for their hides. He added proudly that he had killed a fellow recently with a beer bottle.

George Baggs rode south a piece on the following morning with Meeker, Post and Collom, describing what they would find over the next divide. Bear River was twice as wide and deep as the Little Snake and yet the Bear Valley was relatively undeveloped. The stiff pull up Gore Pass from Middle Park had impeded the flow of people from Denver. And lately the White River Utes were not cordial to ranchers pushing up against their Reservation. The Collom boys lived on Collom Creek; the Morgan tribe was down Bear River. Tom Iles's ranch and Hulitt's place and Peck's store were on the Bear near the mouth of Elkhead Creek. Up Bear River eastward, along the Gore Pass road, were the Smarts. Just beyond them was Major James B. Thompson, trying fresh fields after over-doing things a bit as Denver Ute Agent. Thompson was poli-ticking amiably as clerk of the new Routt County and as United States Timber Agent, whatever that was. James H. Crawford had a spread at Steamboat Springs.

Baggs turned back soon. Joe Collom led the way south along Fourmile Creek through prickly pear and greasewood, over the Little Snake–Bear River Divide and down the richer valley of Fortification Creek. The broken plateau to the west was covered with juniper and serviceberry and piñon. Eastward were tree-less hills and then the sharp profile of Hahn's Peak. They lunched at the odd porphyry dike, Fortification Rocks, the crenelated ridge of which reminded Meeker of Camelot and inspired him to recite, more or less accurately, twenty or thirty stanzas of Tennyson's *Idylls of the King.* And by nightfall they were camping on the Bear by Himley's Ford and Peck's one-room store, a counterless chaos of sacked coffee, sugar, flour, tobacco, guns and bullets. Peck was away but Mrs. Peck sat on some sacks nursing her baby. She told Meeker that she was postmistress and had named her post office Windsor, after the elegant Hotel Windsor then a-building in Denver.

Sixty-five miles still to go. The three men spent May 9 toiling over Williams Fork Mountains and slithering down Deal Gulch to Williams Fork — a winsome waterway, musical, blue-green and bounded on the north by tawny hills so monumental and so uniformly gullied that Meeker was reminded of the long row of elephants which he had seen in Philadelphia standing side by side at Barnum's Circus. Meeker was getting tired now. His zest was gone and his optimism was waning a trifle. A cold drizzle began as the three men made camp in the waisthigh grass along Deer Creek. Their sage fire would burn just enough to boil coffee and cook eggs but not to warm anybody. They dined soggily during a violent electrical storm, slept a little and were off again in the wet dawn, sloshing through the clay ooze of Milk Creek Valley and lunching miserably at Yellowjacket Pass with old Sleepy Cat Peak rising in the misty east like a troubled dream. Then they hurried down Coal Creek Canyon past Danforth's coal mine to Agency Park, and in late afternoon to the Agency, which stood on the sagey bench just above White River.[1]

Inside the two-acre stockade, Meeker and Post gazed on a depressing clutter of six small buildings with dirt roofs. The buildings looked abandoned and ready to collapse before the bitter wind which roared around Adams' Point into the valley from the river canyon. Some dispirited mules in a corral stared glumly at the men. The mules were the only reception committee. Joe Collom said that Danforth's two remaining employees were off hunting near Trappers Lake. Chief Douglas's band lived in an old village a dozen miles down-river in Powell Park. Jack's band was still in winter quarters, probably at Whiskey Gap north of Rawlins.

Heavy clouds overhung the level gray-green valley, which Meeker judged to be two or three miles wide. Cottonwoods and very thick willows lined the river. It was about seventy-five feet across and a foot or so deep with a bottom of large stones over which the water boiled in angry whitecaps. From the Agency it trended west in a sweeping north-to-south curve. The undulating Danforth Hills rose two thousand feet above the valley on the right. They were streaked horizontally with gray sandstone and peppered top and bottom with piñon and cedar. The bleak treeless hills on Meeker's left were half as high.

So this was the end of the road. The loneliness of the place was overwhelming. Meeker described his feelings later in a letter to the *Greeley Tribune:*

> So the sun goes down over the moutains and one looks down the narrow valley, looks along the wagon road where only one track has been made this year, as if some one were coming, tired and ready for a warm supper, looks out through the gap in the range as if a four-horse team might be discovered in a

hurry to make the five or six miles before dark. But not a soul is seen. Nothing moves.

If there were neighbors five miles away, or ten or twenty, it would be quite cheerful and one could ride over for a visit once a month. . . . But it is 65 miles to the nearest house where, by the way, no family is now living, the woman having gone East because it was so lonely. It is lonely, so lonely.

The very end of the road! For a moment, on that bleak late afternoon in May of 1878, Meeker's irrepressible spirit, his incessant creative impulse, faltered. For a frightening moment the fire of his recaptured youth subsided and he felt like a remnant ember of sad futilities — a weary old man with nothing accomplished except the bad verse he wrote for N. P. Willis in Greenwich Village, the debts he made in his failure to put over the theories of Charles Fourier at Trumbull Phalanx, the clothespins he peddled in Illinois, the hackwork he did for Horace Greeley and the family he neglected at Union Colony while promoting an impractical idealism.

But Meeker remained Meeker. He was down only for a moment. He spotted a woodpile poorly stacked and dismounted abruptly to set it straight. Then, shouting a gay order to William Post, he kicked his way into the rotting domicile of the White River Indian Agent.

CHAPTER XII The Adventures of
Captain Armstrong

THE GLOOM LIFTED SOON. The clouds melted off. The sun shone
bright and warm. Amid the fragrance of May flowers and greening sage, Meeker began the happiest year of his life — getting
acquainted with the placid contours, the glowing atmosphere,
the serene climate, the simple joy of living in White River
Valley.

The Colorado setting did not resemble the Polynesian isle
on which Captain Armstrong was shipwrecked in Meeker's
romantic novel. But Meeker knew that he could be his own
attractive hero here on the Western Slope just as well as in the
South Seas. Characteristically, he set about learning things. He
studied geology and F. V. Hayden's maps. William Post had a
book on trout fishing, and Meeker consulted it — to become an
expert angler. He rigged a line on a pole and baited it gingerly
with a grasshopper. On his first cast below the Agency, he
hooked a ferocious two-pound trout which almost pulled him in
the river before he could yank it up on the bank. He described
the event in a letter to the *Greeley Tribune:*

> Spotted, wet, fresh, but oh, how he flopped! I took him in
> my hands, and tried to get the hook out of his mouth. It would
> not come, for it was deep in its flesh, and the blood ran out.
> The only thing to do was to take my knife and cut out the
> hook. While I did so, his prominent eyes looked pitiful on me,
> as much as to say — "How can you?" Alas, fish have been
> caught for ages, and even long ago in Lake Galilee. Still I

could not help saying to myself, "There will be a settlement some of these times for all this cruelty." [1]

He was encouraged from the start by Secretary Schurz's tendency to give him everything he asked for. Such consideration for an Agent was unprecedented. Meeker ascribed it to Schurz's wish to placate Senator Teller, and to his hope that Meeker might really solve his whole Indian problem at White River.

With Schurz behind him, Meeker received most of the long-overdue Ute annuities for '77. The quality of Ute rations improved as Meeker organized efficient weekly distribution of flour and oats and plug tobacco. Post was ration clerk, assisted by a young Uncompahgre Ute named Henry Jim whom Chief Ouray had recommended. Meeker also speeded up the mail service, so that the carrier left the Agency for Rawlins regularly on Monday and returned with the mail on Saturday.

These results impressed Chief Douglas, whom Meeker found to be a wispy, indecisive man with a small following of mostly older people. The results impressed also Ouray's brother-in-law, Johnson, the most distinguished and most muscular Indian Meeker had ever seen. They even impressed the graying Kane-ache, who asked for an Agency job, saying that he was tired of wearing Army uniforms and chasing around the Plains with the Rover boys, Colorow, Piah and Washington.

But Chief Jack reacted differently. He presented himself in late May — neat and dark as a piñon nut; intense, somber. He had a long, earnest nose and he still wore the scout clothes which General Crook had issued to him in '77 — fringed jumper, buckskin pants, cowboy boots, cowboy hat. He wore earrings and, around his neck, the silver medal which President Johnson had given him during his Washington visit with Ouray and Kit Carson.

Meeker told Jack how high were his hopes that he could teach Jack's band how to milk cows and get rich. Jack replied that getting rich might be fine for white men, and maybe even for Ouray who had a Germantown carriage and wore underwear and got a thousand dollars a year to promote the white man's way. For himself and his band he wasn't so sure. He thought they'd better stay Indian as long as the game lasted. His people were afraid of cows. Their hands were too soft for milking, and the smell of milk made them sick.

Furthermore, Jack felt that they were rich enough already, what with an Agent to serve them and the treaty money and annuities and supplies which the government had promised to pay them forever for the San Juan and other lands. And why, Jack asked, couldn't Meeker give them their flour monthly in hundred-pound bags, instead of each Wednesday in twenty-five-pound bags — so that they wouldn't have to stop hunting so often to come in to the Agency? Meeker observed mildly that rules were rules, though he saw that he would have to put Jack straight later on all the changes Congress had made in the treaties to square them up with reality. Indians, Meeker said to himself, would have to stay home and work these days for their emoluments. And the Agent must give the orders.

In June, Chief Douglas guided Meeker and Post about the smiling Valley. They rode fifty miles and more upriver along old Ute trails into the evergreen forests and secret gardens of the Trappers Lake-Marvine Lake flattop area. They rode west down-river forty miles through Powell Park to the start of the yellow plateau region — rolling, barren and dreary — which extended into Utah.

Powell Park, Meeker remembered, was named for F. V. Hayden's rival, the government geologist and ethnologist, John Wesley Powell. Major Powell had lost an arm at Shiloh while Meeker was Greeley's war correspondent there. Losing an arm was just what Powell had needed, psychologically, to achieve one of the most rugged feats of American exploration — the descent in 1869 of the Colorado and Green Rivers through all their terrible canyons.

Douglas told Meeker that, in late October of '68, Major Powell, his wife, his brother Walter and six others came to Powell Park near Douglas's village to spend the winter. The men surveyed some of the valley and studied Ute customs and language before heading toward Green River in mid-March. Douglas had liked the Powells, had called on them often and had learned a little English from them.

Meeker noted that Powell Park began a dozen miles below the Agency. It was separated from Agency Park by a narrowing two miles long where White River cut its way between the Danforth Hills on the north and Grand Hogback hunching up to the river from the south. Douglas explained that Powell Park averaged five hundred feet lower than Agency Park, and for that reason was much warmer in winter, much less windy, and usually snow-free. It looked as large as Agency Park and its grassy upper third seemed to contain at least ten thousand acres of bench land fit for irrigation.

At least two thousand Ute ponies were grazing all over Powell Park. Douglas explained that the Park's grass was a godsend, adding irritably that his band had trouble keeping their ID cattle from poaching on this prime pony pasture. He suggested that perhaps the Agent could exclude the cattle from Powell Park with a fence like the one he had built around Greeley. Near Douglas's village, Meeker noticed a half-mile racing strip which belonged to Johnson. Beside it was a corral of racing ponies munching oats. William Post had distributed the oats, which were supposed to be for the sustenance of nonexistent Ute work horses.

Meeker was beginning to see that the ponies were the essence of his problem. Douglas reiterated that Ute civilization was based on ponies, on food and shelter secured by ponies, on Ute pride in their genius for handling ponies, on Ute kindness and love stimulated by adoration of ponies and on freedom derived from pony mobility. In short, the Utes were the slaves of their ponies. They could never become self-supporting at White River as long as they had so many to care for. At the same time, the ponies made possible the wide-ranging, lazy, wasteful, un-

controllable way of life which Senator Teller had sent Meeker
out to destroy.

Getting rid of the ponies, Meeker realized, would not be easy.
And still he was confident that Captain Armstrong had more
than enough charm and tact and brains to make the Utes
see that their ponies were a millstone around their necks. By
reason alone he would persuade even Chief Jack that white
civilization was the best civilization, for all its absurdities and
conceits.

In an early letter to Schurz, Meeker requested a total of
twenty thousand dollars to begin the transition. He wrote that
as a starter he would set up a model farm with a Grand Canal
for irrigation on the best part of the Powell Park pony pasture
near Douglas's village. He would fence in the farm to allow the
work horses and milk cows and beef cattle to graze inside without having to share the grass with the ponies. He would move
the Agency down-river to the center of the farm, so that the
Indians would have the benefit of his close supervision. The
Utes would not like it when he plowed up Johnson's race track
to plant corn, but they would be pleased in the end when they
got high prices for their crops. As their living standard rose,
they would begin wanting things and they would find that it
was more enjoyable to stay home and work than to traipse all
over Wyoming. Their pony worship would decline and they
would ask Meeker for ID stallions to breed their scrawny
mounts up to work horse standards.

That was enough for Schurz in one letter. Meeker did not
mention future projects like the millions of pine logs to be cut
by Ute lumberjacks, the bull trains of fruit grown by Ute
orchardists, the mountains of coal from Ute mines, the bales
of wool clipped by Ute shepherds, the countless crates of Ute
chickens, the busy railroad and the turnpike running down
Coal Creek Canyon from Rawlins to handle the export of the
new Meekerland. Douglas and Jack would cease feuding and
would unite. Chief Ouray's band, observing the economic rev-

olution at White River, would elect to migrate from the Uncompahgre to have Meeker teach them farming at other Valley points. Presto!

Schurz authorized the twenty-thousand-dollar plan promptly. In July of '78, Meeker headed for Rawlins, Greeley and Denver to buy machinery and to hire an engineering staff. He reached Greeley just as Arvilla and Josie were leaving home for the Agency, escorted by Mary's fiancé, W. S. Fullerton. Joe Collom was waiting at Rawlins with the four-mule wagon to drive the women to White River. Arvilla boarded the cars clutching a huge illuminated volume of *Pilgrim's Progress* nearly as large as she was. Out of Arvilla's hearing, Josie told her father that she had bought Gurnsey's book on obstetrics which he had requested. He had written Josie instead of Arvilla for the book, because obstetrics was a subject one just didn't mention to Arvilla. Meeker felt that the White River birth rate was unsatisfactory, and the textbook would help him to improve the whole Ute pregnancy procedure.

The change of attitude of Greeleyites toward Meeker astonished and delighted him. A few months back, they had avoided him for fear he might ask a loan. He had been regarded, then, as a pretentious failure, always criticizing others though unable to make a go of things himself. Now he was lionized. He was their revered Founder again, their economic and spiritual idol, their editorial wizard. Besides, he was a very special kind of Indian Agent at White River, earning one hundred and twenty-five dollars monthly, with twenty thousand dollars to spend in Greeley and Denver on clothing, machinery and what-all, and vaster sums for hiring a staff.

More than a hundred young men applied for Agency jobs, not so much for the monthly salary of sixty dollars and sixty-five cents as for the honor of working for Meeker, and for the romance of it. Meeker took the cream of the crop. He engaged John S. Titcomb, the original Union Colony surveyor, at seven dollars a day, to lay out his Grand Canal. For lumber expert he picked Ed Clark, a brother of the Greeley tycoon, J. Max Clark. He signed Fred Williams, John Dunbar and Ed Mansfield to build bridges and roads, and Fullerton's brother for masonry and plastering. He drew up a waiting list of bright educated youngsters like Arthur Thompson, Harry Dresser and Fred Shepard.

The fuss made over him at Greeley mellowed his viewpoint and erased much bitterness from his memory. Before going on to Denver he toured the now prospering Colony with his old friend Max Clark and commented: "After all, Max, though the enterprise bankrupted me and brought me much sorrow, yet I am proud to have been the leader. It will be counted an honor to every man who took part in the settlement of Greeley. I am more than compensated in the grand success of the undertaking and I have nothing to regret." [2]

Ed Clark led the new Agency employees to White River by way of the Middle Park-Gore Pass road. Meeker and Engineer Titcomb spent a week in Denver buying implements and lodging grandly at the American House. Meeker's last purchase was a thick volume of the Dr. Mynor Bright edition of the Samuel Pepys diaries, which entranced him on the cars all the way to Rawlins. Here he and Titcomb were pleased to meet a handsome, genial young man named Thomas A. Edison whose inventions had inspired several Meeker editorials in the *Greeley Tribune*. Meeker was faintly depressed to see the golden flush along Edison's lips from chewing tobacco, and he thought of suggesting that there might be a connection between Edison's unfortunate tobacco habit and the deafness in one of his ears. But he restrained himself and said nothing.

Edison explained that he was building a lookout in Rawlins to study the total eclipse of the sun in September. He declined Meeker's invitation to hunt at White River, saying that he couldn't go so far and anyhow his luck was bad. Joe Rankin had driven him to the Little Snake and he'd got only two rattlesnakes, which the wagon ran over. Later at Fort Steele the soldiers had teased him by posting a stuffed rabbit. He hadn't been able to hit even that.

Joe Collom arrived and drove Meeker and Titcomb south. Joe reported that Mrs. Meeker, Josie and Fullerton had survived the wagon trip to White River, though he had had to make camp one night at Fortification Rocks, the worst rattlesnake sanctuary in the region. He had told Fullerton about the snakes — but hadn't told the women, who bedded beneath the wagon and slept well all unsuspecting. The men didn't sleep a wink. Fortunately the snakes stayed away. Joe added that Chief Douglas and his band hadn't been so amiable in ages.

Their amiability was displayed soon and it pleased Meeker as much as his reception at Greeley. As the Agency wagon crossed Williams Fork Divide and descended Milk Creek Valley, a hundred Utes welcomed him with drums beating, children singing, squaws giggling and loose ponies galloping about in wild excitement. Meeker wrote later: "Ever so many hands were shaken and ever so many jokes and laughs went around. And then we travelled over Yellowjacket Pass and down Coal Creek Canyon and just as the sun went down we entered the gate of the Agency stockade."

It was good to be home.

CHAPTER XIII   Woman, the Natural
                Savage

JOSIE MEEKER was the career-girl type. She did not shine as cook
at her Agency boardinghouse. In a letter to son Ralph, Arvilla
wrote:

> Soon after arriving I ate something at Josie's. I ate it three
> different times. and each time immediately after eating I was
> very sick as I never was before. I downed the Graftenberg
> pills, knowing I must do something. I vomited and purged
> and then felt relieved but it was two or three days before I
> got around. I never eat any more of her cooking and I get sick
> no more. Your Father knows this, but no one else.

Arvilla and Meeker both were a bit dismayed by the way
Josie took to Agency life. Within a month she was every Ute's
friend. She discussed their savage customs with almost too much
sympathy and admiration. She taught the girls how to freshen
themselves with eau de cologne and how to keep fastened with
hooks and eyes. She went fishing with Ouray's sister Susan up
Piceance Creek to the top of Roan Plateau through the bee-
plant and fireweed. She wouldn't push her Agency school. Most
parents, she said, opposed the school for fear that their children
might want to leave them if they learned anything, and she
didn't blame them. She had two orphan pupils and Douglas's
ten-year-old Freddie, and Sowerwick's son Henry, and the eight-
year-old daughter of Jane, who worked for Arvilla. Now and
then, lovelorn young Utes came to class, particularly Persune

— who asked Josie often to marry him, even though he had two wives already.

Meeker suspected that Josie played Spanish monte with the men. Once he saw a squaw offer her a cigarette while they sat watching the races at Johnson's track. Everyone went to and bet on the races — the employees, Joe Collom, the Morgans, Joe Rankin, even William Byers's son Frank, trekking up from Hot Sulphur. The boy jockeys rode stark naked without bridles, arms outstretched, beating and kicking and yelling like maniacs. At the finish, the ponies were apt to run away, but nobody cared. If the jockey didn't like it he just fell off. It never hurt.

Ration day was exciting, especially when four to six long-horns were turned loose, run down and butchered by teen-agers pretending to be buffalo hunters. The squaws dressed the steers. They sometimes had fights with hair pulling and slapping. Shoe-fitting Day was a festival. The Utes couldn't remember their shoe size, so Mary's beau, Win Fullerton, the shoe boss, had them lie on their backs with feet up in a great circle. He fitted them from his stock on a wagon moving along with him. In the evenings at the Agency the Utes entertained with concerts and dances. Johnson's tame bear did tricks. Ed Clark sang. There were occasional star performers like Charles Lowry, a sometimes mail carrier who lived at Bibleback Brown's on the Little Snake. He was a wonder on the harmonica and the Utes loved him as much as Uriah Curtis.

Not in years had Meeker found so many interesting things to write about. Through that first summer, fall and winter he spent long hours at his desk composing letters to Commissioner Hayt at the Indian Bureau, to Senator Teller, to William Byers, to Governor-elect Pitkin, even to his old Civil War hero General John Pope, who had military jurisdiction over White River. Twice he wrote futilely to Major Thornburgh at Fort Steele in General Crook's department, asking him to keep Chief Jack from spending months at a time in Wyoming.

He wrote of Ed Clark's pinery twenty-five miles upriver, of

the road Ed and Harry Dresser built to it, of the new Powell
Park road, of the limestone and coal he and young Fullerton
found in The Narrows between Agency Park and Powell Park,
of wells dug, of four Ute homes built, of cookstoves installed.
He told how sweet serviceberries tasted in August, and how Ute
tots hid from their mothers between the shaggy fetlocks of the
ponies.

But his greatest interest was his model farm. Titcomb surveyed a perfect Grand Canal route from White River at The
Narrows and tapering northwest along the bench for two and
a half miles nearly to Strawberry Creek where the creek emerged
from Danforth Hills. Mr. Lithcomb of Bear River began digging Grand Canal. Then Uriah Curtis came in and induced
Douglas and his band to finish the first mile for wages and
double rations. Meeker had plenty of excess rations, since Jack's
group and the ex-Denver Utes were usually away in Wyoming
or in the Colorado parks.

Under Grand Canal, the Greeley boys plowed and planted
forty acres of winter wheat. They grubbed out sage and made
streets for the new Agency. Douglas Avenue began at The
Narrows, crossed Grand Canal on Arvilla Bridge and ran west
for seven miles. Ute Avenue started at Douglas's village on
White River and ran north half a mile, intersecting Douglas
Avenue and ending at Grand Canal. Meeker's L-shaped office
and home would stand at the southeast corner of Ute and
Douglas Avenues. The milkhouse would be close by.

Southward, at the corner of Ute Avenue and Meeker Street,
the Greeley boys built their twelve-bed bunkhouse. They
started Josie's new boardinghouse and living quarters east of the
bunkhouse on Meeker Street. Hay and cattle corrals went up
across Ute Avenue. Below the bunkhouse was the storeroom
and blacksmith shop moved down from the old Agency. They
stood on either side of Josie's Lane, which ran east past Jane's
lodge, vegetable garden and pony corral to Johnson's tepee
several hundred yards away.

All these matters were described in Meeker's letters and in editorials for the *Greeley Tribune*. The editorials were almost unique in American literature of the period. Few writers treated Indians with such objectivity and humor.

Of the White River Utes, Meeker was intrigued most by the medicine man Johnson, Ouray's brother-in-law. He wrote, in an October 2, 1878, editorial:

> Some of the men planted potatoes last Spring. The one who is making most of them is Johnson, a considerable Chief, and one who takes the lead in progress and enterprise. He is not given to politics at all and he devotes his energies to improving his domestic affairs. He has three cows from which he has milk, butter and cheese; and poultry and goats. A table has been made for him at which he and his eat. He has crockery, dishes, and if he had a house he would probably make things shine. Susan, Johnson's wife, is a good genius and she makes her husband do as she bids. She is a large, handsome woman, reminding one of that Boston lady, Louise Chandler Moulton. [Mrs. Moulton, a friend of Meeker's when both wrote for the *New York Tribune,* reigned for years over a Boston literary salon.]

The rest of Meeker's piece suggests that Johnson followed Chief Ouray's lead closely in farming matters:

> When Johnson dug his potatoes he hired his retainers, fifteen or twenty women and children, giving them about half a bushel a day for their work, and they made an interesting sight. He was busy among them to see that they did their work well, and he helped to sack. During much of the time he smoked cigarettes like a first-class business man, but once or twice he got tired and lay down on the ground, back up, and slept awhile, and then was up and busy again.

> He wore a bottle-green flannel shirt, buckskin leggings and moccasins, and a blanket strapped around his middle so as to form a sort of short petticoat. His plug hat was by the fence because he had work to do. His face was painted, first with crimson streaks on his forehead as brilliant as the rays of the autumnal setting sun, and then there was a band of bright

yellow an inch wide, commencing at his left eyebrow and running across his eye, then running diagonally across his nose to the right corner of his mouth. On each cheek were three short bright bands of red, yellow and blue.

You see Johnson is one of those men who lead from the savage to the barbaric life on the way to civilization. He is not quite as far advanced as Cedric, the Saxon, the master of Garth, in Scott's *Ivanhoe,* but he is probably equal to the best among the British chiefs who tried to withstand the invasion of Julius Caesar.

Meeker's deep interest in women found full play at White River, and centered around Arvilla's housemaid, Jane. She was a handsome girl just Josie's age and tall and slender like Josie, but she had none of Josie's gaiety. She was poised and reserved and she dominated her husband, Pauvitz, whose brother Antelope was a subchief of some prestige.

Jane was born a Uintah Ute and she had been a slave child in Chief Tabby's lodge when her parents died. She was unhappy there and ran away so much that Tabby sold her, in the mid-60s, to that high-living Virginian Judge William A. Carter, who took over Fort Bridger in '57 and made two hundred thousand dollars in the next ten years as Army sutler and agent for the Overland Mail. Through most of her teens, Jane waited table in Carter's sumptuous barony amid elegancies of food, wine and tableware unequaled in Wyoming Territory. She learned good English from the visiting Army brass and other celebrities. She admired the flamboyant Carter but went roaming now and then even so. The Utes always brought her back to Fort Bridger because the Judge paid a twenty-five-dollar bounty for her return. At length, she wanted to marry Pauvitz. Judge Carter let her go.

To say that the sulky Jane disturbed Meeker is to understate probabilities. He worried about her constantly and did all he could to please her. Her desire for a second child prompted his sudden interest in obstetrics. He dug a well for her. When she inherited the Danforth half-acre truck garden she asked Meeker to care for it while she went off for the summer. He did so, weeding it faithfully for six weeks and breaking his back carrying countless pails of water to it from the river a quarter-mile off. Then Jane returned; she rewarded him with a sort of smile, and nine beets out of a total beet crop of thirty bushels which he had nursed to triumphant maturity. She gave him no potatoes at all, though he was permitted to buy some from her at three cents a pound.

She tormented him by flirting with Frank Byers, whom he disliked. She probed his sore spots by contrasting his pallid economic status with that of the openhanded Judge Carter. She needled him with tales about the Judge's magnificent threshing machine, and about his square Steinway piano which had been hauled by bull team from his ancestral Bull Run home in Virginia, and about his magic patent medicine, "Balm of Life," which cured everything (it was half alcohol). She implied that Meeker wasn't man enough to grow flowing white whiskers like Carter's.

But there were compensations. Jane was a splendid source of inside information on Ute ladies which he used in his *Greeley Tribune* articles. She explained to him how they put up their tepees and packed their mules and made their moccasins and wore their double-square shawls. She discussed feminine breech-clouts and showed how nursing was made simple by eight-inch slits in their calico dresses which exposed their breasts when they raised their arms. Of this device, Meeker wrote: "The creation and structure of our Ute ladies are precisely the same as that of ladies in New York."

In an editorial, "Woman, the Natural Savage," Meeker presented the facile conclusions of his study of Jane. He wrote in part:

> Each day as the sun descends, she and her daughters come into the village from the timbered valleys loaded with firewood. She rises first in the morning and builds the fire and prepares the

breakfast, in some cases cooked better than many white women cook. Then she is out in the sun stretching buckskin or stroking down beaver or otter skins or cutting garments or ornamenting them with bead work. She has no idle hours.

Meanwhile, the men have nothing to do. The young men often lie sleeping as late as ten or eleven o'clock in the morning, and when they get up and stretch, possibly wash themselves, they go to the camp kettle for meat and to the frying pan or bake-kettle for bread, washing it down with weak coffee. After that, they sit around in the shade or by the fire with their companions, smoking cigarettes and enjoying themselves as much as young men at Newport or Saratoga.

The case is this. The women know as if by instinct that the worker is the master. They are utterly opposed to the men working, and utterly opposed to any change in any respect that shall tend to an abridgment of their power. The Indian man is their subject, their necessary instrument.

Deeper observation leads to the heart and core of the great difficulty that lies in the way of Indian civilization, and this is the blind tenderness which the mother feels for her children. An Indian child, or at least boy, must never be whipped. The mother can't stand it, and she will not. Thus what we know as discipline or training cannot exist among the Indians, and so one has a condition in which the maternal instinct, short-sighted and foolish, is united with energy and force derived from unremitted labor, and this in the woman becomes the master, while effeminacy, affection and idleness combine to make the man a slave. Therefore, woman in the Indian social state is the natural savage.

For some months Meeker hoped that Jane would become a true friend whom he could trust to post him on Ute sentiments and who would help him to evaluate his position. Instead she became a gossipy spy for Douglas and Jack and for disgruntled Greeley employees who objected to working so hard to create Meekerland. In early spring of '79, Meeker decided to coddle her no longer. He had just moved into his new Powell Park office at the corner of Douglas and Ute Avenues. He began their conversation in a gentle vein:

MEEKER: Now Jane, you will be planting your garden soon. I just want to warn you that last Summer's style of gardening is played out.

JANE: Played out? How so?

MEEKER: Well, I'll tell you. After the things are planted, it will not do for you to run off and leave me to plow, hoe and pull weeds. You or some of your family must stay here all three moons and work your crops, for no one will touch them, and in that case you will have nothing.

JANE: You say we must stay three moons? What for? Hoeing the things once is enough.

MEEKER: You must hoe them three or four times, and must keep watch of them and you need not undertake to tell me how the work is to be done.

JANE: But we never done so before and we had heaps.

MEEKER (*warming up*): But I tell you the thing is played out. If you get anything you must work for it.

JANE: Why can't white men do the work as before? They understand it. We don't.

MEEKER: It won't do. Now, I worked your garden last year. I carried hundreds of pails of water. You had a nice garden and got lots of money. But this year we have a big ditch and plenty of water. You must attend to things yourself.

JANE (*sweetly*): But Mr. Meeker, ain't you paid for working?

MEEKER: No. Not to work for you.

JANE: Well, what are you paid money for if not to work for us?

MEEKER: (*momentarily stumped*): Yes, I see how it is. . . . I'll put it this way: I am paid to show you how to work.

JANE: But the Utes have a heap of money. What is the money for if it is not to have work done for us?

MEEKER (*coming to a boil*): I'll tell you, Jane. This money is to hire me and the rest of us to teach you to help yourselves so that you can be like white folks and get rich as they are rich — by work.

JANE: (*black eyes wide*): Ain't all these cattle ours and all this land?

MEEKER: The cattle, yes. The land, no.

JANE: Well, whose land is it, and whose is the money?

MEEKER (*almost yelling*): The land belongs to the government, and is for your use, if you use it. If you won't use it and won't work, and if you expect me to weed your garden for you, white men away off will come in and by and by you will have nothing. Do you understand?

JANE (*very quiet*): Yes. But I can't tell you, Mr. Meeker, how bad you make me feel.

She left the office and Meeker watched her as she walked across the porch, past his hitching rack and down Ute Avenue which ended at Douglas's lodge on White River. She walked stiffly and rapidly, keeping her handsome head straight ahead.

Meeker was aware that he had said too much. He had asserted not only that the Utes didn't own White River Valley, but that they couldn't even stay there if they didn't do what Meeker wanted them to do. He might as well have told Jane that her people were as confined as the convicts at Canon City.

He stood by his big desk and scolded himself for a strategic blunder which would have appalled Captain Armstrong. But, as always, he accepted in the end the wages of his own perversity. He went beyond acceptance, like a small boy who breaks six more windows after recovering from the shock of breaking one. He sat down and wrote out in full the whole conversation for publication in the *Greeley Tribune*.

CHAPTER XIV

Road to Ruin

WHAT MEEKER WROTE about Jane was read with satisfaction in Denver by William B. Vickers, that ardent advocate of Ute extermination. Vickers had edited the *Colorado Sun* for General Cameron in the early days at Greeley to counteract Meeker's liberal Republicanism. After leaving Greeley, he had ridden his Ute hate train to high places, mostly as editor of the *Denver Tribune*. In 1878, he was high also on the strategy board of the Teller-Chaffee Republican command which permitted Frederick W. Pitkin of the San Juan mining camps to be elected Governor of Colorado. Pitkin was a fair-minded tyro politician, and the Teller-Chaffee crowd was a little afraid of him. It put in Vickers as his private secretary to make sure he didn't get idealistic about the Utes.

Vickers deduced from Meeker's harsh words to Jane, that the new Agent had seen the light at last. Vickers had not liked Captain Armstrong's plan for a self-supporting Ute community at White River at a time when a showdown was possible which would destroy Chief Ouray and exile all the Colorado Utes eventually to Indian Territory, where redskins obligingly died like flies. Ouray, Vickers felt, remained the major obstacle to Ute removal. He had thwarted the Ute Commission of '78 by preventing closure of the new Los Pinos Agency on the Uncompahgre and consolidation of his band with the two White River bands as outlined in Senator Chaffee's bill. And he had tried hard to block the sale of Uncompahgre Park, just north of the San Juan camps, for ten thousand dollars, — insolently tell-

ing the commissioners, "We have no land to sell to people who
have not paid for what they bought before."

But Vickers was happy to learn that Ouray's chronic nephritis
was getting worse. His great strength, physical and moral, was
waning. When twenty-one of his Uncompahgre subchiefs overruled him and signed away Uncompahgre Park, he didn't draw
his ivory-handled revolver and shoot anybody as he would have
done a decade earlier. He merely called the twenty-one signers
fools and told them that the ten thousand dollars they were
supposed to get, in the unlikely event that Congress appropriated it, was money still owed to them for the San Juan
Cession.

Vickers knew that the four-mile square Uncompahgre Park
sale eased the way for extinguishing Ouray's "Brunot Treaty"
of '73. A greater help still was the feat of the Ute Commission
in inducing the three Southern Ute bands — Weeminuches,
Capotes and remnant Muaches — to split off from the Uncompahgre and White River Utes, and take their own Reservation
and Agency below Pagosa Springs near the New Mexico line.

Bribery on the Congressional level accomplished this miracle.
The commissioners were Senator Lot M. Morrill of Maine,
Judge N. C. McFarland of Kansas and General Edward Hatch,
commander at Santa Fe of the Ninth Cavalry which served
Army posts in northern New Mexico and southern Colorado.
Senator Morrill got mountain fever at Fort Garland and went
to bed there. Judge McFarland was sick too, but he took
quinine for "sensations" and felt better. So the Judge and the
General crossed San Luis Valley to Uncle Lafe Head's town of
Conejos and on over the Continental Divide to Pagosa Springs.
They had a mule train carrying twenty-eight thousand silver
dollars from the Denver mint which was guarded by Lieutenant
Charles Adam Hoke McCauley, an eager young engineer bris-
tling with thermometers, compasses, barometers and odometers.
McCauley was on detached service from Fort Steele near
Rawlins.

The two commissioners authorized McCauley to give seventeen silver dollars to each member of the three Southern bands who approved the split-off from the other Colorado Utes. A majority of 902 men, women and children did approve and collected their silver dollars. Thus, for $15,334, the three Southern Ute bands gave up their half interest in the undivided 12,000,000 acres of the Colorado Ute Reservation and accepted, in its place, 1,166,000 acres of land below Pagosa Springs. The undistributed 12,666 silver dollars were packed back on the mules and Lieutenant McCauley returned them to the Denver mint. Senator Morrill collected his Commission pay plus mountain fever sick pay of five dollars per diem from August 6 to October 2, 1878.

The Ute Commission's success in enfeebling the "Brunot Treaty" filled William Vickers's cup of joy. The cup overflowed during September when he heard of genuine Ute outrages in Middle Park. It seemed that some ex-Denver Utes — Piah's and Washington's bands, totaling eighteen lodges — camped in Middle Park after hunting buffalo east of Denver and damaged some harness near the ranch of General William A. Hamill. That was a poor place to damage harness. General Hamill was the richest mine owner in the Georgetown area, and he had just replaced Senator Chaffee as Chairman of the State Republican Committee.

Frank Byers and a Hot Sulphur Springs posse went after the Utes, seized Piah's guns and shot Johnnie Tab-biscuit dead as he reached for his knife. Then Frank talked with Piah and Washington and gave Piah back his guns when the two chiefs agreed to leave Middle Park. The Utes rode down Grand River and turned south up Blue River along Gore Range. Piah, who was tippling, saw Old Man Elliott chopping wood outside his Blue River ranch and allegedly killed him with two bullets in the back to avenge Johnnie Tab-biscuit's death. The date was September 3, 1878.

Mamie Elliott got news of the murder to Long Bridge

(Kremmling) and from there it flew to Denver, where consternation reigned. While the city braced itself against invasion by eighteen Ute lodges, General Pope, who was at the American House, alerted all his post commanders. Sheriff Dave Cook and twenty-six stalwarts rushed to Georgetown by train, crossed Berthoud Pass and followed the Utes up the "back White River trail." [1] Soon Sheriff Cook, and fifteen others, got to seeing thousands of Ute sharpshooters behind the serviceberry bushes — and furthermore the coffeepots leaked and there were only ten tin cups and two frying pans for the whole posse. So these sixteen stalwarts turned back.

William Byers was among the ten who did not turn back. On September 9, they camped at Old Squaw Camp near Piceance Creek headwaters and rode north next morning down Flag Creek from Roan Plateau to White River Agency, where Washington and a hundred other Utes told them that Piah had fled to the Uncompahgre. Byers introduced his nine friends to Arvilla and Josie Meeker and he argued a bit with Jane, who told him what he knew already — that the posse had no authority to trespass on the Reservation. Then Meeker arrived from Powell Park. He advised Byers to leave. Young Freddie Douglas broke the tension by raising a tiny American flag on the Agency pole. Utes and whites cheered and shook hands. The posse left White River northward by way of Coal Creek Canyon and Yellowjacket Pass because Byers wanted to try the trout fishing along Milk Creek.

Though the posse men dropped the Old Man Elliott matter, William Vickers didn't. Through fall and winter he filled Governor Pitkin and the *Denver Tribune* with anti-Ute propaganda slanted against Ouray. He asserted that the murderer Piah was a loyal Uncompahgre and Ouray's right-hand man: Ouray and Chipeta were probably hiding him in their palatial Uncompahgre farmhouse. And Piah hadn't murdered just Old Man Elliott alone. Unquestionably he had murdered Rancher Joe McLane, who had vanished on July 30 while chasing white rustlers near Cheyenne Wells, one hundred and seventy-five miles east of Denver. Piah's band had been hunting east of Denver in July, hadn't they? [2] As for Johnny Tab-biscuit — nobody knew how many whites *he* had murdered. Nine North Park miners in '77, for sure. And poor Marksberry in '75, on Pikes Peak near Cripple Creek. A bad actor, Johnnie Tab-biscuit. Vickers claimed to have learned from an unimpeachable source that Johnnie was related to Ouray, or perhaps Chipeta.

All the while, Vickers worked on a definitive summing-up which would show the world with unanswerable logic why the Utes could not be tolerated any longer in Colorado. Meeker's stand, as implied in his published talk with Jane, gave Vickers his clinching argument. His summing-up appeared first in the *Denver Tribune* under the title "Lo, the Poor Indian!" — taken from Alexander Pope's *Essay on Man:*

> Lo, the poor Indian! whose untutor'd mind
> Sees God in clouds, or hears him in the wind;
> His soul proud Science never taught to stray
> Far as the solar walk or milky way . . .

It was reprinted widely under that title or, simply, "The Utes Must Go!" and it became the rallying point for prevailing Colorado opinion. Governor Pitkin was forced to accept it as the official philosophy of his regime. Vickers wrote in part:

> The Utes are actual, practical Communists and the Government should be ashamed to foster and encourage them in their idleness and wanton waste of property. Living off the bounty of a paternal but idiotic Indian Bureau, they actually become too lazy to draw their rations in the regular way but insist on taking what they want wherever they find it. Removed to Indian Territory, the Utes could be fed and clothed for about one half what it now costs the Government.
> Honorable N. C. Meeker, the well-known Superintendent of the White River Agency, was formerly a fast friend and ardent admirer of the Indians. He went to the Agency in the firm belief that he could manage the Indians successfully by kind treatment, patient precept and good example. But utter

failure marked his efforts and at last he reluctantly accepted the truth of the border truism that the only truly good Indians are dead ones.

PUBLICATION OF "LO, THE POOR INDIAN!" marked the turning point in Meeker's White River career. Thereafter, his Utes went definitely against him. Chiefs Douglas and Jack accused him formally of writing the article. Though they accepted his denial of authorship, they were still sure that he held the opinions about good dead Indians which Vickers ascribed to him. They suspected more and more that the Agent who had done so much for them at first was quite capable now of calling in soldiers to drag them in chains to Indian Territory if he couldn't have his way.

All through the warm spring of '79, Meeker had a wan feeling that he was shedding Captain Armstrong as a snake sheds its worn-out skin. He was losing the Captain's kindness, his optimism, his all-embracing love. On the surface, he progressed in his subtle war against the ponies. He had taken over some of the best part of their Powell Park pasture. He plowed and fenced with the new Glidden barbed wire an eighty-acre field between Grand Canal and his new office home at the corner of Douglas and Ute Avenues. Secretary Schurz gave him permission to order a four-hundred-and-nine-dollar threshing machine, a nine-hundred-dollar gristmill, two seventy-dollar wrought-iron breaking plows and some new fangled blue vitriol for preparing seed wheat.[3]

He built a house for Johnson beyond Jane's corral on Josie's Lane, and Johnson moved into it with Ouray's sister Susan and his other wives. Douglas's village revolted one day against the plowing and the barbed wire. The men dumped the new shoes which Fullerton had fitted to them in a big pile on the floor of Meeker's office. With Johnson's help, and by threatening to make Jack head chief, Meeker quelled the revolt and the Douglas men came back for their shoes. Later, Meeker induced Jack and Sowerwick, his henchman, to take up agriculture by promising them a new red wagon. Jack's acreage was in Agency Park near the mouth of Coal Creek, and Meeker called it "the Farm That Jack Built." Along White River, beside the Farm, Jack and Sowerwick set up their village of ninety lodges.

And still Meeker knew that Captain Armstrong hadn't convinced a single Ute except Johnson of the wonders of white civilization. Though he resisted the thought now, a part of him could see that they had come with him a little way merely because they were gentle, kindly people who hated to cross a persistent and weary old man.

In addition, he had other problems. There was Josie, obeying his orders to seek a larger enrollment for her school and yet seeming to side often against him with Utes and employees. Jane withdrew her daughter from the school, and by June Josie had only one pupil left, Freddie Douglas — not counting Persune and other adult admirers. Meeker had the pleasure of paying most of the one-thousand-dollar debt owed to Horace Greeley's daughters, but he feared that too much work had been piled on Josie in the process. Arvilla suggested as much in a letter to Ralph:

> Josie don't look quite so fresh as she did when she first came here. Still, she seems quite well and puts in every inch of her time in doing something. I don't believe one on the place has worked as hard as Josie. The boarding house and school are together and they have been moved down from the Old Agency. She runs the boarding house, buys all the provisions, pays a woman $25 a month for helping, boards and teaches her little girl besides. . . .

Arvilla did not ease Meeker's trouble by urging him to try Methodist missionary methods at the Agency and to enforce a Methodist Sabbath there. She hinted that he could make the Utes work if he accepted the Bible literally. When he debated the point, she wept and wrote Ralph: "Oh, I'm so *glad* you are a true Christian. I'm so glad that all my children are believers in Jesus!"

His staff gave him many headaches. He spent months training some of the Greeley boys, only to have them get scared and go home. The new spring employee crop was more like a kindergarten. It included Harry Dresser's brother Frank — a shy, curly-haired lad hardly out of knee pants, and so homesick that he wrote his mother in Greeley every night. Another novice was Fred Shepard, aged twenty. Fred could play the fiddle and that was about all. Arthur Thompson, also aged twenty, was more promising. He had farmed a little at Greeley, did not drink or smoke, and had "put on Christ by baptism" in joining the Baptist Church.

Fred Shepard had come from Greeley to White River in a wagon with the Shadrach Price family of four. Price's wife, Flora Ellen, was the one to whom Josie paid twenty-five dollars a month to help run the boardinghouse. She was a blandly pretty Illinois farm girl with the voluptuous form of a Rubens nude. Though she had given birth to two children, she was only sixteen years old — and half that age mentally. She threw her wide curves around the boardinghouse with the innocent abandon of a babe in its bath, and Meeker realized that she had no remote notion of how she disturbed the digestive processes of the bachelor boarders. Her husband, Shadrach Price, was a stolid and truculent native of Kansas who liked to boast about how he shot and scalped nine redskins while crossing the Plains with Flora Ellen. But Shadrach could plow.

Meeker's success in persuading Jack to start a farm near Coal Creek had given him a few May days of fresh hope. Then he was thrown off balance by an entirely unexpected and bewildering new situation. It rained just once during that spring, and that was all the rain for many months. Ordinarily, forest fires in the Colorado Rockies caused no concern. They were started by lightning, by careless campers, by ranchers destroying sage and by Utes driving game with fire and clearing underbrush from pony trails. But the forest fires could not die out during the unprecedented drought of 1879. By July, the forests blazed in a hundred places. Smoke from Pikes Peak fires hung heavy even over General Palmer's suave resort of Colorado Springs.

Denver newspaper editors, cued by the popularity of "Lo, the Poor Indian!" went to work gathering testimony so that they could blame all the fires on all the Utes. James B. Thompson told them that Washington's band started fires on Bear River which threatened his home and haystacks. Land Office Surveyor General Campbell said Colorow's band had fired North Park and ordered his transit men to leave the park. Frank Byers said Antelope's band fired Gore Range and that Ouray's Uncompahgres were trying to burn up the silver camps of Irwin and Gothic above the Gunnison. Miners from Hahn's Peak and Leadville and the San Juan told the editors about big "Ute fires" near their diggings. Even Sam Hartzel in South Park said the smoke from Ute-caused fires was making his heifers hard to settle.

On July 5, Secretary Vickers composed a wire for the Indian Bureau which Governor Pitkin signed. It asked for troops to drive roving Utes back onto their Reservation and concluded:

I AM SATISFIED THERE IS AN ORGANIZED EFFORT ON THE PART OF INDIANS TO DESTROY THE TIMBER OF COLORADO. THESE SAVAGES SHOULD BE REMOVED TO INDIAN TERRITORY WHERE THEY CAN NO LONGER DESTROY THE FINEST FORESTS IN THIS STATE.

The Indian Bureau wired Meeker promptly:

GOVERNOR OF COLORADO REPORTS YOUR INDIANS DEPRE-DATING NEAR NORTH AND MIDDLE PARKS. IF CORRECT TAKE ACTIVE STEPS TO SECURE THEIR RETURN TO RESERVATION. THE SECRETARY DIRECTS THAT IF NECESSARY YOU WILL CALL UPON NEAREST MILITARY POST FOR ASSISTANCE.

This message irritated Meeker. As he explained to the Indian Bureau, he had repeatedly reported the absence of the Utes from White River to Major Thornburgh at Fort Steele and had asked him to clear Jack's band and Douglas's band from Bear and Little Snake Valleys. The Major had taken no action, and had not even answered his letters. More troubling still was the fact that the contents of Pitkin's message asking for soldiers and urging Ute removal to Indian Territory reached Douglas and Jack almost as soon as it reached Meeker. They reacted at once by ceasing work on all agricultural projects and by holding long angry meetings at Douglas's village and at the Farm That Jack Built.

For the first time, Meeker began to wonder if he and Arvilla and Josie and the rest were in danger at the Agency.

CHAPTER XV

Almost There

FEARS FOR HIS FAMILY'S SAFETY increased day by day. At last, on July 29, Meeker learned that General Pope was in Denver and he left at once to see Pope about bringing troops to White River.[1] He paused in Greeley to hire replacements. Al Woodbury was quitting soon as Agency blacksmith. Ed Clark, W. S. Fullerton and Ed Mansfield had a month's leave coming to them. In their absence, the Agency would have for protection only William Post, Harry Dresser, Shad Price and the dewy youngsters Frank Dresser, Fred Shepard and Arthur Thompson. In Greeley, he was able to hire only one man, George Eaton, an original Union Colonist, for farm work. In Denver, he called first on David Moffat, cashier of the First National Bank, which had the Agency account, and arranged to pay for the promised threshing machine. Then he hired Wilmer Eskridge, a newcomer from Iowa, as Agency sawyer, and met General Pope at the Grand Central Hotel.

Pope inquired about Agency affairs. Meeker described his failure to imbue the Utes with a desire to be civilized; their great resentment over "Lo, the Poor Indian!"; Major Thornburgh's lack of interest in disciplining Douglas and Jack; and his own fear of a Ute uprising. He concluded that he was about ready to resign as Indian Agent after fifteen months of futile struggle.

But John Pope urged him to be patient. He disclosed that he had sent Captain Dodge and Company D of General Hatch's Ninth Cavalry from Pagosa Springs to Middle Park and Gore Pass to investigate the fires. Dodge's Middle Park camp was on Grand River at the mouth of Troublesome Creek, only one hundred and seventy-six miles from White River — twenty-five miles closer than Fort Steele. Even if Thornburgh remained inattentive, Dodge's forty-four Negro cavalrymen had orders to rush to the Agency at the first sign of trouble. Under these circumstances, Pope felt sure that the Utes would behave.

And so Meeker boarded the Denver Pacific on August 5 feeling somewhat reassured. Still, he doubted that Dodge's small Negro unit could do much if real trouble started. He felt that at least a hundred soldiers would be necessary. He changed to the Union Pacific at Cheyenne and as he sat down in the palace car a strikingly handsome young Army officer entered and took a seat near him. From journalistic habit, Meeker presented himself to the officer, who rose to his feet and grasped his hand in a gesture of pleased recognition. He explained that he was Major Thornburgh, commanding at Fort Steele, and that he had been wanting to meet the Indian Agent at White River for a long time.[2]

They talked pleasantly at first, like old friends. Thornburgh said that he had just served a week on General Court Martial at Fort D. A. Russell. Before that he had had a glorious hunt in the Sierra Madres south of Fort Steele with General George Crook, his department commander, and Webb Hayes, the President's son, and Dr. John Draper, the renowned urologist. The fishing at Battle Lake had been superb. Thornburgh had caught fifty-two red-sides in thirty minutes. General Crook shot a magnificent buck for Webb Hayes, and Thornburgh had helped Hayes lug the head to Cheyenne for mounting. Hayes planned to hang it in his father's library in the White House.

The Major asked if Meeker's Utes were still roaming off the Reservation. Meeker replied sharply that they were indeed, and the reason was that the Major had ignored his pleas to remove them from the Little Snake and Bear Valleys. As a result, he continued, his farm program was failing, because the Utes would not stay home and work. Instead, they pursued their old pony economy, trading their skins for guns, ammunition, liquor, top hats and poker decks. And starting fires.

Thornburgh said that he was sorry. He said that he had forwarded Meeker's requests for help to General Crook in Omaha, who had sent them to General Sheridan in Chicago, who had sent them to General Sherman in Washington. General Sherman had sent no orders back to him to remove the Utes from the Little Snake and the Bear. Without such orders, Thornburgh was unable to take troops ten miles from Fort Steele.

The Major added that in July General Sherman had asked him to investigate Governor Pitkin's complaints about the fires. Though he was busy then with the Crook-Hayes hunting party, he had gathered reports from Wyoming settlers who owned ranches along the North Platte east of the Continental Divide in a sixty-mile stretch southward from Steele almost to the Colorado line. The settlers reported that members of Jack's band had done much hunting on Spring, Brush, French and Beaver Creeks, but had set no fires.

Meeker interrupted to say that Wyoming reports meant nothing since the North Platte country was east of the Divide and from 100 to 250 miles north of the areas where the fires were alleged to be raging. Then he changed the subject by asking Thornburgh his views on transfer of the Indian Bureau to the War Department. Thornburgh replied positively that the Army could conduct Indian affairs very well. He was about to amplify but Meeker got in ahead of him.

He gave a lecture which became progressively more blunt and curt, asserting that West Pointers were suave with ladies and celebrities, fair judges of good wine and versed in math, sports and history; but they knew nothing about teaching Indians agriculture. He said that soldiers were notorious drunkards who gave Indians their bad habits and debauched their women. He contended that Indians were uninclined to be civilized by men savage enough to have murdered women and children wholesale at Sand Creek and Washita. Thornburgh listened in a polite cold fury. When Meeker's monologue ended it was clear that further conversation between the two was impossible.

Just then the conductor arrived for tickets. Negligently, Thornburgh flashed his elegant Union Pacific pass lettered in gold. The conductor acknowledged it with smiling respect and turned to Meeker. From his wallet Meeker drew a soiled and shabby requisition authorizing the Union Pacific to collect twenty-one dollars from the Department of Interior for the Agent's round trip. The conductor studied the shabby scrap of paper for some time. He accepted it at last with a reproving sigh.[3]

THE HEART CAN BREAK before the mind accepts the imminence of disaster. Meeker's outburst at Thornburgh was a symptom of the slow breaking of his heart. It was a stout heart which had carried his eager mind through adolescence on Lake Erie to poetry in New Orleans and Greenwich Village to socialism at Trumbull Phalanx and to fame as a war correspondent and Founder of the greatest agricultural colony in the West. It was a tender heart, too, which sustained his tender if somewhat perplexed love for his children, and for Arvilla toward whom he was now journeying. At Rawlins, he was met by Harry Dresser, who drove him and his new employee, George Eaton, southward. On a late afternoon, as they came down to Williams Fork, the wagon overturned. Meeker was caught beneath it and his left arm was wrenched badly. The wagon was wrecked. Eaton propped him against a rock and there he waited in great pain through the night until Harry returned from the Agency with Ed Mansfield and another wagon.

The symbolism of the incident was ominous — the wrecked vehicle, the injured arm, the worried, weary, unhappy old man unable to proceed along the road on his own. But his tough mind rejected symbolism. In the depth of his frustration he was determined still to succeed. He decided that he had been too good to the Utes. Well, he hated them now. They were a cowardly, dishonest and contemptible race. But they would understand force — the soldiers, the guns, the chains, the noose. He would succeed with force and cruelty where reason and kindness had failed.

With his uninjured right hand he penned an editorial for the *Greeley Tribune* entitled "Almost There," which contained these lines:

> The pleasant part of life is when we are conscious we have nearly reached a desirable object. But often as we pass through life we are taught by experience that little is enjoyed beyond being almost there.

ALMOST THERE. The feel of fall was in the mountains. The myrtle warblers were flocking for migration. Upriver at Meeker's pinery the aspens were turning. The night wind had a melancholy sound as it came down from Sleepy Cat and passed through The Narrows. Meeker spent much time during these late sad August days in his office, losing himself in the adventures of Samuel Pepys or trying to condone his own desperate acts — the ugliness and unfairness of them, their falseness to all his dreams and ideals. He became distant and distrustful of his employees, refusing to discuss his orders to them even when they conflicted. He berated Josie because she still enjoyed watching the pony races. On a wild rumor, he lashed out at Jane's brother-in-law, Antelope, accusing him of running a brothel at Charlie Perkins's hotel.

When he learned that Jack and Sowerwick had gone to Denver and complained of his behavior to Governor Pitkin, he told them that they deserved hanging for their disloyalty. He charged them also with starting more Gore Range fires in reprisal for the presence of Captain Dodge's men in Middle Park. Sheriff Bessey arrived from Hot Sulphur one day with warrants against two Utes, Bennett and Chinaman, for firing James Thompson's barns. Douglas refused to help the Sheriff do his job, so Meeker promised to have him jailed if the soldiers came. He even attacked his favorite, Johnson, accusing him of stealing Josie's school water for his ponies.

The ponies! They were his real enemy. And yet Meeker had enough objectivity left to appreciate their virtues. The ponies were of the wind and rain, of the sun and earth and sky. The laws governing their life, and the life of the Utes who worshiped them, were God's natural laws, eternally just and incorruptible. What inducement could he offer Douglas and Jack to forsake them? Social position? A knowledge of plane geometry? A stone mansion with an iron deer in a half-acre yard? A half-acre yard . . . for a people whose home for countless generations had been all God's wondrous outdoors?

But Senator Teller and Secretary Schurz hadn't sent him to White River to philosophize about Indians. His job was to tame them. Early in September, he gave Shadrach Price peremptory orders to start plowing a new two-hundred-acre field for winter wheat. He chose the tract with great care, to determine once and for all who was stronger, the United States government or the ponies. The tract was rich pastureland along Josie's Lane through Jane's corral and on east as far as Johnson's house.

As Price's plow began tearing up the thick turf, Jane and Antelope hurried to Meeker's office to protest. That tract, they said, belonged to Jane. The Agent could not plow it. Jane's ponies had to have that grass to live. Destroying the grass was murder.

Meeker ignored the protest. Price plowed on. Johnson's son Tim and another young Ute got their rifles and walked along beside the plowing team urging Price to stop. Price did stop, and then resumed at Meeker's command. He plowed several hours, turning up a strip of brown earth seventy-five feet wide and half a mile long. At last, as Price made his far turn, Tim Johnson and his friend exposed themselves in the sage nearby and fired their rifles in his direction. The whistling bullets seemed to pass close to Price's ears. He concluded to stop plowing for good.

A week of long, heated, smoke-filled conferences followed — sometimes in Meeker's office, sometimes in Douglas's lodge, or in Jack's upriver. The summer's tension got much worse. Josie spent much time bickering with Jane. On Saturday, September 6, Black Wilson, the mail carrier, brought the mail from Rawlins. There were several letters from worried parents begging the Greeley boys to come home. Ed Clark and W. S. Fullerton, who were vacationing in Greeley, must have given these parents a disturbing account of Agency conditions. And still the Greeley boys at White River were not afraid. Fred Shepard wrote his mother in part:

> As regards to my getting out of here soon, I have not felt as if I was in any danger so far as my life is concerned since I have been here any more than ever I did in your door-yard. I don't blame the Utes for not wanting this ground plowed up. It is a splendid place for ponies and there is better farming land, and just as near, right west of this field, but it is covered with sage brush.
>
> Douglas says he will have his boys clear the sage brush away if N. C. will only let the grass alone. But N. C. is stubborn and won't have it that way and wants soldiers to carry out his plans. Don't know how it will turn out, but you can bet if they touch anybody it will be the Agent first.

On Monday morning, September 8, Meeker wrote to Commissioner Hayt in Washington a long report of his plowing problems, of the exhausting conferences and of how in the end Douglas and Jack had agreed to let him plow Jane's tract if he built her a house and a corral elsewhere. He addressed the report and gave it to Black Wilson, who took it with the regular Monday morning mail for delivery to Rawlins.

That same afternoon, Arvilla Meeker was in the Agency office reading her huge volume of *Pilgrim's Progress*. Johnson knocked on the door and entered. The big medicine man's

handsome face was full of anger — and that was unusual. He
had always been the most placid and dependable of all the White
River Utes. Meeker had said lately that he could not have endured his troubles without Johnson's support.

Johnson asked for the Agent. Arvilla said that he had just
stepped out. The Indian left and Meeker arrived, sinking
wearily into the pillows which Arvilla had arranged in his desk
chair to make his sore arm more comfortable.

And then Johnson returned. He began talking fast at Meeker,
almost shouting. Arvilla caught only a word here and there.
Johnson seemed to be saying that Meeker was plowing his land
and was sending lies to Washington in the letter which he had
given Black Wilson.

Suddenly Meeker broke in. He said very deliberately, "The
trouble is this, Johnson. You have too many ponies. You had
better kill some of them."

Johnson stared at Meeker for a long moment, utterly dumb-
founded. Then his big brown eyes began blazing with the fire
of a reasonable man who has been assaulted at last with the
consummation of blasphemy. He moved evenly toward Meeker,
grasped him by the shoulders, lifted his thin body from the
pillows and hustled him across the room and onto the porch.
Arvilla ran screaming to the door. She saw Fred Shepard and
George Eaton run up and grab Johnson as he flung the Agent
hard against the hitching rail.

That was all. Johnson did not touch Meeker again. He
walked away without a word. Shepard and Eaton helped Meeker
from the rack and back to his office chair. He felt himself over
and said he was bruised a bit but not hurt internally. What hurt
most, he said, was to have his friend Johnson turn against him.
First it was Jane . . . now Johnson.

He did not sleep at all that night. Next day, he called Josie
and dictated letters to Governor Pitkin and Senator Teller and
a telegram to Commissioner Hayt. The telegram read:

I HAVE BEEN ASSAULTED BY A LEADING CHIEF, JOHNSON, FORCED OUT OF MY HOUSE AND INJURED BADLY, BUT WAS RESCUED BY EMPLOYEES. IT IS NOW REVEALED THAT JOHNSON ORIGINATED ALL THE TROUBLE STATED IN LETTER SEPT. 8. HIS SON SHOT AT PLOWMAN, AND OPPOSITION TO PLOWING IS WIDE. PLOWING STOPS: LIFE OF SELF, FAMILY AND EMPLOYEES NOT SAFE: WANT PROTECTION IMMEDIATELY: HAVE ASKED GOVERNOR PITKIN TO CONFER WITH GENERAL POPE.

N. C. MEEKER, INDIAN AGENT

But now, having composed this formal request for troops, he vacillated, torn by his old habit of trying to be liberal and uncompromising at the same time. He rehashed in his mind his differences with the Utes whom he had planned to conquer by love and whom the telegram would commit him irrevocably to conquer by hate. He reviewed his lecture to Major Thornburgh, wherein he had implied with such certainty that bringing in soldiers only made matters more insoluble where Indian problems were concerned.

He could not decide what to do. The telegram to Commissioner Hayt and the letters to Pitkin and Teller were still on his desk on Wednesday morning, September 10. In late afternoon a visitor arrived from Rawlins — John W. Steele, who owned the Rawlins-White River mail contract. Steele, a forthright man from Wallace, Kansas, was not happy. He told Meeker at supper that he had been losing money on the White River route since July because of the Ute troubles. The experienced riders wouldn't carry mail at all — not Joe Rankin or Charlie Lowry or Mike Sweet, though Black Wilson was on the job temporarily at premium wages. Steele said that his piddling contract had cost him plenty, greasing political palms and getting things set up in Rawlins. And now these redskins threatened to put him out of business. What kind of a government was it that didn't protect its taxpayers?

Meeker answered the question by showing Steele his still-unsent telegram to Hayt. Steele was jubilant. Troops! Why, they were just the ticket! They would solve everything — his problems and Meeker's problems both. Could he deliver the telegram? Good! He would be off for Rawlins with it at dawn. The War Department in Washington would have Meeker's troop request in four days.

John Steele spent the night on an improvised bed which Josie arranged in William Post's storeroom office. He slept badly, partly because the bed was lumpy and partly because the Utes seemed to be having a war dance most of the night in the Agency streets. He was glad to find them gone at dawn as he rode toward The Narrows and Coal Creek Canyon carrying Meeker's letters and his telegram for Western Union in Rawlins.

But Meeker slept long and late. It was the hard sleep of a man who wished that he didn't have to wake up. He knew that his life's dream went north with the telegram.

CHAPTER XVI Help Wanted

JOHN STEELE REACHED RAWLINS safely on September 13 and sent
Meeker's telegram to Commissioner Hayt in Washington. The
Commissioner wasn't there to receive it. He was busy as usual
running the Second National Bank of Jersey City. His assistant,
E. J. Brooks, passed the telegram along to Secretary of the
Interior Schurz. But Schurz was away too, inspecting Indian
Agencies on the West Coast. *His* assistant, A. Bell, wired him
about Meeker's peril and at the same time applied to George
McCrary, Secretary of War, for troops to help Meeker.

Bell's news seemed dire to Schurz, and to his private Secretary, Bob Mitchell, Josie Meeker's friend. It reached Schurz at
a very bad time. He had been trying all summer to clear himself
and President Hayes of blame for events which had disgusted
millions of Americans — the removal of the peaceful Nebraska
Poncas to Indian Territory to placate the troublesome Sioux.
The last thing Schurz wanted just then was more nation-wide
lambasting due to Indian trouble in Colorado. Consequently,
he and Mitchell hastened to San Francisco and caught the first
train east to consult with Governor Pitkin in Denver.

Secretary of War McCrary and General of the Army Sherman
approved Meeker's request for help and instructed General
Sheridan in Chicago to order "the nearest military commander" to forward troops to White River. Nobody in Sheridan's office knew exactly where White River was, or what military
commander was nearest to it. But, after a couple of days of
ludicrous trial and error, the order arrived correctly at Fort

Steele, Wyoming, by way of General Crook in Omaha, who addressed it to Major Thornburgh.

Thornburgh was off hunting again near Battle Lake. His orderly, Private O'Malley, saddled a fast horse and hurried up the North Platte River to find him. He rode out of the Red Desert, passed the obsolete Overland Trail and spent the night in J. T. Crawford's meadow beyond Warm Springs. At dawn he climbed into the Sierra Madres and crossed the Continental Divide at ten thousand feet, before noon. Just below him, on the pine-rimmed talus shore of Battle Lake, he saw Thornburgh's wagons and mules. He rode north a mile or so along the ridge toward the elk grounds under Bridger Peak, and found the hunting party having lunch and enjoying the splendor of the mountains. He dismounted, saluted the Major — and gave him General Crook's telegram. It read:

YOU WILL MOVE WITH A SUFFICIENT NUMBER OF TROOPS TO WHITE RIVER AGENCY UNDER SPECIAL INSTRUCTIONS.

Thornburgh had brought along Taylor Pennock as his guide on this hunt. His first thought after reading the message was that Pennock was the man to guide his White River expedition. Nobody else had Pennock's knowledge of northwest Colorado. But merest chance blocked his wishes. It happened that his guests were two Tennessee bankers and his older brother, ex-Congressman Jacob Montgomery Thornburgh of Knoxville. The Honorable Jake was an imposing person — a Civil War colonel, a brilliant lawyer, a first-name friend of President Grant, who had sent him in '72 as U. S. Commissioner to the International Exposition in Vienna. His success as a charmer of ladies had been demonstrated when, at thirty-eight, he wooed and wed the prettiest teen-aged belle in Washington, Laura Pettibone.[1]

The younger Thornburgh had always been very proud of and awed by Jake. It was natural for him to pass Crook's message on to him for comment. Jake didn't like what he read. He said so heatedly for some minutes. The United States Army, he declared, was not going to bust up this hunt. He hadn't brought two of his best friends all the way from Tennessee just to play poker at Fort Steele. The Major would have to go to White River. But the hunting party was staying with the elk under Bridger Peak. All Jake needed was one wagon, a fortnight's food and a little Guckenheimer for snakebite. And Taylor Pennock, too, of course.

The Major explained that he needed Pennock himself. He argued the point. But he had never crossed Jake in his whole life and he gave in at last. He and his detail of soldiers started back to Fort Steele without his guests and without the guide in whom he had so much confidence.

THOUGH MAJOR THORNBURGH'S FATE would be determined by the same forces which would determine the fates of Chief Ouray and Nathan Meeker, he was the product of a world utterly different from their worlds. He grew up in a Southern tradition with Yankee overtones. His mother, Olivia Anne, taught him cavalier manners, New England morality and deep reverence for women. His father, Montgomery, taught him love of nature, how to hold his bourbon and deep reverence for horses. Montgomery also made him an expert on Irish setters and a crack shot able to hit half-dollars tossed up fifty feet away.[2]

He was born Thomas Tipton Thornburgh in 1843 in New Market, East Tennessee, where the Thornburghs of Virginia had been prominent since periwig days. The family had opposed slavery. At the start of the Civil War young Tip was already over six feet tall and he would have joined the Union Army except that his mother said he was too young. His father must have been a man of epic courage and idealism. He was an Andrew Johnson Democrat in the State Legislature and he risked death throughout his long parliamentary battle to keep Tennessee in the Union. His Secessionist colleagues outvoted him and betrayed him into captivity. So he died of starvation, as a political prisoner at Andersonville, when he was only forty-five.

Meanwhile, Tip had run away from his mother and joined the Sixth Tennessee as a private. He galloped all over Kentucky and fought with General Sheridan's men at Stone River. His brother Jake watched over him as a substitute father and got him appointed in '63 to West Point. He graduated twenty-sixth in his class and was assigned to the Second Artillery at the Presidio, San Francisco. He attended artillery school at Fortress Monroe, Virginia, where he proved himself to be, if not brilliant, still an ambitious and conscientious officer. Besides, he could shoot at and hit those half dollars. In regimentals he was so delightful to look at that he found himself assigned as Aide to the Grand Marshal in President Grant's second inaugural parade down Pennsylvania Avenue.

At a Fortress Monroe hop, a friend of Thornburgh's, Lieutenant Alpheus Clarke, had a young sister on his hands. She was a tiny thing, just graduated from St. Clair Hall in Wisconsin. Her name was Lida and she was the eighteen-year-old daughter of Major Robert D. Clarke, an Army paymaster at Omaha.

Lieutenant Clarke dumped Lida on Lieutenant Thornburgh. The date didn't seem favorable. When Lida looked shyly up at the great profile it was almost a foot above her. Thornburgh was twenty-six — practically an antique. But he had young ways. Soon the little blonde wanted this smooth-shaven giant with gentle black eyes and curly black hair. During the hop, they held hands in the moonlight at the Postern Gate and watched the yellow cabin lights and romantic silhouettes of the schooners sailing out of Chesapeake Bay.

Thornburgh and Lida were married at Fort Omaha on the evening of his twenty-seventh birthday, December 26, 1870. It was a big wedding adorned with a great deal of brass, all West Pointers of course. Major Clarke, the bride's father, was a popular old Army man and a distant cousin of General Sherman. Paymaster General Benjamin Alvord was his best friend. Among those crowding into the post chapel were old General Innis Palmer, bowed down with the weight of many medals, and General Christopher Augur, one of the country's top dozen military leaders. General and Mrs. Eugene Carr came from Fort McPherson, three hundred miles away. General Nelson Sweitzer was an usher.

Lida's train of white grosgrain silk was eight feet long. Her satin dress was short-sleeved and low at the bodice, with short points at the waist. Her hair was wreathed in orange blossoms. The maid of honor, her sister Robertine, and the bridesmaids wore white tarlatan dresses and overskirts. The groom wore his blue regimentals, epaulettes, gilt buttons, sidearms and gleaming black boots. Standing with him were Lieutenant Frank Nye and Alpheus Clarke. The service was High Episcopal and the couple gave their *I do*'s in "clear, unfaltering voices." Or so wrote the society editor of the Omaha paper.

Several hundred people attended the reception afterwards at the residence of General Sweitzer. General Alvord contributed ten cases of champagne. The crowd danced to the music of the Second Cavalry Band. Alph Clarke and Frank Nye watched champagne consumption and decided at midnight that the newlyweds could slip off unnoticed to the Union Pacific train. They changed clothes and did slip off and were about to draw the green curtains of their sleeping section when the whole bridal party boarded the train with the declared intent of chaperoning them all the way to California. As the train rattled off from Omaha, the chaperones gave toasts and sang "Listen to the Mocking Bird" and "The Man on the Flying Trapeze." But they disembarked at Gilmore a few miles out and left the Thornburghs alone. It had been a very nice wedding.

After their San Francisco honeymoon, the couple were stationed briefly at San Diego and at Alcatraz where they received as a late wedding present a bear cub named Dick Bristen. In '71, Thornburgh went to Knoxville as military science teacher at East Tennessee University. Then it was Fort Foote, Maryland, until '75. By that time he was a First Lieutenant of Artillery and had covered his chin with a fine set of muttonchop whiskers. One day a vacancy occurred in his father-in-law's Paymaster Corps, which had no rating lower than Major. Thornburgh discussed it with Major Clarke and with General Alvord and agreed to join the Army paymasters in Texas. General Alvord jumped him over one hundred older lieutenants and two hundred and fifty captains to become, at thirty-two, one of the youngest majors in the service.

Major Thornburgh was glad in that summer of 1875 to receive the extra pay and added allowances. His family was growing. He had two small children, Bobby (aged three) and Olivia (aged one). Lida was pregnant again. He had two Irish setters, Tom and Bill — by Elcho out of J. G. Lester's Lula — and they ate a great deal.[3] He was a man of normal vanity and he got pleasure out of his higher rank and out of the realization that he was bound to wind up at least a major general if he behaved himself and didn't get killed.

But soon he made a dismaying discovery. Carrying money around the Texas posts was not the most stimulating branch of military science. It was even less stimulating in Omaha after his transfer there in '77 to work with his father-in-law. Still, he was outdoors and that was the main thing. He could hunt and fish and train his dogs. His shooting skill improved as he grew older and his reputation as a marksman spread. He had not been stationed at Omaha long when, just for fun, he agreed to appear in a shooting match with the renowned Dr. Frank Carver.

This Carver was supposed to be an intimate of people like Wild Bill Hickok and Calamity Jane and Liver-Eating Johnson who, however, wouldn't eat just anybody's liver; it had to be a

Sioux's. Carver claimed to be a dentist but nobody ever saw him pull a tooth. He had fought Indians, hobnobbed with Kaiser Wilhelm and he had shot out the gas lights in the bar of the Waldorf-Astoria in New York to amuse General Sheridan. He was said to have killed thirty thousand buffalo during the 1870s. In a single fortnight he shot two hundred and fifty elk and eighty deer. He regarded himself as unquestionably the best rifle shot on earth.

The Carver–Thornburgh match lasted an hour. For a time the two marksmen stayed even, and it was only near the end that the Major began missing the glass balls and lost out. But Carver was impressed. General George Crook was present, and he was impressed too. Soon after, Crook put Thornburgh up for membership in the Omaha Gun Club and began to take him along on hunting trips as far west as Fort Bridger, where they were guests of Judge Carter, the convivial plutocrat whom Meeker's housemaid Jane admired so much.

Crook, a tall, shy, laconic man, was the greatest of United States Army Indian fighters. He had fought Indians in California and Oregon and Idaho and Arizona. He invented the Indian scout service, developed fast mobile attack based on mule pack trains, improved the art of night fighting and brought peace to the Gila River Apache region. During the Sioux-Cheyennes uprisings, he was sent to the North Platte. The Sioux leader Crazy Horse beat him badly on the Rosebud in June, 1876. But his casualties were only eight killed. The defeat was a victory compared to the stunning disaster on the Little Big Horn a few days later when General Custer and two hundred and sixty-four others were killed by Crazy Horse's men.

One day during the spring of 1878, General Crook called Thornburgh to his desk in Omaha. He had a proposition. Major Henry G. Thomas, the commander at Fort Steele, was feeling too old for further service in the field. He was looking for a place in the Paymaster Corps. Thornburgh, Crook knew well, was bored with paymastering. How would he like to trade jobs with Thomas and take over at Fort Steele?

Thornburgh wasted no time accepting the offer.

FORT STEELE WAS SITUATED on a bend of the North Platte sixteen miles east of Rawlins at the east edge of the Red Desert. It stood in a desolate semicircle of sand ridges which protected it slightly from the incessant wind. The ridges lifted in bands of pink, yellow and black. They had some beauty in the rose of dawn as the sun prepared to appear over the Medicine Bows. But by day they were ugly and oppressive.

The fort was named for General Frederick Steele who was valorous at Chapultepac and at Vicksburg. He died the year Fort Steele was built, 1868. His widow and home-town Congressman got busy and had him memorialized. Many Army posts got their names that way. Sometimes they were named twice, thereby soothing two widows. Fort Sanders, east of Steele on the Union Pacific, was Fort Buford first, honoring General John Buford. Then it was renamed for Captain William P. Sanders who died at Knoxville. In '67, the new railroad fort at Cheyenne was called Fort D. A. Russell after a general killed in Virginia. They call it Fort Francis E. Warren now, for a Wyoming Governor.

Steele was built by Colonel Richard I. Dodge, author of the Western classic *Our Wild Indians*. Its purpose was to guard Union Pacific construction crews working across the Red Desert during the late 1860s. Troops at Fort Sanders had guarded these crews from Laramie to the Medicine Bows. Steele's garrison had guarded them through Rawlins to the next railheads, Rock Springs and Green River.

After the Union Pacific began running and the settlers poured in, there were no railroad crews to guard any longer and no warlike Indians in Carbon County for the soldiers to fight. Consequently, when Thornburgh came to Fort Steele in

July of 1878, he found the post falling to pieces. The biting dust
eddied about the ramshackle barracks, the stone hospital,
Union Pacific depot and the Hugus sutler store. The only really
fresh thing in sight was the Virginia creeper which struggled up
the lattice on the porch of the many-gabled Commander's
Quarters. General Crook had told Thornburgh frankly that the
post served no military purpose whatsoever. It was just a cheap
place to house troops. Crook expected to abandon it at the first
opportunity and transfer Thornburgh to a spot where he would
have some adventure.

Under these decaying conditions, Steele's new commander
should have had a morale problem. But he always got along well
with enlisted men. He kept up discipline without being a
martinet. He issued passes freely so that the garrison could let
off steam on Lower Row in Rawlins. He allowed dances at the
post. He excused everyone from duty on September 10, 1878, to
see the total eclipse of the sun. He arranged post schedules to
permit the garrison to watch the passing emigrant trains with
the thirty-ton eight-wheel engines pulling the boxcars at twenty
miles an hour. The arrivals of the two daily passenger trains
were pleasant events. Lida and the children joined the soldiers
in waving at the swells in the palace cars.

Thornburgh found plenty to do during his first year at
Steele. His roster was constantly expanding and contracting and
that made for desk work. And there was that ill-fated junket to
Nebraska in the fall of 1878 which he led for General Crook,
to stop two pitiful bands of Cheyenne Indians escaping northward from Indian Territory. In Nebraska, Thornburgh's troop
train had a hotbox and crept along. When it reached the Platte
crossing, the two Cheyenne bands — babes, pregnant mothers
and all — had slipped by. Thornburgh mounted his infantry
and went in pursuit. But Crook's quartermaster had failed to
provide the usual Indian scouts and mobile pack train. The
supply wagons mired down. The cattlemen scouts were useless.
The soldiers got lost in a fog, followed false trails and nearly

died of hunger. They marched two hundred and fifty aimless miles over the sandhills and had to be rescued by the Third Cavalry.[4]

The Major was not criticized too harshly for this Nebraska fiasco because he was not to blame for transport failure. But he took it very much to heart. He felt that he had let his friend Crook down. That was why, as he left Battle Lake and hurried down the North Platte in mid-September of 1879, he made meticulous plans for a successful White River expedition. He was determined not to let Crook down again. At Fort Steele, he went furiously to work, hardly sleeping for two nights. Crook's "special instructions" gave him two Fort Steele companies, which would be joined in Rawlins by two companies of cavalry from Fort D. A. Russell, Cheyenne. On Sunday morning, September 21, the Fort Steele companies were ready to move and they marched in review across the dusty parade ground while Thornburgh watched from his porch with Lida and the children.

The men didn't look like much. They were not the cream of American youth but mostly imported McNamaras and Donovans from Ireland and other immigrants with names like Eichwurzell and Schickendonz who hardly spoke English. Their uniforms were motley and of a thousand shades of blue caused by bad dyes. Their rifles were out of date. Their campaign hats were those shallow 1872 affairs which the Quartermaster Corps palmed off as new by peeling away part of the brim and reducing the crown to three inches at a cost of fifteen cents each.

And yet the men thrilled Thornburgh as they marched past in the bright Wyoming sun — smiling, brisk, brave, willing fellows. He loved them and had complete faith in them and he said as much as he took Lida in his long arms and kissed her and told her not to worry. He would settle the White River trouble and would be back with her in a month.

He could speak with such conviction because he was not actually worried himself. Except, perhaps, the veriest touch. The cause was an odd little note which he had just received, place-marked New Market, Tennessee. It was from his ancient grand-father, who could not have known about the expedition when he had dictated it to Jake's pretty wife, Laura Pettibone. The note read:

MAJOR T. T. THORNBURGH
DEAR GRANDSON:
I have but a few words to say. As you have dealings with a treacherous people (the Indians, I mean) be on your guard and remember Braddock, Saint Clair and Harrison, how they were served. I will be 88 years old on the 7th of October and enjoy tolerable good health but am totally blind. If convenient, write me something of the country, the Indians and yourself.
Your grandfather,
AI THORNBURGH
per Laura [5]

CHAPTER XVII Troopers South

THORNBURGH AND HIS FORCE arrived in Rawlins that same Sunday afternoon and found the two Fort Russell companies from Cheyenne waiting for them in camp on the south side of town. Many of the Cheyenne soldiers knew Thornburgh's men well, having served at Fort Steele themselves in the past year. There was a period of greeting and good-natured ribbing among the four units. And there was a general mild perplexity as to what this White River expedition was all about, and why it was any concern of theirs.

The perplexity derived from the way the Army was organized in 1879. There were three main Divisions under General Sherman, comprising a total of 24,262 enlisted men and 2127 officers. The Atlantic and Pacific Divisions didn't amount to much. The guts of the Army was General Sheridan's Division of the Missouri, which spent most of $50,000,000 which the Army cost annually, and absorbed three quarters of its personnel. The main job of Sheridan's Division was to ride herd on 250,000 western Indians by means of 19 regiments of infantry, 8 of cavalry, 4 companies of artillery and 200 Indian scouts, a total force of 15,517 men scattered among 71 forts. The Division's territory measured 1,600,000 square miles, which spread over an immensity of plain and mountain, desert and high plateau, from the Mississippi to the High Sierras, from the Rio Grande to Canada. It was a land of infinite variety, traversed by a single railroad, the Union Pacific.

The Division of the Missouri was subdivided into four Departments: Texas, Dakota, Platte and Missouri. General George Crook at Omaha commanded the Department of the Platte, which had 17 posts and a total of 3000 soldiers, mainly members of the Third and Fifth Cavalry and of the Fourth Infantry, which was Thornburgh's regiment. General Crook's Department took in Iowa, Nebraska, Wyoming Territory, Utah Territory and part of Idaho. It did not include Colorado.

The White River Agency, therefore, was not in Crook's Department at all, as Thornburgh's puzzled troopers kept telling each other, even though Thornburgh was "the nearest military commander" stipulated in Sherman's original order. White River was in the remote northwest corner of General Pope's Department of Missouri. But all of Pope's twenty forts were far from Meeker's Agency; for instance, five hundred very tough miles lay between White River and Fort Lewis at Pagosa Springs, which was home base for Captain Dodge's Negro company currently guarding Middle Park.

No member of the White River Expedition had ever journeyed to White River from Rawlins. That is why Thornburgh needed Taylor Pennock so badly. On that Sunday evening of September 21, Major Thornburgh went to see Rawlins's first citizen, James France, for help in getting a substitute guide and for general advice. The half-pint pioneer said that Joe Rankin was able and willing to guide the White River expedition inasmuch as the Major couldn't take Pennock away from his brother. At the Little Snake, the Major could engage Charlie Lowry to go on in ahead to tell Meeker that the troops were coming. The Utes wouldn't bother Charlie because they were so fond of his harmonica.

As for the Utes in general, France told Thornburgh that they seemed more threatening than ever. His Agency freighters had been leery of them all through August while delivering to Meeker twenty-six thousand pounds of flour, a ton of seed wheat, some blue vitriol, six cookstoves, platform scales and two pairs of field glasses. And now he was very much worried about the fate of fifteen thousand dollars' worth of Ute annuity supplies which he had put on the road to White River.

France explained it all in loving detail. On September 14, he had sent along two four-mule wagons containing four thousand pounds of flour. He asked Thornburgh to watch out for these wagons, as the teamsters were inexperienced — a small and elderly Jew peddler, Carl Goldstein, and a teen-aged boy, Julius Moore. On September 16, John Gordon's long bull train of ten wagons in tandem and thirty-three oxen had left Rawlins with three bullwhackers helping John. The train carried ten thousand pounds of flour, as well as tin pans, washtubs, washboards, meat cleavers, red flannel shirts from Wanamaker's, emery paper, a wheelbarrow for Johnson and two Denver saddles for Josie Meeker and Flora Ellen Price.

The next day, France had dispatched John Gordon's brother, George, and two drivers with three four-horse wagons. The first wagon carried delftware and china. The second — a special, low truck-wagon — contained something few Rawlinsites had seen before. It was Mr. Meeker's threshing machine. Its big pulleys, grain chute and long folded straw-stacker gleamed in the sun. George Gordon's third wagon, also low, carried a steam engine to run the thresher. Finally, on September 18, Al McCarger and his son drove south in a wagon loaded with saws, spades, axes, paper bags, lamp chimneys, coal oil and thirteen thousand feet of barbed wire for more fencing-out of ponies at Powell Park. Also there was a sack of play hatchets which Josie had ordered at her own expense for her school children.[1]

France was winding up now. He mentioned that Secretary Schurz had just rolled through Rawlins on the Union Pacific en route to Denver. He figured that Schurz must be going there because of the White River trouble. And then, like Thornburgh's grandfather, France concluded by urging the Major to be on his guard.

MONDAY, SEPTEMBER 22, dawned bright and warm. The whole town of eight hundred turned out for the troopers' departure, the biggest event in Rawlins's brief history. Soon after sunup the men were moving south in cheerful bunches stretching out for two miles and more. The total number of men was 153 soldiers and 25 civilians; there were 220 mules and 150 horses. At the head of the column with Thornburgh were Joe Rankin, Captain J. Scott Payne, Thornburgh's subcommander from Fort Russell, and Lieutenant Samuel Cherry, also from Fort Russell, who had a greyhound along. Cherry, a gay young West Pointer from Indiana, was Thornburgh's adjutant. He limped slightly, having once let a half-ton cannon fall on him instead of on a friend whom he had pushed out of harm's way.

Behind the leaders was the Major's mule-drawn ambulance, driven by Private O'Malley. It contained Thornburgh's rifle, trout rod, diarrhea mixture, photos of Lida in her wedding gown, witch hazel for mosquitoes, Holland gin and lemon extract for ague, a box of Reina Victoria cigars and a small leather Bible which his sister had given him at West Point with the flyleaf inscription, "To Brother Tip from Livvie. Please read *one* chapter every day." Riding with O'Malley was Captain Payne's surgeon, Dr. R. B. Grimes.

Payne's Company F, Fifth Cavalry, followed at some distance. It consisted of forty-three brisk and well-groomed soldiers some of whom basked in the glory of many Sioux battles. Next came twenty-nine members of Fort Steele's Company E, Fourth Infantry, all eligible for discharge soon. Their leader Lieutenant Butler Price, liked to collect rare specimens for the Smithsonian and was currently seeking burrowing owls. The supply train was half a mile behind Price, made up of thirty-three six-mule wagons, not counting Charlie Davis's sutler wagon. Thornburgh's quartermaster was Lieutenant Silas A. Wolf, a dazed lad a year out of West Point. The supply train was guarded by twenty-seven men of Company D, Fifth Cavalry, from Fort Russell. Its officer, Lieutenant James V. S. Paddock, was a small, shy shavetail as green as Lieutenant Wolf.

The rear guard, Fort Steele's Company E, Third Cavalry, was jauntily led by Captain Joe Lawson, a shriveled old-timer of sixty years, his crab-apple cheeks ablaze with sun and bourbon and his whiskers crawling around his tobacco-stained mouth like weeds. Joe had fought as many Indians as George Crook. His troop numbered forty-nine profane, shabby, grinning veterans. They carried their whisky without concealment and swore in mixed Irish, German and Swedish.[2]

For all its unevenness, Thornburgh was satisfied with his force. His only mild reservation concerned Captain Payne, his subcommander, who was in poor physical shape. Payne's health had failed in 1877 during the Chief Joseph campaign. Six months of café sitting in Paris had not restored it. He joined Thornburgh still pale and flabby after long invalidism back East. Though he was the Major's age, thirty-five, his corpulence and stiff bearing made him seem older. Temperamentally, he was Thornburgh's opposite.[3] To him, fighting Indians was purely a tactical problem in time, space and fire power. Thornburgh, by contrast, had General Crook's tendency to see the Indian's point of view and to wonder what kind of a mind and spirit his bullets might be destroying.

Joe Rankin led the expedition on the same scenic route which Meeker had taken in the spring of '78. But it was a golden route now, with splotches of orange aspen, copper oak and red serviceberry as the troops rode into Little Snake Valley early Tuesday afternoon. The Major and Sam Cherry went visiting upriver that evening, as Meeker had done. They met Jim Baker at his blockhouse, and Jim's squaws. They found Charlie Lowry at Bibleback Brown's and Thornburgh hired him as his courier. On Wednesday morning, the four companies climbed over the divide and moved sixteen miles down Fortification Creek before lunchtime to its junction with Little Bear Creek. The grass was knee-high here and the water was excellent. Thornburgh decided to camp over Thursday. That would give him time to set up Lt. Price's infantry and eight of the thirty-three wagons as the expedition's supply depot.

But first they would all rest. The six officers lazed the golden hours away. At twilight Thornburgh stirred himself and dictated a letter to Adjutant Cherry, which Charlie Lowry would carry to White River Agency seventy-five miles south. The letter read:

HEADQUARTERS, WHITE RIVER EXPEDITION
CAMP ON FORTIFICATION CREEK *Sept. 25*

MR. MEEKER
U. S. INDIAN AGENT
WHITE RIVER AGENCY:
SIR:

In obedience to instructions from the General of the Army, I am en route to your agency, and expect to arrive there on the 29th instant, for the purpose of rendering you any assistance in my power, and to make arrests at your suggestion, and to hold as prisoners such of your Indians as you desire until investigations are made by your department. I have heard nothing definite from your agency for ten days, and don't know what state of affairs exists; whether the Indians will leave at my approach or show resistance.

I send this letter by Mr. Lowry, one of my guides, and desire you to communicate with me as soon as possible, giving me all the information in your power, in order that I may know what course to pursue. If practicable meet me on the road at the earliest moment.

Very respectfully, your obedient servant,
T. T. THORNBURGH
Major, 4th Infantry, Commanding Expedition

As Sam Cherry copied out the letter, Charlie Lowry entered the big Sibley tent of the officers. He told them that he had been scouting in the brush around camp and had spotted a Ute spying on them. Thornburgh was startled. He stepped from the tent and gazed over the burnished brush. He saw no sign of spies. The scene at sunset was serene and beautiful beyond belief.

But Charlie Lowry was right. There were spies. Chief Jack's band had left White River on the same day that Thornburgh had left Fort Steele. The Utes had taken the Rawlins road, bound for their fall hunt in Wyoming. When Jack found Thornburgh's troops on the Little Snake he was furious at the invasion and canceled his hunt to watch it. He sent his band back to White River and shadowed the soldiers with his sub-chief Sowerwick and a few others. Jack had seen Thornburgh gazing over the brush on Thursday, even if Thornburgh couldn't see him. He saw Charlie Lowry set out for White River late that night. On Friday, September 26, Jack and Sowerwick trailed the three cavalry companies and their twenty-five wagons for a dozen or more miles south through the deepening beauty. Lieutenant Price's company of infantry stayed behind on Fortification Creek as Thornburgh's supply depot. At Tom Iles's ranch, on Bear River near the mouth of Elkhead Creek, Jack saw Thornburgh call a halt for that day. Soon the banks of the lovely stream were lined with fishing troopers.

Jack slipped a mile downriver and crossed at Himley's Ford to Peck's store, where he bought ten thousand rounds of cartridges from Mrs. Peck. Two of Jack's men hefted the cartridge box on a pony and rode south along the Agency road toward the Farm That Jack Built. Then Sam Cherry and Joe Rankin arrived at Peck's, shook hands with Jack, and asked Mrs. Peck if she had any fixed ammunition. She said that the Utes had bought her last cartridge for their fall hunt in Wyoming.

At 2 P.M. Jack and Sowerwick rode with Lieutenant Cherry upriver past the fishing troopers to talk with Thornburgh in the big Sibley.

Jack controlled his anger but did not try to conceal it. He told the Major that the soldiers had no business coming to White River. Everything was peaceful there. Then he explained how Meeker was trying to force plowing and schooling on his people by withholding supplies which were theirs by treaty. Meeker had notified them that they could not hunt off the

Reservation as punishment for setting fires, which everyone knew had been caused mostly by the drought. And the Agent was keeping them up in the air by saying one thing one day and contradicting himself the next. Finally, Meeker had promised Jack and Sowerwick a new red wagon for starting the Farm That Jack Built. When the wagon arrived, it was an old green model with the paint flaking off. And the Agent said that they could use it only one month.

Major Thornburgh liked Jack's directness, and sympathized with him. But, as a government official, he did not intend to express himself on the subject of Nathan Meeker. He told Jack that General Sherman had ordered him to White River to check rumors, and he hoped that Jack would go in with him. Thereupon, Thornburgh ended the interview. On an impulse, as the Utes rode away, he sent Private O'Malley running after Jack with some Reina Victoria cigars. Then he dictated a wire to General Crook which would go by courier to Western Union at Rawlins:

HAVE MET SOME UTE CHIEFS HERE. THEY SEEM FRIENDLY AND PROMISE TO GO WITH ME TO THE AGENCY. SAY UTES DON'T UNDERSTAND WHY WE HAVE COME. HAVE TRIED TO EXPLAIN SATISFACTORILY. DO NOT ANTICIPATE TROUBLE.

T. T. THORNBURGH, MAJ., 4TH INFANTRY

Jack and Sowerwick stayed at Peck's store until dark and then set out riding fast for White River, sixty-five miles south. At midnight, they stopped near the Milk Creek boundary of the Reservation where Eugene Taylor ran a summer sutler tent for Charlie Perkins. Jack was surprised to find Ed Mansfield, Meeker's employee, there. He asked Mansfield if he carried messages from Meeker to Thornburgh or to Captain Dodge in Middle Park. Mansfield said that he carried no messages. He was just going to Greeley on vacation.

The two Utes thought that Mansfield was lying but they did not harm him. They continued through Yellowjacket Pass and down Coal Creek Canyon. At his White River village, Jack rested and tried to make up his mind what Thornburgh's mission was. He could not believe that all those soldiers would come so far just to talk. He reviewed the past, remembering the massacres of Indians at Sand Creek and Washita, the humbling of the mighty Sioux, the tragic roundup of the Cheyennes. He reviewed what William Vickers had written about the Utes in "Lo, the Poor Indian!" and Meeker's frequent mention during this past unhappy summer of manacles and handcuffs and nooses.

By dawn on Saturday, September 27, Chief Jack had made up his mind. Accordingly, he sent a dozen Utes up Coal Creek to prepare a guard camp at the Beaver Creek springs five miles south of the Reservation line overlooking Milk Creek Valley. Then he left his village at the mouth of Coal Creek and rode through The Narrows to Chief Douglas's tepee. He woke the old man and told him that the crisis was here. They must stop feuding and stand together now. Thornburgh's troopers were approaching. They came at Meeker's bidding to arrest the White River Utes and to drag them in chains out of their beloved mountains to Indian Territory.

CHAPTER XVIII

Death in the Morning

THE WHITE RIVER EXPEDITION was late starting from Bear River on Saturday morning. The troopers had overtaken George Gordon's train bearing Meeker's threshing machine and Al McCarger's wagon. One of George Gordon's trucks had broken down, and Thornburgh's wagonmaster, William McKinstry, spent two hours fixing it. Then the force rode over the divide to Williams Fork and camped in a meadow where Deer Creek came in.

The men were forty-five miles from the Agency now, by way of Milk Creek, Yellowjacket Pass and Coal Creek Canyon. They were thirty miles beyond Lieutenant Price's supply depot on Fortification Creek. Captain Dodge and his Negro company were camped presumably in Middle Park, one hundred and twenty miles eastwards. There was no hurry. Major Thornburgh could only mark time until Charlie Lowry returned from the Agency with an answer from Meeker to his letter of Thursday.

At dusk, Thornburgh watched several horsemen as they trotted up to the officers' tent. He thought that the leader must be Lowry, but he wasn't. He introduced himself as Wilmer Eskridge, a new Agency employee. With him was the Agency interpreter and a Ute guide. Standing apart was old Chief Colorow, who had trailed in with the others from Eugene Taylor's sutler's tent near Milk Creek at the edge of the Reservation. Colorow said that he was representing Chief Jack.

Eskridge reported that Meeker had not received Thorn-

burgh's letter, since Charlie Lowry hadn't reached the Agency
yet. He gave Thornburgh this message:

September 27, 1879

SIR:

Understanding that you are on your way hither with United
States Troops, I send a messenger, Mr. Eskridge, and two Indians, Henry Jim (interpreter) and John Ayersly to inform
you that the Indians are greatly excited and wish you to stop
at some convenient camping place and then that you and five
soldiers of your command come into the Agency when a talk
and better understanding can be had. This I agree to.

But I do not propose to order your movements, but it seems
for the best. The Indians seem to consider the advance of your
troops as a declaration of real war. In this I am laboring to
undeceive them, and at the same time to convince them that
they cannot do whatever they please. The first objective now
is to allay apprehension.

Respectfully,

N. C. MEEKER

Thornburgh studied the message and called Captain Payne,
Lieutenant Cherry, Captain Lawson, Henry Jim and Wilmer
Eskridge to discuss it. Chief Colorow waddled over to the Major,
saluted him as gracefully as his great bulk allowed and got his
permission to sit in.

Eskridge reviewed Agency affairs since September 11, when
John Steele had left for Rawlins with Meeker's request for help.
Things had been surprisingly peaceful for a fortnight. Meeker's
biggest worry had been the shortage of twenty-five pound flour
sacks. And he had complained mildly to Commissioner Hayt at
the Indian Bureau that plowing was still unsafe and "it remains
to be seen if the business and industries of this Agency are to
be conducted under the Indians or yourself."

Yesterday, Eskridge said, the Agent had begun to think that
perhaps he didn't need troops after all. As Ed Mansfield had left
for Greeley on vacation, Meeker had asked him to go toward
Middle Park and report the lull to Captain Dodge. But the
appearance of peace had been an illusion, and the illusion was

shattered this Saturday morning. The cause, apparently, was the arrival of Chief Jack at Douglas's tepee with news of the approach of Thornburgh and his soldiers. So now Meeker felt that the Agency was in great danger. The employees were standing guard over the storehouses, which were half full of annuity goods. The amateur freighters Carl Goldstein and Julius Moore were there unloading. The Gordon trains were expected Monday.

Meeker, Eskridge concluded, had talked with Douglas and Jack and the result was his message asking Thornburgh to leave his troops outside the Reservation and to ride in with only five soldiers for a conference. Chief Colorow picked up the talk here and stated that he was authorized by Chief Jack and his band to guarantee Thornburgh's safety at the Agency. And Colorow added that this grassy spot on Deer Creek, not fifty miles from White River, was a fine camp for the troops and their animals.

Thornburgh considered, and then spoke up in favor of Meeker's suggestion. Lieutenant Cherry and Captain Lawson favored it too. Captain Payne opposed it emphatically. The Army, he said, was supposed to settle Indian Bureau troubles, not mediate them. But Thornburgh overruled his subcommander. Lieutenant Cherry wrote out his return message and gave it to the interpreter, Henry Jim, for delivery to the Agent.

> CAMP ON WILLIAMS FORK
> *September 27, 1879*
>
> N. C. MEEKER
> SIR:
>
> Your letter of this date just received. I will move my command to Milk Creek or some good location for camp, or possibly may leave my entire command at this point, and will come in as desired with five men. Mr. Eskridge will remain to guide me to the Agency.
>
> I will reach your Agency some time on the 29th instant.
> Very respectfully, your obedient servant,
> T. T. THORNBURGH
> *Major, 4th Infantry, Commanding Expedition*

Sunday was Bad Rumor Day in the column as Thornburgh
led his force leisurely up Deer Creek from Williams Fork, closing the forty-five mile gap to the Agency by ten miles. Eugene
Taylor came in from his Milk Creek sutler's tent. He was
frightened. The Utes, he said, had confiscated all his ammunition. And they had intercepted Black Wilson, the mail carrier,
at Peck's store on Bear River and made him drop Saturday's
Agency mail there.

Wilson, Taylor went on, had figured that the Utes must be
on the warpath. He had hurried to Charlie Perkins's other sutler's tent on Good Spring Gulch west of Deer Creek and had
helped Perkins's trader, Mike Sweet, to bury his guns and ammunition. Then Joe Collom had come over from Collom
Gulch and had asked Wilson to sell two hundred tons of hay
for him to Major Thornburgh. Wilson had started for Deer
Creek and had been halted by Chief Jack and other Utes, who
had forced him to go back to Mike Sweet's sutler tent with
them; the Utes had hunted for cartridges, didn't find the buried
stuff and went off mad.[1]

On Sunday evening, Thornburgh encamped his nervous soldiers and put out pickets near the head of Deer Creek. One of
John Gordon's bullwhackers, Columbus Henry, paid an excited call on the Major from Gordon's big bull train just ahead.
He reported that he had just talked to Chief Colorow, who had
said that the Utes would fight if the troops crossed the Milk
Creek line into the Reservation. Then Henry produced a rum-
pled paper which he had found planted on the road — a pen-
ciled sketch seeming to portray four Army officers riddled with
bullets. Thornburgh gave it to Captain Payne who put it in his
duffel along with a tourist photo of Colorow.

To the Major, the outlook was ominous. And late Sunday
night here came his courier, Charlie Lowry, at last. Charlie was
apologetic. He had been a little slow reaching Meeker, having
played some monte at Peck's and having had a drink or two at
Eugene Taylor's. He had arrived at the Agency on Saturday

evening and all hell had seemed about to break loose. Since
Eskridge was with the troops on Deer Creek, Meeker had only
seven white employees to guard Josie and Arvilla, Flora Ellen
Price and her two youngsters. Chiefs Douglas and Jack were in
a state. They had sent all the squaws and children — ninety
lodges of them — south, past the Old Squaw Camp and over
Roan Plateau toward Grand River. The two bands had war-
danced Saturday night and had told Lowry that they were going
to fire the Ute Agency and kill Meeker for ordering troops
from Steele. Lowry had tried to calm them by playing his
harmonica. In the end, Douglas and Jack had promised him to
do nothing drastic for the present.

Thornburgh was ready for bed, but Charlie Lowry's alarm-
ing tale required an immediate staff meeting. The Major admitted morosely to his officers that Captain Payne had been
dead right the night before and that he had been dead wrong.
He should not have approved Meeker's plan for him to come
in without troops. Because of his delay, Jack and Douglas now
seemed to be holding the Meeker women and Mrs. Price virtu-
ally as hostages. He asked for suggestions on what to do next.

Captain Payne took the floor. He had learned from Joe Rankin and from Lowry that the danger point to the troops for a
Ute ambush on the Agency Road was the three-mile stretch
through Coal Creek Canyon. It began on the south side of
Yellowjacket Pass eight miles from the Milk Creek Reservation
line. Its walls in spots came in close to cramp the road and the
stream. The walls rose abruptly as high as a thousand feet. Ute
marksmen on top had a clear view of the road and they could
roll boulders down upon it. The foot of Coal Creek Canyon
was near Chief Jack's big village on White River. If the troops
were attacked by day in such a trap they could be destroyed.

Well, Payne continued, suppose the troops camped on the
edge of the Reservation at Milk Creek on Monday? Major
Thornburgh, Charlie Lowry and five soldiers would go on alone
over Yellowjacket Pass and down Coal Creek to the Agency

just as the Major had agreed to do in his Saturday letter to Meeker. Chief Jack's spies would follow the Thornburgh party on in, believing that they now held more hostages. But, after dark on Monday, Captain Payne would lead the troops quietly after Thornburgh out of Milk Creek Valley and over Yellowjacket Pass. By dawn they would be safely through Coal Creek Canyon and in position to control Jack's village. From there they could lope a few miles down White River to the Agency, if the Major needed them.

Payne's plan was tricky if not entirely dishonest. Thornburgh argued with himself a little before deciding that the trickery was justified by military necessity. He approved it, wrote a letter to Meeker alluding to the new plan in veiled terms, and sent Wilmer Eskridge hurrying south with it through the night. This last letter read:

HEADQUARTERS, WHITE RIVER EXPEDITION, DEER CREEK
September 28, 1879

MR. MEEKER
SIR:

I have, after due deliberation, decided to modify my plans as outlined in my letter of the 27th in the following respects:

I shall move with my entire command to some convenient camp near and within striking distance of the Agency, reaching such point during the 29th. I shall then halt and encamp my troops and proceed to the Agency with my guide and five soldiers as communicated in your letter of the 27th. Then and there I will be ready to have a conference with you and the Indians so that an understanding may be arrived at and my course of action determined.

I have carefully considered whether or not it would be advisable to have my command at a point as distant as that desired by the Indians who were in my camp last night and have reached the conclusion that under my orders, which require me to march my command to the Agency, I am not at liberty to leave it at a point where it would not be available in case of trouble. You are authorized to say for me to the Indians that my course of conduct is entirely dependent on them. Our

desire is to avoid trouble and we have not come for war. I
requested you in my letter of the 25th to meet me on the road
before I reached the Agency. I renew my request that you do
so and further desire that you bring such chiefs as may wish to
accompany you.

T. T. THORNBURGH

Major, 4th Infantry, Commanding

THE MAJOR AND HIS MEN were up and over the frosty divide by
8 A.M. on Monday morning. Thornburgh, momentarily the
sportsman, drank with delight at the first chalky trickle of Milk
Creek. Southeast of him he could see the Gothic grandeur of
spruce forests with old Sleepy Cat nine miles away brushing
the bright September sky. Beyond Sleepy Cat was Pagoda Peak
and the sweeping Flattops enfolding Trappers Lake. It was
game country to dream about, and Thornburgh knew that the
elk and deer would be moving down soon into Milk Creek Valley for the winter.[2] Below Thornburgh, the valley was an oval
dish a mile wide and running five miles southwest to the red-
green folds of the Danforth Hills. The grass was thin because of
the drought, but there was plenty of blue sage two to three feet
high. The fragrance of the sage rode up to Thornburgh on the
breeze with a tang as joyous as the joy he felt in life itself. There
was rabbit bush everywhere too, almost tawny with autumn,
and in the air was the melancholy squawk of Steller jays calling an end to summer.

The Agency road twisted along Milk Creek, ran straight
a piece over the bench and veered south to cross the creek one
last time in a haze of golden cottonwoods and red willows. Then
it climbed through the scrub oak toward Yellowjacket Pass.
Meanwhile, Milk Creek curved northwest away from the road
and vanished behind a noble pile, a triple-knobbed eminence
which rose fourteen hundred feet above the bench and the
straight stretch of Agency road. The mountain, unpretentious
and serene, was dusted on top with juniper and piñon. Its sides

were banded yellow sandstone and along the two miles of its
base was more juniper. Lying at its foot was a series of five gray
sand dunes, and from them the sagey bench ran gently down to
Milk Creek. This noble pile had no name, though it would be
known in time as Thornburgh Mountain.

The long line of troops was like a great snake wiggling four
miles down to the valley floor. There were four creek crossings.
Milk Creek itself averaged seven feet wide, with banks six feet
high. Thornburgh noted that the stream flow was decreasing
steadily as they moved along. At the start of the straight stretch
of road along the bench, he called a halt to water the animals
before the water ceased altogether.

The troops were about to pass John Gordon's ox train. The
Major sent Joe Rankin and Lieutenant Cherry to reconnoiter at
the Reservation line in the cottonwoods near the last Milk
Creek crossing. When they returned, Rankin told Thornburgh
that he had seen fresh campfire ashes. He said also that the water
in Milk Creek near the crossing was so low that it stood in
stagnant pools.

That, Thornburgh said, was dismal luck. They would have
to change the plan. The troops and their three hundred and
seventy horses and mules would not have enough water at the
Reservation line to last them even from now until dark. Where,
he asked Rankin, was the nearest good supply of water? Rankin
said that the nearest was at Beaver Springs, up the road just
short of Yellowjacket Pass and five miles inside the Reservation.

Thornburgh conferred with Captain Payne. Then he ordered
the soldiers to advance.

Lieutenant Cherry, Joe Rankin and three privates led the way
over the last Milk Creek crossing and through the golden cottonwoods. Behind them the White River expedition and John
Gordon's bull train raised a great cloud of dust for more than
two miles on the bench in front of the long mountain. Major
Thornburgh, his ambulance, Private O'Malley and Charlie
Lowry were a quarter-mile behind Cherry's party. The Major

rode with Joe Lawson at the head of Lawson's rough-and-ready Company E, Third Cavalry. Next, at a two-hundred-yard interval, came Captain Payne and his Company F, Fifth Cavalry. Far back of Payne were Quartermaster Wolf's clattering supply wagons and Lieutenant Paddock's Company D, Fifth Cavalry. Surgeon Grimes rode with Charlie Davis on Davis's sutler's cart. They brought up the rear with John Gordon's ponderous ox train.

The unusual two-mile length of the stretch-out did not worry Thornburgh since everyone had agreed that the ambush point was Coal Creek Canyon, ten miles further on. But he felt the thrill of danger crossing the Milk Creek line and entering the Ute Reservation. As he emerged on the other side of the cottonwoods, he saw Cherry and his companions suddenly rein up ahead. They had forked left off the Agency road on a pack trail which ascended a small treeless ravine. The south-running road shifted west a little at the point of the fork to pass around the base of a long grassy ridge, also south-running.

Charlie Lowry explained to Thornburgh that Rankin was taking a short-cut trail which rejoined the Agency road at the end of the long ridge a mile farther on. That was normal. Thornburgh had instructed Joe to take short cuts when possible to spare the cavalry horses. But Lieutenant Cherry's gestures were not normal. First he pointed at the long ridge. Then he motioned violently to Thornburgh to retreat. The Major focused his field glasses on the ridge and saw fifty or more Indians, mounted and unmounted, spaced along the top.

For a minute or two the Major studied the ground while Captain Payne and his company closed up behind Joe Lawson's veterans. Cherry's advance party stayed at the base of the ridge staring up at the Utes in their cowboy hats. Then Joe Rankin turned back from them and trotted toward the Major. Thornburgh sent Lawson and his men deploying in the sage at the right side of the Agency road. He placed Payne's company similarly at the left of the road as Rankin came up to him.

Stolid Joe was shaken. He told Thornburgh that the Utes were members of Jack's band and that they must have planned an ambush from the top of the long ridge, expecting the cavalry-men to pass below them on the Agency road instead of on the higher short-cut trail. He urged the Major to start shooting. Thornburgh replied calmly that he would have to try peaceful means first. He rode out a few yards clear of Payne's skirmishers and waved his hat at the Utes on the ridge. Several of them waved their hats back and some soldiers waved. And then all waving stopped. For an interminable five minutes nobody moved while Thornburgh felt the inexorable rise of tension. At last, two Utes [3] took a few hesitant steps down the ridge to-ward Cherry. The tall adjutant began walking up toward them, limping slightly. As he did so, he waved his hat.

What Thornburgh saw next was the exploding of the giant cap that set off the dynamite of the scene. Perhaps it was simple mischance. Or perhaps it was the inevitable result of processes which began long ago when red men and white men first recog-nized their incompatibility. At any rate, someone chose to mis-construe Cherry's waving hat as a battle cue. A rifle pinged far down at the right to interrupt the autumn clatter of grass-hoppers and the *cheer!* of volplaning goldfinches. A Lawson trooper might have fired it, or a Ute in that sector. An instant later, Payne's men began firing fast without orders.

The battle of Milk Creek was on. Amid the rattle of Army Springfields, Thornburgh heard the sound of assorted Ute rifles — Winchester repeaters, cheap Ballards, Spencer carbines, old tip-ups. He saw three Utes fall, and two of Payne's men. Then he observed mounted Indians crossing Milk Creek and slipping north behind the sand dunes at the base of the long mountain. That meant that it was time for him to see how Lieutenant Pad-dock and Lieutenant Wolf were protecting the supply train.

He was quite aware of the grave situation but he was per-fectly cool and entirely confident that this would not be another Cheyenne fiasco. This time he would bring credit to General

Crook. He trotted briskly into the cottonwoods back along the road, calling to his orderly to follow him with the ambulance. Private O'Malley remembered later that the Major was carrying his Colt revolver in one hand as he passed from his sight — the gun his men in Maryland had given him on his thirty-first birthday, with his name engraved in silver on the butt.

And so Thomas Tipton Thornburgh, aged thirty-five, sportsman, "socialite" and conscientious officer, spent the final minutes of his pleasant life wholly preoccupied with his responsibilities as commander of the White River Expedition, pursuant to telegraphic instructions from Fort Omaha, Department of the Platte, dated 9/16/79. In that, he was fortunate. He had no time to rue the pleasures he would have enjoyed while rising by seniority to the ultimate eminence of a major general. He had no time to look back on the sweetnesses of his past — kissing little Lida at the Postern Gate, drinking champagne on the Union Pacific honeymoon train, raising nice children and blooded setters, matching shots with Doc Carver, catching fifty-two redsides in thirty minutes at Battle Lake.

He was riding alone in the tall grass short of the Milk Creek crossing when a big slug from some Ute's Sharps rifle struck him above the ear. He was probably dead before his long lithe frame toppled from his horse to the ground.

CHAPTER XIX Red Man, White Man

PRIVATE O'MALLEY could not follow Thornburgh with the ambulance because a Ute sharpshooter killed one of his mules. He cut loose the other mule and rode it back to Captain Payne, whose Company F still held the left side of the Agency road near the start of the long ridge. Payne was seated on the ground with a painful arm wound. His mount lay dead near him. He was intensely disturbed when O'Malley told him that Thornburgh was alone in the cottonwoods. He sent old Sergeant John Dolan and Joe Rankin to check on the Major's safety and on conditions at the wagon train.

Dolan returned soon with a horse and with very bad news for the exhausted subcommander. Thornburgh, Dolan said, must be dead. He had seen his riderless horse in the cottonwoods. The supply wagons were desperately disorganized. Young Lieutenant Paddock was trying to fort them up and to drive Ute marksmen from the sand dunes at the same time. Paddock was wounded; Quartermaster Wolf, the West Point greenhorn, was completely at sea.

By sheer power of will, Captain Payne got on his feet to cope with his frightening predicament. He saw now that he had been too preoccupied with Coal Creek Canyon, the presumed danger point ten miles further on. When he had entered Milk Creek Valley it had not occurred to him how easily Jack's band could hold the soldiers here like rats in a well.

Besides the actual enemy, Payne had trouble with his own thoughts. Like all Army officers of the period, he suffered a recurrent nightmare in which he dreamed that his entire force was destroyed by Indians as General Custer's force had been destroyed by the Sioux on the Little Big Horn. And he knew that the Custer massacre was simply the outstanding demonstration of the dilemma which confronted white men always in Indian warfare.

The horn of the dilemma was that the whites had to fight in the red man's environment. That environment sustained the Indian because he accepted its laws and abided by its rules. He could thrive on its bugs and snakes and toads if necessary. He could drink from its plants. When he was wounded he could make poultices and sedatives from its pressed herbs. He permitted its weathers to make his skin as tough as leather so that he didn't have to have clothes, winter or summer. He had no set times for anything. He ate when he was hungry, slept when he was tired and woke up when he was rested. All Indians were born completely educated, possessing innately the knowledge of their world which a lucky handful of white men acquired only by a lifetime of study.

On the other hand, the white soldiers had to haul their environment around with them and to use a great deal of their strength to guard it, as Lieutenant Paddock's men were guarding the supply wagons now. Their lives were burdened by an infinitude of complex necessities. Their food required fixing and they had to have many implements to get it down their throats. To sleep well they needed blankets and rubber mattresses and tents. Their health required doctors and pharmaceuticals without end. Finally, in their secret hearts they admired the red man for his independence of spirit and for his refusal to be imprisoned in a web not of his own making. Soldiers could not entirely enjoy killing Indians.

These were general aspects of Payne's problem. Specifically, at Milk Creek he was fearful of his inexperience. On the Little Big Horn, Custer had fought an enemy whose ways were familiar to him. Payne did not know the ways of these Utes and he began to think that their fighting qualities surpassed those of the Plains Indians. He had observed already their genius for concealed and subtle movement. They seemed to be attacking by pervasion instead of head on. They were avoiding foolish bravado. They were fine marksmen and they were saving their ammunition.

For all his fears, Payne took firm command. He sent Sergeant Edward P. Grimes galloping toward the supply train to get cartridges for Captain Lawson's company who still held the right side of the Agency road. When Grimes returned with the cartridges Payne withdrew Company F from the left side of the road into the cottonwoods and rode ahead of it to the supply train. He had hoped to rest a minute at the train but the situation was too critical. Surgeon Grimes was wounded and getting himself drunk at Charlie Davis's sutler wagon. Payne sobered him with coffee, locked up the sutler wagon and took whisky bottles from several tippling soldiers. He ordered Corporal Hampton M. Roach to direct the digging of a big central triangular pit for the wounded men of Company F.

Payne's difficulties multiplied. Lieutenant Paddock and Lieutenant Wolf had been forced to corral the twenty-five wagons one hundred and fifty yards away from the meager water supply in Milk Creek. They had forted in too small an area — an oblong some two hundred and twenty-five feet across the bench and only seventy-five feet deep. Paddock had left a one-hundred-and-twenty-five-foot gap on the stream side, expecting freighter John Gordon to fill the gap with the ten wagons of his ox train. But the Utes had forced Gordon and his men to abandon the ox train fifty yards off and join the soldiers. Closing the gap in the corral was a sickening task. Payne directed the lining-up of mules and horses in the gap, where they were shot to form an animal breastworks. In the process, one mule jerked loose and had a bucking spree in the pit of the wounded.

Nevertheless, by noon of that bright September 29 the weary subcommander began to think that a second Custer massacre could be avoided. He had managed to get the wagons dismantled and reinforced by breadboxes, forage sacks and ration barrels. Lieutenant Wolf's crew finished the construction of seventeen pits two feet deep, each manned by two lookouts. Sergeant Jacob Widmer had led forty-five volunteers back through the cottonwoods and they had brought in Joe Lawson's Company E.

Then came the worst of all. Payne foresaw it when a stiff breeze began blowing north. At 2:30 P.M., Jack's warriors fired the sage and grass. An eight-foot screen of fire raced toward the corral. Payne sent Sergeant John A. Poppe crawling thirty yards in the sage to set a counterfire. Poppe raced back with his own fire chasing him. It entered the corral and the canvas wagon tops blazed. Ute bullets rained in as troopers beat at the flames. Five soldiers were killed.

Poppe's counterfire passed on and enveloped John Gordon's bull train. Payne watched Agent Meeker's red flannel shirts go up in black smoke. Gordon's oxen escaped the fire by crossing Milk Creek, where mounted Utes out of range wrangled them south toward Yellowjacket Pass. A lull followed. Dr. Grimes laid out ten bodies in the animal breastworks and had them covered with loose dirt. Among them were old Sergeant Dolan and the Utes' harmonica-playing friend, Charlie Lowry. Captain Payne rested briefly until Joe Rankin disturbed him to point out wisps of smoke curling above the Danforth Hills. The Utes, Joe said, were burning White River Agency.

At twilight, Payne rallied his men once more to meet a sudden wild surge of Utes toward the corral. The pit sharpshooters were prepared for them now. The charge petered out. The Utes faded away. Something about the quiet which settled over the bench gave Payne hope that the battle of Milk Creek was over.

And still, big problems remained. Payne directed Corporal Roach to set up a water detail between the creek and the corral. Lieutenant Cherry reported that ninety-six men were still on their feet out of the original force of one hundred and forty-two.

They had fifty horses and mules left. Payne realized that Gordon's captured oxen would serve the Utes for food indefinitely. This was Monday. The rations of his own force would be gone by Thursday. The Utes would starve them to death unless messages went quickly for their relief.

Only two men, Joe Rankin and John Gordon, had enough knowledge of the country to find their way out. The risk was immense. Payne was sure that the Utes were guarding the trails. In their present mood if they caught a white man they would probably give him Plains Indian treatment — castration at least, and maybe death by slow torture.

Rankin and Gordon volunteered to take the risk. So did two Fifth Cavalry corporals — George Moquin of Company F and Edward F. Murphy of Company D. The plan was Rankin's. The quartet and their horses would slip up Milk Creek under the protection of the water detail which would cover them upstream as far as the Agency road crossing. Then they would run for it. If they met a road block, Rankin would take to the brush and move cross-country while the others delayed the Utes. If not, they would use the Morapos Creek trail to Peck's store on Bear River, where John Gordon would ride east on the Gore Pass road to find Captain Dodge. Rankin would put the two corporals on the Fortification Creek road to Price's supply depot, and push on ahead of them north toward Western Union at Rawlins.

Captain Payne prepared messages for Lieutenant Price and Captain Dodge, and a telegram for General Crook which read:

MILK RIVER, COLO., SEPTEMBER 29, 1879
8:30 P.M.

THIS COMMAND, COMPOSED OF THREE COMPANIES OF CAVALRY, WAS MET A MILE SOUTH OF MILK RIVER BY SEVERAL HUNDRED UTE INDIANS WHO ATTACKED AND DROVE US TO THE WAGON TRAIN WITH GREAT LOSS. IT BECOMES MY PAINFUL DUTY TO ANNOUNCE THE DEATH OF MAJOR THORNBURGH,

WHO FELL IN HARNESS: THE PAINFUL BUT NOT SERIOUS WOUNDING OF LT. PADDOCK AND DR. GRIMES, AND KILLING OF TEN ENLISTED MEN AND A WAGON MASTER, WITH THE WOUNDING OF ABOUT TWENTY MEN AND TEAMSTERS. I AM CORRALED NEAR WATER, WITH ABOUT THREE FOURTHS OF MY ANIMALS KILLED. AFTER A DESPERATE FIGHT SINCE 12 N. WE HOLD OUR POSITION. I SHALL STRENGTHEN IT DURING THE NIGHT, AND BELIEVE WE CAN HOLD OUT UNTIL RE-ENFORCEMENTS REACH US, IF THEY ARE HURRIED. OFFICERS AND MEN BEHAVED WITH GREATEST GALLANTRY. I AM ALSO SLIGHTLY WOUNDED IN TWO PLACES.

PAYNE, COMMANDER

With the messages on their way, Payne turned the command over to Captain Lawson and fainted. Dr. Grimes put him to bed in the hospital pit with the other wounded.

THERE IS NOTHING quite like a hero on horseback. Millions have thrilled to

I sprang to the stirrup, and Joris, and he;
I galloped, Dirck galloped, we galloped all three . . .

Robert Browning's hero brought the good news from Ghent to Aix in maybe sixteen hours, which seems too fast for one hundred and seventy-five miles even nonstop. Who cares? The poem is great, especially at the end when poor old Roland, the noble steed, collapses from his effort and is revived by a bottle of vintage Riesling voted to him on the spot by the grateful burgesses.

Longfellow immortalized Paul Revere whose midnight ride was not much farther than around the block. But no poet has written "The Midnight Ride of Joseph Rankin." And yet Joe and his companions deserve a classic too. Joe was not a colorful man. He seemed like just an ordinary cracker-barrel citizen when seated outside his livery stable in Rawlins or when disciplining the chippies on Lower Row. But at Milk Creek his true quality emerged.

He was nearly as worn out as Captain Payne on that anxious Monday night. At 10:30 P.M., he led his quartet up the creek. The great full moon bathed the valley in light. To the tense soldiers bottled up in the corral, it seemed that a horned toad could be observed in such silvery brilliance. For an hour, the soldiers barely breathed, listening for gunfire which would mean that the couriers had been discovered. Even the wounded refused to groan.

The gunfire was not heard. The four men met no Utes — not at the Deer Creek Divide or along Morapos Trail or in Deal Gulch above Williams Fork or at Peck's store on the Bear. At 7 A.M. on Tuesday, Rankin changed horses and breakfasted at the Fortification Creek depot of Lieutenant Price. He lunched and borrowed another horse at George Baggs's ranch on the Little Snake. He had late supper Tuesday night at Sulphur Springs, Wyoming.

At 2 A.M. on Wednesday morning, October 1, his mount trotted along the Front Street railroad tracks in Rawlins. It had been a slow night on Lower Row. When Joe stopped in Foote's Saloon for a couple of stiff ones, a mere dozen drunks and girls gathered around him as a welcoming committee. He had ridden one hundred and sixty miles in twenty-seven-and-a-half hours, but nobody thought of a bottle of vintage Riesling for the horse. Joe left the saloon soon, woke up Carbon County clerk J. B. Adams and went with him to Western Union where he sent the telegram which shocked the nation.

From Department of the Platte Headquarters at Omaha, Captain Payne's telegram was forwarded to General Crook who was with General Sheridan at Division Headquarters in Chicago. Crook wired back instructions to his adjutant, General Robert Williams. By 4:30 A.M. on Wednesday, Colonel Wesley Merritt, commander of the Fifth United States Cavalry, began assembling his relief force at Fort D. A. Russell near Cheyenne.

At the same time, General Sheridan's office called for two thousand more soldiers from forts throughout the Division of the Missouri.

First stories of the Milk Creek battle filled the nation's newspapers next day. Excited crowds thronged telegraph offices across the land and read about the plight of Captain Payne and his helpless men and about the flight of settlers from the Western Slope of Colorado. Within a few hours, Major Thornburgh and Milk Creek were as famous in the United States as General Custer and the Little Big Horn.

All the news stories featured Joe Rankin's opinion that the wrathful Utes had gone on from Milk Creek to destroy White River Agency and to murder the whites there. People who had forgotten about Horace Greeley's popular agricultural editor recalled Nathan Meeker and read long articles about his Union Colony career and about Arvilla and Josie, the Prices and their two small children and the Agency staff. Reports from Greeley stressed the town's anguish — especially that of Mary and Rozene Meeker and the mourning parents of the Agency's young men.

Speculation about the Meekers' fate was endless. But two questions were of more immediate interest to the nation's millions. Would Colonel Merritt's force get to Milk Creek in time to prevent another Custer massacre? And where were Captain Dodge and his colored boys?

CHAPTER XX

Colonel Merritt Takes Over

THE AMERICAN PUBLIC could not have been more confused on
the whereabouts of Captain Dodge and his company of Negroes
than was the Captain himself. This is not to say that Dodge was
lost on Monday, September 29, while the Milk Creek battle
raged unbeknownst to him. He and forty-three of his men were
camped halfway between his Middle Park base and White River
Agency in a pretty spot called Twenty-mile Park. The trail
through Twenty-mile bypassed Steamboat Springs on the Gore
Pass road to Hayden and Peck's store.

Dodge wasn't lost exactly. He just didn't know whether he
should be coming or going. That was what his men had been
doing — coming and going — ever since July when General
Pope had given him standing orders to keep an eye on the Utes
and to go to White River if Nathan Meeker needed him.

There had been frequent complaints of Ute misbehavior
but they had failed to prove out. In mid-September, Dodge had
heard rumors of mayhem at White River and had taken his
company all the way to Peck's store only to learn from Black
Wilson, the mail carrier, that all was sweetness at the Agency
after the September 8 squabble between Meeker and Johnson.
Festive, in fact. While delivering the mail, Wilson had seen
Frank Byers and Joe and John Collom enjoying the pony races
and flirting with Josie Meeker and Flora Ellen Price.

So Dodge's Company D, Ninth Cavalry, had returned to
Middle Park . . . and then they had set out to save Meeker again,
this time by order of General Sheridan. And now, September
29, in the aforementioned Twenty-mile Park, Dodge's courier

galloped up with a second order from Sheridan countermand-
ing the first. Dodge wasn't needed at the Agency after all. An
expeditionary force under Major Thornburgh was en route
from Rawlins to settle the trouble.

Very well. For the third time, Company D faced about and
camped Monday night near Gore Pass in Egeria Park. But
early Tuesday, Dodge met flocks of terrified Bear River settlers
rushing past. They told him that the Utes had ambushed
Thornburgh at Milk Creek, burned up the Agency and probably
planned to kill every white man on the Western Slope. The
befuddled Captain Dodge strove to appraise this latest intelligence. He concluded at length to head west for White River
once more. Next morning back in Twenty-mile Park his men
spotted a note on a bush beside the trail. It read: "Hurry up.
The troops have been defeated. (Signed) E. E. C." The
Negroes hurried. At noon Wednesday, they entered Hayden
village on Bear River and found John Gordon, fresh from the
besieged troops at Milk Creek, and three others, including
Meeker's employee, Ed Clark. Ed had spent Tuesday night at
Steamboat Springs on his way back to work after his vacation
in Greeley. He was the man who had put the "Hurry up" note
on a bush in Twenty-mile Park.

With growing concern, Dodge listened to Gordon's account
of the Monday Milk Creek battle and of the events preceding
it. His interest centered only partly on the importance and
peril of his mission to raise the siege with his tiny force before
Payne's troopers starved to death in the corral. What struck
him most was the realization that here was what he had been
waiting for through his Army career. Here was the chance to
prove the great conviction of his life. That conviction, repudi-
ated by average Americans in 1879, was that the Negro made
at least as good a soldier as the white man.

Captain Francis Safford Dodge was not the conventional
Army officer. He had been raised a genteel New Englander and
had found himself by accident leading a unit of the Second

United States Colored Cavalry through the Civil War siege of Petersburg. Negroes had been banned from the Army since Andrew Jackson's time, but Frederick Douglass, the Negro journalist, got the ban lifted in '63. A total of one hundred and seventy-nine thousand Negroes were recruited. After the war, the Negro ban had been resumed and Dodge had lost his colored unit. Then in '66, Congress had authorized six Negro regiments (today's Ninth and Tenth Cavalry and Twenty-fourth and Twenty-Fifth Infantry). Dodge, recalling his admiration for his Petersburg men, had asked to be given command of Company D, Ninth Cavalry.

For a dozen years, Dodge and Company D had toured the Southwest on escort duty, scouting, Indian fighting and border patrol. No other company, white or black, had made a better record for high morale and devotion to duty. But somehow Dodge had never had the chance to lead his colored men into the sort of crisis which would show their courage and fighting skill for all the nation to see.

Never until now. Dodge gave them a quick little talk, stressing the danger ahead and the huge odds against them, and was moved nearly to tears by their eagerness to do him proud. They sang and joked their way down the Bear from Hayden. At 4:30 P.M. Wednesday, they reached Tom Iles's ranch at the mouth of Elkhead Creek. Dodge called a halt to strip down for the last forty-mile run to Milk Creek. He put eight soldiers on Company D's supply wagons which Ed Clark would lead to Lieutenant Price's depot on Fortification Creek. Three-day rations and one hundred and twenty-five rounds of ammunition were distributed to the thirty-five remaining cavalrymen.

FOUR HOURS later the thirty-five rode off in the chill bright night on their great adventure, with John Gordon as their guide. Dodge set a fast pace, hoping to reach Milk Creek before the Utes were awake. At the junction of Deer Creek and Williams Fork, the Negroes began to understand the extent of Ute fury when they came on the ruins of Al McCarger's wagon, with the cargo destroyed except for Josie Meeker's play hatchets.

They ascended Morapos Creek past Monument Butte and just before dawn arrived at the fearful scene around George Gordon's three wagons. Meeker's threshing machine, gleaming symbol of Captain Armstrong's hopes, was smashed to pieces.[1] The steam engine had been toppled down a ravine. Near it, hideously bullet-ridden, were the bodies of George Gordon and his two helpers.

Captain Dodge watched John Gordon a moment as he knelt by his dead brother. Then he turned to observe his Negroes. They were as stunned as he was by the ghostly sight of the corpses in the ravine. But they showed no fear. With dawn breaking, they crossed the Williams Fork–Milk Creek divide and descended to the sage bench in front of the future Thornburgh Mountain. Near the silent corral, John Gordon hallooed softly. A sentry recognized his voice and his dim form. Within seconds every soldier in the fort was awake. Rifles went up at the stinking animal breastworks to lay down a barrage if the Utes began shooting. But Chief Jack's warriors above the valley at their Beaver Springs camp had not seen the Negroes until it was too late to stop them. As sunrise flooded the bench, the last black man rode to safety.

Within the corral, all was joy, back-slapping, grins, gratitude, and temporary suspension of the color line. Captain Payne and forty-two of his men had painful wounds and the rest were in pitiful shape from the effects of bad water, too much sun, lack of sleep and the awful stench of death. But it was all right. The Negroes had broken the siege and more help would be along soon from Rawlins. Captain Lawson made a speech saying, "You men of the Ninth Cavalry are the whitest black men I have ever seen."

No member of Company D was happier than Captain Francis

Dodge. He felt like a father at his son's graduation, *magna cum laude.*

BEFORE NOON of that same Thursday morning, Colonel Wesley Merritt, the able, bushy-haired leader of the Fifth United States Cavalry, left Rawlins on the twin missions of relieving the Thornburgh force and, if possible, of saving the Agency people at White River. He had with him four companies of cavalry, one hundred and fifty foot soldiers in wagons and a cart full of newsmen including John C. Dyer of the *New York World.* He hired old Jim Baker as his guide at Baggs's ranch and he picked up Lieutenant Price's supply company on Fortification Creek. Early Sunday morning, October 5, his long column reached the corral, where Payne's men and Dodge's men waited patiently. Again there was no Ute resistance. Though the coming of the big force caused a glad flurry in the corral, it was something of an anticlimax. The most exciting event took place when Charlie Lowry, who was supposed to have died six days ago, rose shakily to his feet from his grave of loose dirt in the animal breastworks. He murmured, "What's the matter, boys?" took a sip of coffee and died for good as Merritt's surgeon, Dr. A. J. Kimmell, probed for the bullet in his head.

Merritt had things moving toward good order quickly. The ten dead men were removed from the breastworks and buried temporarily near the corral. Payne's two dead privates were recovered from the battlefield. The forty-three wounded were made comfortable in a new camp, away from the stench and a mile upstream where the water was better. Two of Captain Dodge's Negroes found Major Thornburgh's long body in the cottonwoods, the engraved Colt revolver still held in his hand. No part of his uniform had been removed, but his gilt Union Pacific Railroad pass and other papers were scattered near him. Someone had pinned Payne's tourist photo of Colorow to his breast. Dr. Kimmell embalmed the body and wrapped it in dirt for shipment to Fort Steele.

Colonel Merritt's frame of mind was quite different from that of Major Thornburgh when he had left Fort Steele on his vague errand for General Crook in General Pope's Department. There was nothing vague about this errand of Merritt's. He was here as the leader of a national mobilization, engaging the full energy of the War Department and all the resources of the American people. Though Jim Baker had informed him that the total population of the two bands of White River Utes was only seven hundred men, women and children, he was prepared to quell a major uprising of all the Colorado Utes and assorted Indian allies against the United States. He believed it possible for Chief Jack to have been reinforced already by Ouray's powerful Uncompahgres and by hundreds of Southern Utes under Chief Ignacio. Therefore he would not risk an immediate mercy dash of twenty-five miles to the Agency through Coal Creek Canyon. Instead he would stay a few days at Milk Creek waiting for more troops and setting up supply depots and a hundred-and-sixty-mile courier line on the Rawlins road.

He assumed that these Indians had forfeited their treaty rights in attacking Thornburgh, and that President Hayes had removed them from the jurisdiction of Carl Schurz and the Interior Department and had transferred them to the War Department. Consequently, he had the authority to round them up — all six bands of them — without civilian interference, and to put them somewhere out of the white man's way. General Sherman himself had suggested the strategy. The Utes would be caught like fish in a giant net formed by Merritt's troops pushing south and other troops pushing north under General Edward Hatch from New Mexico, west from San Luis Valley and east from Fort Douglas in Utah.

Before noon on Sunday, Lieutenant Cherry showed the Colonel the September 29 battleground and remained near the long ridge while Merritt returned to headquarters for a nap. While Cherry and his company stood there below the ridge in the open, two shots rang out and bullets kicked up dust ahead of them. Then they saw the heads of a hundred Utes sticking up over the top of the ridge seven hundred yards away. Cherry's bugler signaled for help. As two more companies came up, Cherry was astonished almost out of his wits to see a white man detach himself from these murderous savages who had been fighting white men all week and ride down the ridge to him.

The white man carried an enormous flag of truce fashioned out of a bed sheet tied to a tepee pole. He apologized to Cherry for the two shots, which he claimed had been accidental. He added that Chief Ouray's brother-in-law, Sapovanero, and his bodyguard, Captain Billy, had brought him to Milk Creek from the Uncompahgre Ute Agency with messages for the commanding officer and for Chief Jack. Cherry led the white man back through the cottonwoods to Merritt's headquarters. The Colonel was napping underneath a wagon. He woke up, glanced incredulously at Cherry, took the messages from the stranger and studied them carefully, his head supported by his forearm.

The first message read:

LOS PINOS INDIAN AGENCY
October 2, 1879

To THE OFFICERS IN COMMAND AND THE SOLDIERS AT WHITE RIVER AGENCY:

GENTLEMEN:

At the request of the chief of the Utes at this agency, I send by Joseph W. Brady, an employee, the enclosed order from Chief Ouray to the Utes at the White River Agency.

The head chiefs deplore the trouble existing at White River and are anxious that no further fighting or bloodshed should take place, and have commanded the Utes there to stop. I hope that you will second their efforts so far as you can, consistent with your duties, under existing commands. This much for humanity,

Very respectfully, your obedient servant,

WILSON M. STANLEY
U. S. Indian Agent

The second message, also dated October 2, was the order:

To THE CHIEF CAPTAINS, HEADMEN AND UTES AT WHITE RIVER
AGENCY:
- You are hereby requested and commanded to cease hostili-
ties against the whites, injuring no innocent persons or any
others further than to protect your own lives and property
from unlawful and unauthorized combinations of horse-thieves
and desperadoes, as anything further will end in disaster to
all parties.

OURAY

In flat, tired tones, Joe Brady told Colonel Merritt that he
had reached Chief Jack's camp the night before and that Jack's
men would obey Ouray's order. Jack had requested Brady to
inform the Colonel that the White River Utes wanted peace —
and Uriah Curtis as their new agent. Jack argued that the score
between Indians and whites was even. Many Utes [2] and many
whites had died.

Then Brady gave Merritt the first hint of the news which the
whole country was waiting to hear. Jack had told him nothing
directly, but he had implied that Nathan Meeker was dead.
So were all the Agency employees and the freighters, Carl Goldstein and Julius Moore. Douglas's men had shot Meeker and
the others Monday afternoon when they had learned that the
soldiers had crossed the Milk Creek boundary and had begun
killing Utes. Brady believed further that the Utes were holding
Arvilla and Josie Meeker, Flora Ellen Price and her children
as hostages deep in the mountains.

Merritt rose from beneath the wagon, ran a perplexed hand
through his graying hair, and took Lieutenant Cherry to one
side. In exasperated undertones he told Cherry that he had
never seen the like of this situation. Here were murderers and
kidnapers blandly sending an employee of the Indian Bureau to
him to make absurd propositions on their behalf! God only
knew what was happening to those poor women in the meantime. He ought to arrest Brady for conspiracy or something, but

it was probably more fitting to ignore him. Cherry could give the fellow to understand that the United States Army, not Chief Ouray or this Agent Stanley, was in charge of the Utes. Brady must realize that only the fate of the white women and the Utes' unconditional surrender interested the Colonel. If Chief Jack had any helpful ideas on these matters, he and his henchmen had better surrender to headquarters at once.

Without deigning to look at Brady again, Merritt lay down once more beneath the wagon and closed his eyes. Brady listened to Cherry for some minutes and then crossed Milk Creek through the cottonwoods and went back up the long ridge to report to Jack. Through field glasses, Cherry watched the Indians milling around the white man. Twice a small group of them seemed on the point of coming down the ridge. But in the end they trotted away with Brady toward Yellow-jacket Pass.

FOUR DAYS LATER, Merritt's force at Milk Creek was increased to nine hundred by the arrival of Colonel C. C. Gilbert and six companies of the Seventh Infantry from Fort Snelling, Dakota Territory. The incoming men passed the outgoing members of the original Thornburgh force who were being escorted with their dead and wounded to Fort Steele and Fort D. A. Russell by Captain Dodge's Company D.

And on Saturday, October 11, red-whiskered Jim Baker and Eugene Taylor, the Milk Creek trader, led Merritt and his cavalry through Coal Creek Canyon to the Farm That Jack Built and on down White River. Near the old Danforth coal mine in the middle of the canyon, some soldiers followed a trail of blood up the stream bank to the mine where they found the body of a curly-haired white boy, a coat folded under his head and a Winchester cocked and clasped in his hand.

One of his legs had a bullet wound in it and both feet were bound in pieces of buckskin. Apparently he had crawled down to the creek for water several times and had died at last from a wound in the right breast. He wore Harry Dresser's coat and vest. A pocket contained a letter from Meeker to the Indian Bureau stating that Thornburgh would leave his troops fifty miles away and come in for talks. On a mine timber the boy had managed to post a scrawled message: "Have been here twenty-one hours. All killed at the Agency. Send my money to my mother at Greeley. Frank Dresser."

Five miles short of the Agency the soldiers passed a burned wagon and Eugene Taylor identified the bodies of the two amateur freighters, old Carl Goldstein and his teen-aged companion, Julius Moore. On some rocks in The Narrows was the dead body of Meeker's messenger, Wilmer Eskridge, with a dispatch to Thornburgh from Meeker in his pocket.

As the long column moved into Powell Park, the men gazed curiously at the charred ruins of Meeker's model farm, the end product of his lifelong effort to lead men to happiness. Rising above the golden beauty of the countryside was the Agency flagpole with the American flag waving in the light breeze. Beneath it was utter contrast — the stark wreckage of a wave of demonic hate. Only William Post's storeroom still stood, with tons of flour scattered around it. Elsewhere, the furious Utes had burned what could be burned. They had smashed the rest and strewn the smashings far and wide — plows, wheels, gears and wagons, rakes, mowers, washtubs and hardware.

Clearly each article from the white man's world had been set upon by each Ute with the accumulated rage of many months of bitter resentment and helpless frustration. It had been hacked at and thrown and stamped on and torn as though it were a human — perhaps a white human mouthing contempt of ponies and making threats at red humans for not being white and for defending what they believed in, the ideals they upheld, the achievements which nourished their pride and the kind of love which gave their lives savor and meaning.

Colonel Merritt viewed the scene with disgust and ordered

the column to march into the Agency. Grimly he surveyed the treeless terrain rising southward to the top of Roan Plateau. He knew that Jack's band and Douglas's band must be watching his troops from up there, and he felt a great eagerness to start his drive toward them and Grand River. He was sure that, if President Hayes and his civilians let him alone, he could round up Meeker's and Thornburgh's murderers and rescue the white women before snow came and closed up the Ute Reservation. Thus he would end forever the problem which the Interior Department had been mishandling for a decade.

Eugene Taylor identified the first body found within the Agency as that of Arthur Thompson, the nondrinking, nonsmoking young Baptist whose gun still lay beside him. Close by was the corpse of the truculent Kansan, Shadrach Price, whom the Utes had forced to stop plowing. In the storehouse doorway was the body of William Post, Meeker's old friend from Yonkers, twenty-five-pound flour sacks still clutched in his arms. Near Post were the bullet-riddled bodies of young Fred Shepard, the fiddle player, Harry Dresser and George Eaton, his face chewed by animals.[3]

A hundred yards further on, the soldiers came upon the nude and battered body of the dead Agent, a bullet hole in his head. Around his neck someone had put a heavy logging chain, so that a Ute pony could drag the dead body about the compound in simulation of the way Utes imagined themselves being dragged off to Indian Territory. A stave from an Agency flour barrel had been jammed down Meeker's throat.

Doom and Moonlight

THE LOGGING CHAIN AND THE BARREL STAVE were signs of barbarism which would have been utterly inconceivable to anyone at White River during the week before the September 29
massacre. The tension existed but whites and Utes worked hard
to ignore it and went about their affairs with that heartrending
optimism on the brink of calamity which makes people so pathetic and endearing. Everyone knew that Meeker was sick with
depression and that he had asked for troops on September 11.
But everyone hoped that his mood would change and that the
farming issue could be solved without the soldiers coming into
the Reservation.

Meeker stayed in his office preparing year-end reports, writing Governor Pitkin and trying to ease his despair by rereading
Samuel Pepys. He had some moments of pleasure on Monday,
September 22, when he wrote a check and gave it to Black
Wilson to mail to Horace Greeley's daughters. It was the last
payment on the one-thousand-dollar debt which had plagued
him since 1870. He had some debts left but he figured that he
would be in the clear soon if Mary and Rozene kept on with the
Greeley boardinghouse and if Ralph continued to send Arvilla five dollars a week out of his *New York Herald* salary.
The prospect of being debt-free set him to planning his triumphant return home to resume his place as the Colony's
founder and as a sound business and family man.

He spent a quarrelsome hour with Chief Jack on Tuesday
discussing his refusal to issue annuity blankets in advance so
that Jack's men would have them on their fall hunt to Wyo-

ming. On Wednesday he took a tongue-lashing from Jane because he denied guest rations to Yanko from Chief Ouray's
band, who was up courting a White River girl. Thereafter, Jane
was always hanging around his office and he knew that she was
eavesdropping for Douglas.

All that late-September week the daytime temperature was
unseasonably in the high 80s. Josie and Flora Ellen Price each
stripped down to the limits of modesty — a thin calico dress,
summer corset, light chemise and pants and a single petticoat.
They wore moccasins which Johnson's squaw Susan made for
them, and no stockings. The heat gave to the placid White
River Valley the atmosphere of an uneasy dream. At the big
log boardinghouse where Josie and the Prices slept, the Greeley
boys stretched out their meal hours in somnolent horseplay
with the dozen Utes who loved to loaf there smoking, joking
and begging Josie for bread and sugar.

If the warm days were lovely, the crisp cool nights were superb. At the start of the week, the moon reached first quarter,
rising before sunset behind old Sleepy Cat and bathing the
valley in silver through the evening. The moon grew rapidly.
Just before the week end it was almost full and Meeker read his
American Almanac by its light. But the tension grew with the
growing moon. On Saturday morning, September 27, Douglas
came to Meeker greatly upset over Jack's report that soldiers
from Fort Steele were crossing Bear River. Meeker calmed him
somewhat by saying that he had no knowledge of these troops
and that he would try to stop them short of the Milk Creek
boundary and to arrange a meeting at the Agency between their
commander and the Utes.

From then on, the White River community was in a ferment
of alarm. The squaws of Douglas's village knocked down their
lodges and vanished across White River toward Roan Plateau.
Hopes for peace rose and fell with each Ute courier, and couriers seemed to come every few hours — from Middle Park and
Bear River, from Jack's guard camp above Milk Creek, even

from Chief Ouray on the Uncompahgre south beyond Grand
River and Grand Mesa. On Saturday night, Charlie Lowry arrived belatedly with Thornburgh's stale first message from
Fortification Creek. When Charlie disclosed that the Utes had
detained Black Wilson and the Agency mail at Peck's store,
Meeker doubled the guard of Greeley boys on the storehouse,
which bulged with annuity goods. Next morning he received
Thornburgh's Williams Fork note approving the Ute request
that the Major come in without the soldiers. He read the note
to Jack, who expressed relief, saying that his warriors were
poised to ambush the soldiers in Coal Creek Canyon if they
should pass Milk Creek.

Charlie Lowry, spending Saturday night on the lumpy cot in
William Post's office, was frightened by Ute warwhoops outside
his window. The whoops were ignored by the Greeley boys both
that night and Sunday night, when Douglas staged a full-dress
war dance. In the bunkhouse, young Frank Dresser, he of the
golden curls, wrote his mother as usual by the light of a kerosene lamp. His letter concluded:

> It is now half-past ten, and I must close as I must stand
> guard part of the night. Meeker is afraid they will fire the hay.
> As regards danger, don't fret, Mother. We are as safe and sleep
> as soundly as if in your quiet town of Greeley. Tomorrow the
> soldiers will be in and the plowing will go on, for Meeker must
> carry out orders or resign.

More Utes than usual loitered about Josie's big kitchen begging scraps on Monday morning. Their squaws were gone south
and they had nothing good to eat. Josie and Flora Ellen Price
put Arvilla to work helping them through the breakfast chores.
Meeker wrote a telegram to the Indian Bureau for Harry
Dresser to take later to the Rawlins Western Union:

> MAJOR THORNBURGH, FOURTH INFANTRY, LEAVES HIS COM-
> MAND 50 MILES DISTANT AND COMES TODAY WITH FIVE MEN.
> INDIANS PROPOSE TO FIGHT IF TROOPS ADVANCE. A TALK WILL
> BE HAD TOMORROW. CAPTAIN DODGE, 9TH CAVALRY, IS AT

STEAMBOAT SPRINGS WITH ORDERS TO BREAK UP INDIAN
STORES AND KEEP INDIANS ON RESERVATION. SALES OF GUNS
AND AMMUNITION BRISK FOR TEN DAYS PAST. WHEN CAPTAIN
DODGE COMMENCES TO ENFORCE LAW, NO LIVING HERE WITH-
OUT TROOPS.

N. C. MEEKER, AGENT

At 11:00 A.M., Flora Ellen went into her bedroom to change
little Johnnie Price's pants. Her burly husband, Shad, entered
with his Winchester. He placed sixteen cartridges in the magazine and one in the chamber, laid the gun on the bureau and
told Flora Ellen not to worry. He was loading up just in case.

Meeker, preoccupied and wan, passed Josie's kitchen window
to get from her the key to lock up the government gun closet
in Post's storehouse. He walked with a stoop again, as in his
worst Greeley days, and there was a bemused smile on his handsome face. And still he retained enough of his old spirit to ask
Josie if she knew what September 29 was. When she shook her
head, he said jauntily: "On this day in 1066 William the Conqueror landed in England!" He moved off and soon the three
anxious women in the kitchen saw a courier galloping hell-bent
from The Narrows toward Douglas's lone tepee. Arvilla said,
"Just see that Indian run! It must be he has news."

The courier did have news, and Douglas wasted no time taking it to the Agent in his office. The soldiers, Douglas said bitterly, were at Milk Creek. Some of them were already inside
the Reservation. That, Meeker replied, was possible. The soldiers were strangers in the land and they couldn't know exactly where the line was. But he promised that there would be
no trouble. They would come in no further than Milk Creek.

And at that moment, Wilmer Eskridge entered the office with
Thornburgh's Deer Creek message agreeing again to come in
alone, but hinting that his troops would follow after dark through
Coal Creek Canyon. Meeker passed over the hints. He told
Douglas merely to choose his chiefs for the proposed talks.

Major Thornburgh and five soldiers, he said, were riding in now. It would be polite to meet him on the road. The effect of his words was magical. The strain in Douglas's small dark face disappeared. He grinned widely, shook Meeker's hand and hurried to Josie's boardinghouse where he gave the good news to Jack's henchman, Sowerwick.

Douglas went on down to his tepee for lunch. Meeker, reliving his days as an astute Civil War correspondent, wrote a crisp note to Thornburgh:

WHITE RIVER AGENCY
September 29, 1879 — 1 P.M.

MAJOR T. T. THORNBURGH
WHITE RIVER EXPEDITION, IN THE FIELD, COLORADO
DEAR SIR:

I expect to leave in the morning with Douglas and Serrick to meet you. Things are peaceful and Douglas flies the United States flag. If you have trouble getting through the canyon let me know. We have been on guard three nights and shall be tonight, not because we know there is danger but because there might be. I like your last programme. It is based on true military principles.

Most truly yours,

N. C. MEEKER, *Indian Agent*

He addressed the note and sat down for lunch in Josie's kitchen with Sowerwick, Wilmer Eskridge and some of the Greeley boys. Soon Eskridge was ready to return to Major Thornburgh with the note. Two Utes, Ebenezer and Antelope, would guide him. Josie packed supper for all three men in an old copy of the *Springfield Republican* which she found in the milkhouse wrapped around butter. After their departure, Meeker returned to his office to read his Pepys. The Greeley boys went out to continue work on a new building. Douglas, still all smiles, came in the kitchen to bum bread and butter for dessert. He shook Arvilla's hand and patted Josie, who asked him when he would put Freddie back in school. He said "This afternoon," and Josie said "You had better!" and Douglas said

"I will." They laughed together and Douglas left to visit William Post at the storehouse.

Only the women were in the kitchen now, washing and wiping dishes, languidly in the 1:30 P.M. heat. A small Ute boy stopped to borrow matches, announcing proudly, "Now I go smoke." Josie winked at Arvilla and said, "I'll warrant he'll set something on fire." Flora Ellen stepped out to fetch her three-year-old May and was disturbed to find Ebenezer, who ought to have been riding north with Eskridge, hitching his pony to the bunkhouse rack. On the roof of the new building she could see Arthur Thompson spreading dirt, which Frank Dresser and her husband threw up to him. Beyond them on the street to White River she saw Douglas walking up to a dozen or so Utes, armed and unarmed. Among them were Pauvitz and Antelope and Persune and Johnson's son, Tim.

And then doom came.

It came without prearranged signal. It came without apparent volition on anyone's part. It came with that awful finality which blunts the senses, like a body in suicide hurtling down from the top of a building. Several Utes simply raised their rifles and began blasting at their unarmed friends, the Greeley boys. The Utes might have been dolls in a puppet show, pulling triggers at the bidding of an unseen cosmic force. Flora Ellen had a benumbed impression that Art Thompson died first, falling headlong from the roof. She heard William Post begging someone not to shoot him. Then her own Shad Price staggered and collapsed holding his abdomen. Frank Dresser raced toward the boardinghouse in his bare feet and Flora Ellen grabbed the screaming May and darted into her bedroom. Frank followed her, picked up Shad Price's Winchester and fired at the Utes through the dining room, putting a bullet into his friend Jata, who was Johnson's brother. Then Flora Ellen and May ran into Josie's bedroom and joined Arvilla, Josie and little Johnnie under Josie's bed.

Soon they smelled smoke. Frank Dresser took them from the

burning boardinghouse and across the street to the adobe milkhouse, the small window of which faced north on Meeker's
fenced field. Frank piled bread jars and cans against the milkhouse door and Arvilla dressed a bullet wound in his leg.

They stayed in the damp and airless room from 2 P.M. until
sunset at six o'clock. They sat there too stunned, too helpless,
too hopeless, to sense much, or to believe the horror which had
come upon them all. How could they believe the unbelievable?
Mrs. Meeker picked at her dress, wept and stopped weeping,
wondered what had happened to her husband and tried not to
think of the unhappiness his quest for a better world had
brought them. Josie was all gentle compassion for the Utes she
had learned almost to love. She told herself that the evil of the
massacre could not be in them. It must be something from
outside operating through them. Flora Ellen was pure terror.
She died the deaths of a thousand Indian-ravished heroines
whom she had met in fiction. Curly-haired Frank listened
numbly to the fitful firing and when the sound was heavy he
would say, "There goes a storehouse gun." The children sobbed
themselves to sleep. At last they ran out in the cooling twilight
to Meeker's house nearby. In the office, peaceful as a vicarage,
Josie stood a moment, a tall, slender, white-faced girl, her mouth
wide open in anguished query. She was looking at the Pepys
Diary lying open on her father's desk. Through the blinds she
saw Utes looting the storehouse. She said to the others, "Let's
try to escape north while they are busy."

They went through the gate into the fenced field. Arvilla
was lame from an old hip injury and could not hurry. Frank
Dresser ran like a deer and disappeared in the sage beyond the
fenced field. But the Utes saw the women and children and
came for them. Arvilla fell when a bullet grazed her thigh, and
lay still on the ground, her eyes like a trapped rabbit's. A young
Ute named Thompson reached her.

"I am sorry," he said. "I am heap much sorry. Can you walk?"
Arvilla whispered, "Yes, sir."

The Ute helped her to rise, offered her his arm politely and led her toward White River. As they passed the Meeker house, he asked if she had money inside.

"Very little."

"Please go and get money. And hurry up. We have to ride a great ways tonight." [1]

She went in the quiet house calling "Nathan! Nathan!" and somehow found twenty-six dollars in bills and four dollars in silver. Then Thompson helped her to walk to Douglas near his tepee and she gave the old chief the money. Not far off she saw Josie seated on a pile of blankets with May Price on her lap. Standing guard over Josie was her grown-up lovelorn pupil, young Persune, and one of Persune's squaws. Farther away were Flora Ellen and Johnnie Price. The big farm girl looked comically huge beside her captor, the small Uncompahgre Ute Ahutupuwit. Arvilla limped from Ute to Ute. Where, she asked, was Meeker? The Indians shrugged.

And yet, after these hours of horror, Arvilla began to feel something almost like relief. She was ashamed of the feeling and asked her Methodist God to forgive her. But they had been unspeakable, those terrible weeks of tension after Johnson had pushed Meeker against the hitching rack. At least she needn't worry now about the awful things that might happen. They had happened. Most of them had happened. And she observed that old Douglas was suffering too. He was tippling from a pint bottle of whisky, but he was not drunk. Arvilla judged him to be merely bewildered and sad. She had a notion that Douglas and the rest, who were preparing for travel, were as stunned as she was by what they had done. They seemed torn by opposing impulses — the impulse to protect their captives tenderly, and the impulse to brutalize them as required by ancient rules of Ute warfare. Where — oh, where was her husband?

Arvilla began to shiver as night came on. She watched the great full moon turning yellow in the east above Sleepy Cat. She spoke to Douglas about her thin garments and those of the girls. He sent her on a horse with Thompson and a lantern to get some things. The Agent's house was burning at one end. Entering, she called "Nathan!" But low this time, almost to herself. . . . Then she loaded Thompson up with towels, blankets and a small box of medicines. She donned her hat and shawl, put a handkerchief and a needle packet in her pocket and walked out hugging her illuminated volume of *Pilgrim's Progress*.

A hundred yards south of the house she came suddenly on a man's body, startlingly white in the moonlight, and clad only in a shirt. It was Nathan Meeker. He had been shot in the side of his handsome, youthful head, and blood trickled still from his mouth. But he lay entirely composed, straight as he stood in life, his arms at ease beside him, as though he were about to explain what had happened to William the Conqueror on September 29, 1066. Arvilla wept softly and knelt to kiss him. But she did not actually kiss him. Thompson was beside her and she realized that no Indian could understand such a morbid gesture. She decided that it would be better not to displease Thompson. She left the white body, hoping that Nathan Meeker's Utopia would be easier for him to come by in the land where he was now.

And soon the strange caravan began leaving Powell Park on the Grand River trail which ran up stream to the White River ford and south toward Old Squaw Camp on Piceance Creek. Arvilla watched Flora Ellen Price ride by with Johnnie in her arms. The small Uncompahgre Ute who had captured her had hung William Post's gold watch around her neck as a mark of possession. Douglas lifted Arvilla on a raw-boned nag with no saddle and mounted the same animal in front of her. They rode off a quarter-mile behind Flora Ellen. Josie and May followed half a mile behind Arvilla and Douglas. Persune had given Josie a fine horse with a good saddle and he had knelt on his hands and knees so that she could mount by stepping on his back.

Later, the caravan ascended Flag Creek in the moonlight toward the divide. Douglas tippled often from his whisky bottle, sighting it against the moon to see how much liquor remained. With drunkenness, he became obscene and rough, threatening Arvilla with sexual attack, holding his pistol to her head and singing Negro spirituals in a raucous voice. But she was beyond fear now. She thought mostly of her sweet virgin child, Josie, the Sacred One. She prayed that Persune would not violate Josie's person, being certain that the experience would drive her insane, or that she would kill herself rather than to yield.

And then at times she dreamed, with a wild surge of hope, that Frank Dresser had escaped up Strawberry Creek, had reached Thornburgh's troops already. This was Monday night. An Army courier from Milk Creek could arrive at Rawlins by Thursday, and telegrams of their plight would fly that day to Governor Pitkin, to Secretary Schurz, to President Hayes!

In the meantime, if the Utes didn't burn them to death, she would pray and read her *Pilgrim's Progress.*

"The Damned Dutch
Secretary"

By the odd workings of fate, the government's effort to rescue
Arvilla Meeker and the girls derived from a series of events
which began more than three weeks before Chief Douglas and
his men carried them off into the Grand River wilderness on
September 29.

Early in that month, Secretary Schurz, Bob Mitchell and a
tall young German nobleman, Count August Dönhoff, stopped
briefly in Manitou near Colorado Springs to rest and to drink
soda waters on their way to inspect California Indian agencies.
Governor Pitkin came to call and took them to see General
Charles Adams so that Schurz could have his countryman's
views on the White River situation.[1]

By this time, Adams owned a pleasant clapboard home with
a pet carp pond in the cottonwoods near Manitou. Things had
worked out well for him. After having spent the early 1870s as
Indian Agent at White River and at Los Pinos, he had endeared
himself to thousands of naturalized Germans by insisting that
the new State of Colorado print all its laws in German as well
as in English and Spanish. He was valued as an organizer of
the German vote by Governor Pitkin, whose election he had
sponsored in '78, and by President Hayes, who had made him a
United States Post Office Inspector of contract mail routes in
Colorado and New Mexico.

Adams enjoyed the excitement of policing the remote mail
routes and exposing crooked contractors. The job kept him out-

doors where he could keep his powerful body in shape, strengthen the arches of his flat feet, hunt often and have respite from the shrill piping of his Pekingese-like spouse. Also, he could stay in touch with old friends like Sowerwick of White River, the ailing Chief Ouray on the Uncompahgre, and Otto Mears, the mighty mite who had become the biggest political and financial figure in the San Juans.

For the past two years, Adams had been distressed about Ouray and his intolerable burden of Ute problems. He had heard of Chief Jack's visit to Governor Pitkin in August to complain that Meeker was trying illegally to force the Utes to farm. And he had learned that Jack and the old Muache toper, Kaneache, had begged Ouray twice to seek Meeker's dismissal before something gave way.

The General realized that the Uncompahgre and White River Utes could not retain much longer the ten million acres which still remained of their beautiful Reservation. White pressure mounted with the daily boundary disputes, phony alarms and complaints about fires. Climaxing all the pressures was the discovery of the richest silver deposits in the world at Leadville — only thirty-five miles from the Reservation line. The overflow of Leadville prospectors pushed up to and over the east boundary at a hundred places. Adams yearned to do what he could to help his Indian friends. He hoped that Ouray's band could keep their ancient lands along the Uncompahgre River and that the Douglas-Jack bands would submit peaceably to practicing agriculture in the Powell Park-Piceance Creek area. He knew that the only alternative was their removal, to a living death on a desert reservation.

Adams was thrilled to meet the gay and witty Carl Schurz and his tall friend, Count Dönhoff, Secretary of the German Legation in Washington. For a time the three Germans reminisced — and even sang for Pitkin a drinking song of the University of Bonn, which Schurz and Dönhoff had attended.

Then they talked about Indians. Adams described the perilous state of White River affairs and warned Schurz that it would not be safe to send troops there until the Meekers left. The Secretary remarked with disarming frankness that a White River calamity would delight Senator Teller and other Grant Republicans, who longed for a good reason to dump President Hayes (and with him their arch enemy, Schurz) from the 1880 ticket. Also it would delight the Army, who would use the calamity as a basis for new demands to transfer the Indian Bureau. Finally, Schurz said, it would put a crimp in his pet scheme to complete civilizing the Colorado Utes by giving them title to lands as individuals instead of assigning large tracts to them as a tribe. He estimated that it would take only five hundred thousand acres of the twelve-million-acre Ute Reservation (including the Southern Ute part) if each adult Ute accepted a good one-hundred-and-sixty-acre farm like Ouray's plus eighty acres for each Ute child. Then, the remaining eleven million, five hundred thousand acres could be opened for white settlement — and everybody would be happy.

. . . Presuming, General Adams pointed out, that the Secretary could convince the Utes that the settler influx would so increase the value of their five hundred thousand allotted acres as to make them worth more than the huge terrain they would be giving up.

Governor Pitkin expressed polite opposition to any such allotment plan. He argued that, if white settlers were to make land more valuable by their initiative, they were entitled to every last bit of benefit. Besides, he was irrevocably committed to his private secretary's — and Senator Teller's — "The Utes Must Go!" policy. And yet, as Adams told Schurz later, the Governor was not a Teller puppet. The fact was that Adams admired Pitkin, and found something appealing about the way he tried to square his own integrity with the strange stands he was obliged to take as Governor. After eight months in office, he was still surprised to find himself there. He came of aristocratic Connecticut forebears, was graduated with high honors at Wesleyan University and had practiced law with great success in Wisconsin until he broke down with consumption in 1872. Two years of sanatoriums in Europe and Florida had merely brought him to death's door. He had arrived in Colorado thin as a rail and had lived briefly at Evergreen near Denver. Then, as a sort of last gallant gesture before giving up the ghost, he had ridden a horse four hundred miles to the San Juans. Instead of killing him, the ride and the rugged mining life had cured him. In addition, he had made a quick fortune in the Prince Albert group of mines.

He became a close friend of Otto Mears. Canny Otto knew Colorado politics as well as he knew his own precipitous toll roads. He knew how frightened the Denver Republicans had been when Thomas Patterson, a Democrat, was elected Territorial delegate in '74. Mears decided in '78 to exploit their fear and name his own Republican candidate for Governor by threatening to throw the San Juan vote to a Democrat if his wishes were not granted.

Mears asked the frail, reserved Pitkin to be his candidate. Pitkin declined, and then accepted, following an impulse to achieve something in spite of his physical handicap. Mears told the Denver Republicans about his gubernatorial candidate. They snubbed his suggestion and went on with plans to renominate the incumbent Governor, John L. Routt. Mears did not snub easily. In retaliation, he informed the Denver crowd that San Juan voters were tired of taking orders from Senators Chaffee and Teller and were setting up their own State with Del Norte as capital. The Denverites capitulated, needing the support of San Juan Republicans to defeat the Denver Democrats. Mears let his statehood movement expire. Pitkin was nominated for Governor in place of Routt and won the election. His first official act was to give his salary to charity.

Pitkin enjoyed his early September visit in Manitou with Schurz and Adams though he remained firm for Ute removal. As Schurz left Adams's home, he asked the General to be pre-

pared to go to White River if Schurz sent word to him. He sent
no such word, but on September 19 he did wire Adams from
Cheyenne to meet him in Denver at once. He added that he
feared possible Ute resistance to Thornburgh's expedition, and
had interrupted his California tour to confer with Pitkin. The
news about Thornburgh disturbed Adams too. And, as he met
the Schurz party that evening at the Colorado Central depot in
Denver, he was dismayed further to note that the Secretary was
not going to have much time to concentrate on the problem of
White River.

Schurz was busy socially, for one thing. In Cheyenne his party,
including the elegant Count Dönhoff, had been joined by Webb
Hayes, the President's son, who stepped off the train in Denver
hugging the deerhead for the White House library which General Crook had bagged for him on the Thornburgh hunt. They
all dined with Governor Pitkin at the Grand Central Hotel and
then attended a large conclave of State Republicans. The appearance of "the damned Dutch Secretary" on the platform
drew faint applause [2] in contrast to the ovation given Senator
Teller for his speech demanding removal of the Utes. Schurz
and Dönhoff spent the following morning with two other Denver visitors, Edward Everett Hale, the author, and an old Washington friend, Walt Whitman, who had lost an Interior Department job once for having written *Leaves of Grass*.

That afternoon, the celebrities and a trainload of Denver Republicans went sightseeing; and it was not until Monday, September 22, that Schurz, Pitkin and Adams managed a White
River conference. They accomplished little. Adams asked for
action, but Schurz was preoccupied by his impending interview in Omaha with Bright Eyes, the Ponca heroine, and by
an Indian policy speech which he would deliver on October 1
during the International Fair of Five Nations at Muskogee.
And Pitkin was bedazzled by a long talk he had just had with
the West's most powerful man, Jay Gould, who controlled ten
thousand miles of Western railroads. Gould, Pitkin said, agreed

to spend countless millions on new Colorado railroads as soon as Pitkin got rid of the Utes and opened their Reservation to settlers and miners.

On Tuesday, Schurz and Webb Hayes left for Omaha. Count Dönhoff stayed behind to tour Central City gold mines and Adams boarded the cars of General Palmer's narrow-gauge for New Mexico on Post Office business. For the rest of the week Adams was restless and uneasy, plagued by vague forebodings. He blamed them on the bright moonlit nights which spoiled his sleep. On October 4, at a stop halfway between Albuquerque and Santa Fe, he met the southbound stage and learned from the passengers about the Milk Creek ambush and rumored massacre.

The devastating news struck him with sickening force. It was not the ambush against Thornburgh which perturbed him: after a century of Indian wars, most Americans granted red men the right to fight soldiers. The awful thing to Schurz was this rumor of Ute murder at the Agency — the thought of friends of his like Douglas and Sowerwick being driven to such madness. And that thought led to another, still more shattering. What had happened or what was happening to Arvilla and Josie Meeker?

He had lived for years with these Utes. He had observed many times how they tended under stress to revert to ancient ways, as tame wolves go wild from fear. If they had been impelled to murder the Agency's male employees, then the white women would be their captives, and subject to sexual outrage. As Adams understood it, custom made outrage obligatory, symbolizing abasement of the enemy. Even if the Ute men were reluctant to honor custom, some of their squaws might require it. And Adams could imagine how the American people, steeped to a neurotic degree in notions about the sanctity of a white woman's person, would rise in uncontrollable violence if they heard that the Utes had raped two prominent females serving the United States Government. All the horror and inhumanity of the Sand Creek Massacre might be repeated, stimulated this time by the mob fury of two hundred thousand Coloradans instead of the mere thirty thousand or so who had inhabited the Territory in 1864.

At Santa Fe, Adams read the Denver papers and perceived that Governor Pitkin and his alter ego in Ute affairs, William Vickers, had grasped this great chance to justify all the propaganda which Vickers's "Lo, the Poor Indian!" had inspired. Pitkin had authorized his private secretary to release the Milk Creek battle news in the form of a telegram, wonderfully slanted in the right direction, which he had received on October 1 from Laramie, Wyoming:

THE WHITE RIVER UTES HAVE MET COLONEL THORNBURGH'S COMMAND SENT TO QUELL DISTURBANCES AT THE AGENCY KILLING THORNBURGH HIMSELF AND KILLING OR WOUNDING MANY OF HIS OFFICERS, MEN AND HORSES WHEREBY THE SAFETY OF THE WHOLE COMMAND IS IMPERILED. I SHALL WARN OUR PEOPLE IN THE NORTH PARK AND TRUST THAT YOU WILL TAKE SUCH PROMPT ACTION AS WILL PROTECT YOUR PEOPLE AND RESULT IN GIVING THE WAR DEPARTMENT CONTROL OF THE SAVAGES IN ORDER TO PROTECT THE SETTLERS FROM MASSACRES PROVOKED BY THE PRESENT TEMPORIZING POLICY OF THE GOVERNMENT WITH REFERENCE TO INDIAN AFFAIRS IN ALL TIME TO COME.

COL. STEPHEN W. DOWNEY
DELEGATE TO CONGRESS, WYOMING TERRITORY

Along with this telegram, Vickers gave reporters a copy of Pitkin's wire to Secretary of War McCrary:

DISPATCHES JUST RECEIVED FROM LARAMIE CITY AND RAWLINS INFORM ME THAT WHITE RIVER UTES ATTACKED COLONEL THORNBURGH'S COMMAND 25 MILES FROM AGENCY. COLONEL THORNBURGH KILLED AND ALL HIS OFFICERS BUT ONE KILLED OR WOUNDED BESIDES MANY OF HIS MEN AND MOST OF HIS

HORSES. DISPATCHES STATE THAT THE WHOLE COMMAND IS
IMPERILED. THE STATE OF COLORADO WILL FURNISH YOU
IMMEDIATELY ALL THE MEN YOU REQUIRE TO SETTLE PER-
MANENTLY THIS INDIAN TROUBLE.

> FREDERICK W. PITKIN
> GOVERNOR OF COLORADO

In succeeding stops at Las Vegas, Trinidad, Canon City, Denver and Leadville, Adams followed the papers anxiously from
battle to massacre to Colonel Merritt's report that the Meeker
women and Flora Ellen Price and her children were captives
of the Utes. The more he read the more he longed to participate
in events. He noted with wry amusement and exasperation the
strategy of Pitkin, which ignored everything Adams had told
him about Ute society. Though the Governor knew well that
the ambush and massacre must have been caused by the White
River Utes alone (population, 700), he gave Vickers a free hand
to convince the nation that Ouray's 1500 Uncompahgres, Ignacio's 1300 Southern Utes and even Tabby's 500 Uintah Utes
from Utah were equally guilty and were massing for a bloody
showdown.

Vickers's technique was crude, cynical and effective. The reporters who camped in Pitkin's Denver office received from
Vickers every wild rumor from any Colorado settler anywhere,
no matter how absurd, for prominent publication as the gospel
truth. The *Denver Tribune* related:

> The Governor's office is besieged by sturdy old pioneers and
> hot-blooded young men offering their services to the State in
> defense of their homes and to exterminate the savage horde.
> They beg to join the volunteer movement to drive the Utes
> from Colorado soil — or into it. Among others to call on the
> Governor was General Samuel E. Browne who commanded
> the militia and Government troops on the road from Denver
> to Julesburg when the Cheyennes and Arapahoes sacked the
> route. The General spoke with fire: "Governor, I offer my
> services in any capacity I may be needed in wiping out these
> red devils and in protecting our people."

Pitkin set himself up as a military man of no mean ability. He called militiamen to arms under General Hamill at Georgetown, under General Joe Wilson at Leadville, under General Dave Cook at Lake City. He sent sage advice to General Hatch at Santa Fe warning him that Merritt's southward push was pressing maddened Ute legions under Ouray, Jack and Douglas against the defenseless mining camps of Ouray, Rico and Silverton. He dispatched couriers to urge the evacuation of the Eagle River and Elk Mountain mining districts. He demanded from General Pope one thousand friction primers, one hundred thousand rounds of ammunition and hundreds of Springfield rifles to defend Leadville, Hot Sulphur Springs and Denver from Ute destruction. Pope learned from Pitkin that Breckenridge on Blue River had been razed and that Chief Ignacio and one hundred warriors were galloping down the Dolores to join one of Ouray's crack fighting units.

All through that post-massacre fortnight, the fuming and frustrated Adams watched Colorado and the rest of the nation lapping up Vickers's propaganda and palpitating with vicarious dread. But he suspected that the Governor and his private secretary might be overplaying their hand. There were dampening items. General Pope announced from Fort Leavenworth that he was sending troops to Pagosa Springs, "not because an outbreak among the Southern Utes is at all likely, but to prevent the possibility of one." Blue River residents denied that Breckenridge was in ruins.

General Joe Wilson sent a telegram to Pitkin:

YOUR INFORMATION ABOUT MEN BEING KILLED AT KOKOMO IS NOT RELIABLE.

General Hamill wired him:

I DO NOT PLACE MUCH RELIANCE ON RUMORS OF INDIANS NEAR HOT SULPHUR.

General Palmer's *Colorado Springs Gazette* stated treasonably that Pitkin's theory of a general Ute uprising was nine tenths political hot air. The *Gazette* insisted that Ouray had had no connection with the trouble except to save the soldiers at Milk Creek from total annihilation after they had trespassed on the Reservation for no good reason.

On October 13, General Adams journeyed from Leadville toward Denver and at Como received a telegram as he rode the Denver and South Park Railroad. It was from Secretary Schurz in Washington, asking him to penetrate the Ute wilderness and try to rescue the captive women as an Interior Department special agent. If Adams would go, Schurz wrote, President Hayes would have an order issued by General Sherman halting further troop movements by Colonel Merritt until Adams completed, or failed in, his mission.

Immeasurably relieved and stirred, Adams wired back his acceptance and wired Ouray via Del Norte that he would arrive on the Uncompahgre soon. He sent a third wire to Mrs. Adams at Manitou, instructing her to bring his Winchester and spare blankets to a southbound train at the Colorado Springs depot. Next evening he dined in Denver with Count Dönhoff and granted his plea to be taken along on the Western Slope adventure. Then he saw Governor Pitkin at his Welton Street home, outlined his plan to find the captives through his friendship with Ouray and Sowerwick, and got his promise to soft-pedal his Ute-removal campaign until the rescue occurred.

THE TWO TEUTONS made a striking pair in the morning of October 15 as they boarded the cars for San Luis Valley. Adams, the two-hundred-and-fifty pound six-footer whom Governor McCook had hired as bodyguard a decade ago looked spectacularly stalwart still at thirty-five. The aristocratic Dönhoff was an inch taller, more slender and a year younger, and in fine physical condition too. They would need all their stamina, for they were undertaking one of the most rugged and extraordinary treks in

Western history, equally wearing on the emotions and on the body. The rail trip to Alamosa, General Palmer's year-old terminus in the middle of San Luis Valley, would be relatively easy. Even so, the distance was two hundred and fifty miles and life was grim when the five booster locomotives began burying the passengers in cinders during the grind over La Veta Pass. Thereafter, they would travel mostly by horseback over an interminable labyrinth of mountain roads and Indian trails, lashed by hail and chilled by snow flurries. They faced nine hundred miles of this horseback existence and they hoped to cover it all in ten days' time.

The Count's aristocratic bearing came naturally to him. He belonged to an East Prussian noble family eight centuries old whose members had excelled as feudal landowners, monks, soldiers, diplomats and matchmakers. Dönhoff's father had been a delegate to the liberal Frankfort Parliament of German States and young Dönhoff himself had entered the Prussian diplomatic service in '71. He had served throughout Europe before having himself sent to the Washington Legation in April of '79 to avoid having to marry Prince Bismarck's only daughter, Countess Marie.

Dönhoff left Denver with Adams wearing a green velvet hunting cap and matching coat bearing the Dönhoff coat of arms — a wild boar's head on a shield. He told Adams that helping to rescue the Meeker women would be in line with family tradition: the Dönhoffs had got their coat of arms from the King of Poland when a Dönhoff knight had saved the life of the King's daughter by severing the head of a charging boar. The Count was eager to meet some polygamous Utes. Polygamy intrigued him because his great-aunt, Sophie-Julie Dönhoff, had married a thorough polygamist — Frederick William II, King of Prussia — whose royal home was blessed with two royal wives, two morganatic wives and one official mistress.[3]

General Adams was fully aware of the trials and dangers ahead of them, but Dönhoff went along blandly and blindly. He showed no realization of his strange position as a high German official. He must have known, but he did not seem to care, that he was incomprehensibly taking a vital part in one of the most delicate American domestic crises since the Civil War. He did not visualize the international furore which would occur if by chance the Utes should murder the Secretary of the German Legation, who happened to be also the favorite candidate for son-in-law of the Iron Chancellor of the German Empire.

Their cindery rail trip ended that night. At dawn, they rode up the Rio Grande through Del Norte and Wagon Wheel Gap. They grew increasingly preoccupied with future perils and hardly noticed the fading gold of foothill aspens and the soaring San Juan peaks ahead already touched with snow. They passed Lake Santa Maria and over the Rio Grande-Gunnison divide to Lake City. At Lake San Cristobal, Adams eased their state of mind by talking about the cannibal Alfred Packer and showing Dönhoff where the five skeletons had been found in '74. From Lake City they rode north on Otto Mears's rough toll road down Lake Fork and west past the breath-taking Black Canyon of the Gunnison. They were on the century-old North Fork of the Spanish Trail now. As they moved over the divide to Chief Ouray's farm on the Uncompahgre, Adams spoke of travelers who had passed that way during the 1830s, Antoine Robidoux and Kit Carson. He talked of Captain Gunnison's sad traverse in '53 and of Captain Marcy's December crossing in '57 to get supplies for Johnston's army stalled at Fort Bridger in the Mormon campaign.

At the farm, Adams found Chief Ouray deeply depressed and looking very ill. He wore full Ute regalia, as he always did in times of trouble, but his beaded buckskins fitted badly because he had lost so much weight. Chipeta had changed from a plump, dimpled beauty to a harassed middle-aged woman.

Both of them were overjoyed to see General Adams. Ouray related in fluent Spanish that he had come close to suicide on

October 2 when two couriers had arrived at his home a few hours apart bringing news of the battle and massacre. The first courier was Yanko, coming directly from Milk Creek. Ouray's sister, Susan, sent the second from White River Agency during the massacre. Ouray was hunting up the Gunnison at the time but Chipeta was at home and she led Yanko to Ouray's camp.

Ouray had been sure that the two catastrophes meant the end of his Ute world which he had worked all his life to preserve. He had passed a night of torment and had considered turning aboriginal and joining Douglas with his band and Chief Ignacio's and fighting until the whites exterminated them all. His common sense brought him around and he sent the Los Pinos Agency employee, Joe Brady, to stop Jack's band from further battle. Other couriers had gone to Douglas and to his sister Susan to see that the white women had good care. He had sent a runner to Ignacio to keep the Southern Utes at home and he had quarantined his own men in their winter village near his farm.

He was, he said, despairing still, and yet Adams's arrival gave him a flicker of hope. Everything depended on Adams now. If Douglas and Jack would release the women to him, the whole nation might be relieved and less inclined to hang every kind of Ute from a yellow pine. Ouray knew about Schurz's scheme for treating Utes individually instead of as a tribe. Here again, the results of the Adams mission could be decisive. If Adams found the captives unharmed and well treated, then Schurz might find it politically feasible to test his new approach to the Indian problem by naming a commission to decide what handful of men should stand trial for murder, instead of punishing the whole Ute tribe.

They talked on and on over a bottle of Ouray's Spanish wine, discussing trails and picking guides to take Adams and Dönhoff to the camp of the captives. The talk and the wine made them feel better. They began to see possibilities. If commission hearings should be held, the advance of Merritt's soldiers could probably be delayed until snow closed the Ute country and gave the nation time to cool off.

But just after midnight, their happier mood turned black again. A runner from the women's camp came to report that Douglas's and Jack's war drums were beating along Grand River. Merritt's big force had begun moving south on a new wagon road which the Colonel was building from White River to the top of Roan Plateau. Jane and her husband Pauvitz were among the angry clique demanding death for the captives (and for General Adams, too, if he showed up) unless the soldiers stopped their advance and returned to White River.

CHAPTER XXIII Ordeal on Grand Mesa

MOST PEOPLE'S LIVES contain a brief passage so dramatic as to make the rest of their days seem like sideshows, trifling and unremembered. Such a passage for Adams and Dönhoff began Sunday morning, October 19, when their party of five whites and thirteen Indians, organized on Saturday at Los Pinos Agency, said good-by to Ouray and Chipeta and rode downstream toward Grand River.

Their mission was the climactic event of a racial crisis which had been maturing for centuries. But Adams did not bother to review the tangled skeins of history. He did not think of Spanish governors or of the gay Escalante or of Zebulon Pike or of Kit Carson or of the pious Felix Brunot. Mostly he tried not to think at all, substituting an exaggerated levity.

He found distraction in his personnel. The thirteen Utes led by Ouray's brother-in-law, Sapovanero, wore typical Ute garb — black felt hats with feathers sewn in the bands, hair cropped short at the top of their collars, striped cotton shirts, black vests, buckskin leggings and miners' shoes. The buckboard for returning the women was driven by an old friend, Captain M. W. Cline, a trader who had staked out the San Juan town of Ouray, in '75. The supply wagon carried two Los Pinos Agency employees, George Sherman and W. F. Saunders, who were doubling as *Denver Tribune* reporters. When the mules balked, Sherman beat and cursed them until exhausted and then burst into tears. Ouray's runner, Yanko, got them moving with his horse as bell mare. Yanko told Adams, "White man heap goddam!"

Toward evening the men came to the Gunnison, forded it

near the site of Antoine Robidoux's trading post and camped below the vast purple bulk of Grand Mesa. At dawn they were away again, and paused for supper at the mouth of Whitewater Creek, ten miles short of the Gunnison-Grand River junction. There two runners, Cojoe and Henry Jim, loped in from the camp of the captives with electrifying news. Merritt's soldiers were advancing south and Jack's band were working up to a new high pitch of fear and rage as they forted on Roan Plateau to stop the soldiers. The lives of the white women were in greater danger than ever.

Adams, Sapovanero and Ouray's war chief, Shavano, held an urgent meeting and agreed to push on this night. They figured that the distance to the captives was almost sixty miles by the regular route — ten miles on northwest to Grand River and thirty-five miles east up the Grand to Plateau Creek and fifteen miles back south along Plateau to the north rim of Grand Mesa.

Old Shavano, a small, gentle man whose proud bearing was enhanced by the fine Navajo blanket looped about him, eyed the slice of rising moon and said softly that he knew a deer trail. It was a precipitous short cut, up Whitewater Creek to the top of Grand Mesa and across it to Plateau Creek. The trail was a man-killer and a horsekiller. The buckboard and supply wagon would have to be left behind on Whitewater, but the deer trail would save them twenty miles.

They voted to take it — a nightmare of twisting defiles and sandy shelves which climbed the towering cliffs. On top at ten thousand, five hundred feet they entered Thigunawat, home of departed Utes. Everything seemed eerie and ominous — the flatness of Grand Mesa, the hooting owls, the convulsive scattering of deer and scaled quail. The men were silent and fearful as they rode past limpid lakes dotted with ducks and mirroring the slice of moon. The General lost control of his well-disciplined mind. He recalled having seen the Meeker women in '76 when Meeker had sought a postmastership, and now he tortured himself imagining how they fared, knowing how other white women had fared with other Indians inflamed by similar injustice — the Kansas farm wife nailed alive to her cabin door, the Nebraska bride roasted in a slow fire, the pregnant New Ulm woman whom the Sioux let live but whose unborn child was ripped out and destroyed.

Adams prayed for captives and captors both. He knew that the American people had taken awful revenge for Indian atrocities. What would they do to the Utes, and to their defender, Carl Schurz, if Adams discovered the mutilated bodies of Arvilla Meeker and her graceful daughter?

The quarter-moon set. Dawn came. The party reached a crystal pond and a brook. Shavano said that the captives were camped on that brook near its junction with Plateau Creek twelve miles farther. They had breakfast — beans and coffee — and pressed on. And suddenly they topped a rise, and Adams saw the camp in the widening valley a mile ahead.

He reined up and stared spellbound, trying to readjust his hideous imaginings to fit the lovely scene below. The thirty-odd white tents shimmered innocently in the morning sun. Beyond them, Grand Mesa fell away, and under it spread the golden valley of Grand River framed by the red-and-gray Book Cliffs and Roan Plateau in back. In the grassy meadow, sheep, goats and ponies grazed. Brown naked boys with bows stalked chipmunks and ground squirrels. Some girls were picking dried berries. A line of squaws strolled picturesquely down the ridge with packets of piñon wood. There were no men in sight.

Yanko rode to Johnson's lodge and returned to report that Douglas and Sowerwick would be back soon from Douglas's big Grand River camp. Adams's head ached with excitement. He spurred his horse toward the tents, with Cline and Dönhoff behind him. By an odd hunch, he passed the first tents and rode half a mile down the line to Johnson's lodge and then to the very last tepee where two squaws were holding a blanket

over the opening. Captain Cline yelled, "There she is!" Adams
answered "Keep an eye on her!" and dismounted at Johnson's
lodge, which he found empty. Then he hurried on foot over
to the last tepee just as a white woman pushed the squaws aside
and emerged from the tent, holding the hand of a little white
girl.

The woman was Josie Meeker. Adams studied her face anxiously and his hopes rose. She was deeply tanned, but her blue
eyes shone and her face showed no special sign of hardship.
Her long blond hair was bobbed now at the shoulders. She held
a needle and thread in one hand and she wore a warm skirt and
close-fitting jacket with red cuffs and a black border around
her slender hips — a costume obviously cut from a brown twill
annuity blanket. Her clear voice had only a slight tremor. "I'm
so glad to see you, Mr. Adams!"

He was far less composed than she. He mumbled, "Poor
child." Then, to end his suspense, he said, "Are the others all
right?"

"Quite well, considering."

"Forgive me, Miss Meeker. I must ask something painful
right now, before the Utes come. Do you know who killed your
father and the rest?"

"We couldn't see. We could only guess."

He took a deep breath. "Tell me this. How did the men
treat you?"

"Better than we expected. Especially since Saturday when
we arrived here."

"I mean — you know how the Utes are, Miss Meeker. Did
they commit any indignity to your persons?"

Her glance was sidelong but she spoke quickly, as if she had
prepared her answer. "Oh, no, Mr. Adams. Nothing of that
kind."

Adams relaxed. "I am greatly relieved," he said. "That will
make it easy to get you on your way home."

BUT IT WASN'T EASY. Douglas and Sowerwick arrived in truculent mood and the conference was stormy. Adams, Dönhoff and Sapovanero sat on one side of Douglas's big lodge. Across from them were thirty White River Utes. Over and over, Douglas said that the women would be released as soon as Adams went to White River and stopped the advancing soldiers. Over and over again, Adams refused to go north to see Merritt until the captives were given to Captain Cline.

After five weary hours, Adams began to have a sick feeling that he had failed in his mission. And then Sapovanero rose. He announced to Douglas's men that he had heard enough. He said that he was official spokesman for Chief Ouray, head of all the Utes, and that he brought an ultimatum. This day was Tuesday. If the white women did not arrive safely at Ouray's farm by Friday, Ouray would lead his Uncompahgres north in full strength to seize the captives and to drive the White River Utes into the guns of Merritt's troops.

There was a strained silence. Finally, Douglas asked Adams, "Are you sure that you can stop the soldiers?"

"I am on this mission by the authority of President Hayes. I think Colonel Merritt will listen to me."

And so Sapovanero won his point. At 5 P.M., the release of the women was approved and Adams promised to start for White River after supper with Dönhoff, Sapovanero and Sowerwick. In the morning, Captain Cline and his Ute escort would take the women and children to the wagons at Whitewater Creek and on to Ouray's home, Lake City and Alamosa railhead.

As the two white men left the tent, dizzy with fatigue and relief, they saw Mrs. Meeker, in calico dress, shawl and sunbonnet, limping toward them from the silvery creek willows where Johnson had hidden her. Beside her were Josie and the plump Flora Ellen Price, wearing a garment like Josie's and a floppy sombrero. Behind them was the smiling squaw Susan with Johnnie Price tied on her broad back, grinning like a monkey as he sucked a piece of roast meat. May Price skipped gaily after Susan.

Mrs. Meeker was pale and gaunt. And yet Adams thought that she didn't look too badly after the awfulness of the past three weeks. He took her thin hand and described the results of the conference. She thanked him brokenly and sobbed a little and said that she was glad to be freed, for Josie's sake. "For myself," she said, "I don't care. Mr. Meeker is gone. I have nothing to live for. I am sixty-four years old, Mr. Adams. An old lady, you might say."

THE GENERAL prepared a telegram for Yanko to carry to Western Union at Del Norte by way of the Elk Mountain trail and Cochetopa Pass:

CAMP ON PLATEAU CREEK
OCTOBER 21, 1879

C. SCHURZ
SECRETARY, WASHINGTON, D. C.

ARRIVED HERE THIS MORNING AND HAVE SUCCEEDED IN PERSUADING INDIANS TO RELEASE MRS. MEEKER, MISS MEEKER, MRS. PRICE AND TWO CHILDREN WITHOUT CONDITION WHO WILL LEAVE HERE TOMORROW WITH SUFFICIENT ESCORT. I GO TO WHITE RIVER TO COMMUNICATE WITH GENERAL MERRITT. THE INDIANS ARE ANXIOUS FOR PEACE AND DESIRE A FULL INVESTIGATION OF THE TROUBLE.

CHARLES ADAMS
SPECIAL AGENT

He had a little time then to hear some of the women's story with its contrasts of Ute behavior compounded of their frustration and despair. The women had seen cruel days and kind days.

Persune had bestowed on Josie the gallantry of a Galahad, giving her his best ponies and saddles and blankets and kneeling for her so that she could mount her horse by stepping on his back. Susan had defended them all throughout and had shown her esteem by offering Flora Ellen the fantastic price of three good ponies for little Johnnie. But Jane had enjoyed distressing them by saying they would be shot soon and asking how they liked being ordered around by Indians for a change. Arvilla had suffered most. Douglas's squaws had tossed her about like a sack of meal and he had been childishly mean, stealing her only handkerchief, hiding her packet of needles and threatening to burn her beloved *Pilgrim's Progress*. He had spit on her, lunged at her with knives and assigned to her his boniest horse without a saddle. But later his baby fell sick and Arvilla had cured the baby with homeopathic pills. Thereafter, Douglas saw to it that Arvilla had an extra blanket and a catskin pillow.

Practical Josie told of making warm clothes in case they were held all winter, and she described the daily confusion of alarms and indecision, with warriors shuttling aimlessly to their Roan Plateau lookouts. The weather had been pleasant except for a hailstorm and a night of howling wind. During the first two weeks, they had been in separate camps but Johnson and Susan had got them together. They had changed camps with each threatened advance by Merritt's force — seven camps in all, passing from the Agency along the Hogback to East Piceance Creek, down Rifle Creek to Grand River and down the Grand with one long stay at Douglas's main Roan Creek camp.[1]

AFTER SUPPER on that memorable Tuesday of October 21, Adams, Dönhoff and Sapovanero headed north. As they left, the General had a chance to ask Flora Ellen Price if she had been outraged. Her prompt denial, like Josie's, had a rehearsed sound that disturbed him vaguely through a second conference that same night with Jack and Douglas in Sowerwick's Grand River lodge. The two Germans slept late on Wednesday morning and did not get away until noon.

As they rode up Grand River with Sowerwick's escort, a Ute runner arrived to report a new crisis. He said that two Utes and two of Merritt's men had been killed in a skirmish on Roan Plateau. The runner glowered at Adams and implied that perhaps he had planned the skirmish to make things look still worse for the Utes.

From then on, Adams and Dönhoff felt entirely insecure until they entered Merritt's camp Thursday evening. But nobody trusted them there, either. Merritt had retired. The soldiers were in a state over the Roan Plateau killings and most disagreeable to two white men who had ridden into Army lines escorted by the enemy. A sergeant even hinted that Adams must be a Ute spy and ought to be hung.

But in the morning Colonel Merritt greeted the visitors cordially, having known Adams for years. He praised him for saving the women and said that of course troop movements were out of the question until the Meekers reached civilization. He went on to explain with rueful humor that he was "tied hand and foot" anyhow. On October 19, just as he had begun his southward push to settle these Utes for good, General Sheridan had wired him to halt the advance until Carl Schurz had time to mess things up and give the Army permission to proceed. Spitting mad to be thwarted again by "the damned Dutch Secretary," he had recalled his cavalry and had started writing a hot letter to Sheridan protesting this muddleheaded interference.

In the middle of it, a courier ran in to tell him about the Roan Plateau affair. It seemed that Lieutenant William B. Weir and a civilian, Paul Humme, had left a scouting party to do some hunting by themselves. Weir had wounded a deer near a hidden Ute look out. A Ute boy had exposed himself in his curiosity to see if the deer was going to fall. Humme saw the boy and shot him dead. The Ute lookouts then killed both Humme and Weir.

The incident, Merritt said, was both tragic and embarrassing. The embarrassing part was that neither Weir nor Humme officially belonged to his expedition. They were just friends of his: Weir was Chief of Ordnance at the Cheyenne Arsenal; Humme was his civilian assistant. They had begged Merritt to be allowed to go along for the hunting, and he had signed them on, naming Humme "chief of scouts." Merritt had warned them not to go off alone on Roan Plateau, and they had disobeyed his orders.

DURING THAT AFTERNOON, Adams wrote a long telegram to Secretary Schurz which Army couriers would take to Western Union at Rawlins. In it he described his Grand River conference with Douglas and Jack. He outlined their view that the Milk Creek battle began because the soldiers had crossed the Reservation boundary unexpectedly; that Meeker was killed in reprisal for twenty Ute casualties at Milk Creek; that the other employees were killed because Frank Dresser had shot Johnson's brother; and that those guilty of murder at the Agency should be punished. The wire continued:

> IT IS HARD TO SAY WHO WOULD BE PUNISHED, AND ONLY AFTER EXAMINING MRS. MEEKER AND THE OTHERS CAN THE FULL GUILT BE FASTENED ON ANYONE. I SHALL RETURN TO-MORROW TO DOUGLAS' CAMP AND ON TO CHIEF OURAY. SHALL INSIST AND ADVISE THAT HE BRING THE LEADERS TO JUSTICE AND I THINK THAT PART MAY BE SAFELY LEFT WITH HIM. . . .

Here Adams paused and considered deeply his suspicion that Josie Meeker and Flora Ellen Price might have lied when they had denied so promptly that they had been outraged.

This question of outrage had plagued him ever since October 4 near Albuquerque, when he had heard rumors about the massacre. Its importance had grown in his mind, particularly since Josie Meeker's remark on Tuesday that none of the white women had actually seen any Ute shoot anybody. That meant simply that no Utes named by the women as murder suspects need be afraid to give themselves up and stand trial — provided that no outrage had occurred. But if the women had been outraged and would testify to the fact, then the Utes would feel their goose was cooked. They would refuse to stand trial for anything on the grounds that public opinion would be convicting them in advance.

With all his heart, Adams hoped that Josie and Flora Ellen had told him the truth on Grand Mesa. Otherwise, he was sure that he could not prevent the people he had come to know and love from being robbed of their homeland and exiled to some soul-killing barren. Meanwhile, he decided to wire Secretary Schurz what he himself wished to believe. He ended his White River telegram:

. . . AND I THINK ALSO THAT THE UTES SHOULD BE GIVEN CREDIT FOR THEIR GOOD TREATMENT OF THE CAPTIVES AND THE DELIVERY OF SAME TO ME. GENERAL MERRITT WILL KEEP THE TROOPS HERE. AND I WOULD REQUEST IN ANSWER TO THIS A FINAL PROPOSITION DIRECTED TO OURAY WHICH MAY BE SENT ME VIA DEL NORTE TO LOS PINOS AGENCY, AND WHICH I WILL COMMUNICATE TO HIM. I SHALL BE BACK AT LOS PINOS BY OCTOBER 30 AND EXPECT FURTHER INSTRUCTIONS THERE.

CHARLES ADAMS
SPECIAL AGENT

ADAMS AND DÖNHOFF said good-by to Colonel Merritt on the twenty-fifth, talked to Douglas again at his Grand River camp [2] and reached Los Pinos on the twenty-ninth. They were worn out and frazzled by their incredibly arduous ten-day trip, mostly without sleep. But they were happy to learn that the women and children had arrived safely on the twenty-fourth at Ouray's home and had been overjoyed to find Ralph Meeker waiting there to take them on at once to Lake City bound for Alamosa and Greeley.

Wilson Stanley, Los Pinos Agent since July, had two telegrams for Adams and a sheaf of stenographic testimony which the women had given at the Agency to William J. Pollock, an Indian Bureau inspector who had arrived with Ralph Meeker.

The first telegram read:

DEPARTMENT OF THE INTERIOR
WASHINGTON, D. C.
OCTOBER 26, 1879

GENERAL CHARLES ADAMS, SPECIAL AGENT
LOS PINOS AGENCY, VIA DEL NORTE, COLO.

DISPATCH OF 24th FROM WHITE RIVER RECEIVED. YOUR DISPATCH FROM PLATEAU CREEK ALSO RECEIVED. PRESIDENT HAYES DESIRES ME TO EXPRESS HIS VERY HIGH APPRECIATION OF THE COURAGE AND GOOD JUDGMENT DISPLAYED IN THE PERFORMANCE OF YOUR TASK.

YOU WILL NOW INSIST UPON THE FOLLOWING TERMS: THE WHITE RIVER UTES ARE TO MOVE THEIR CAMP TEMPORARILY TO THE NEIGHBORHOOD OF LOS PINOS AGENCY. A COMMISSION CONSISTING OF GENERAL HATCH, YOURSELF AND OURAY TO MEET AT LOS PINOS AS SOON AS POSSIBLE TO TAKE TESTIMONY TO ASCERTAIN THE GUILTY PARTIES: THE GUILTY PARTIES SO ASCERTAINED TO BE DEALT WITH AS WHITE MEN WOULD BE UNDER LIKE CIRCUMSTANCES. THE WHITE RIVER UTES OR AT LEAST THE MISCHIEVOUS ELEMENTS AMONG THEM, TO BE DISARMED. THESE TERMS, APPROVED BY THE PRESIDENT AND GENERAL SHERMAN, ARE FAIR, AND THE MOST FAVORABLE THAT CAN BE OFFERED. STATE THIS TO OURAY.

C. SCHURZ, SECRETARY

So far, so good. Adams noted that Schurz was backed not only by the President but also by the Army's highest official in his revolutionary determination to treat the Utes just as though they were white Americans. Schurz's second telegram, marked "confidential," was inspired obviously by Adams's sentence, "And I think also that the Utes should be given credit for their good treatment of the captives." The Secretary suggested that Utes who would accept farms "according to plan discussed by us at Denver" could probably remain in Colorado, regardless of the Meeker massacre. The hold-outs would have to go to Utah or to Indian Territory.

When Adams read the first telegram to Ouray, the ailing chief expressed great pleasure at being named as a member of the proposed peace commission. But something about the second telegram seemed to make him apprenhensive. Several times he asked Adams to reread it and then to translate it into Spanish. And suddenly the General realized that Ouray, too, was worrying about the possibility of outrage. The realization came to him when Ouray inquired if it were customary in American court trials to accept the testimony of women.

Why was Ouray apprehensive? Had he picked up some gossip which Adams hadn't heard? Worriedly, Adams went to his room and took out Inspector Pollock's sheaf of testimony which the women had given to him. It was addressed to Indian Commissioner Edward A. Hayt "covering the period from the time of the massacre at White River to the day of their deliverance at Ouray's house, October 24, 1879." It was a voluminous document and an hour passed before Adams reached the end of all the things Mrs. Meeker, Josie Meeker and Flora Ellen Price had told the Inspector about those twenty-six terrible days.

When he had read the very last page, the General put the sheaf face down on the desk. He was smiling broadly. Though the women had described many unpleasant things, there was no slightest hint of outrage in all those pages. They had told

Pollock just about what they had told him, except in more detail.

And then Adams happened to notice writing on the reverse side of the back page of the testimony. It read:

(COPY)
October 29, 1879

COMMISSIONER HAYT:

I have also a statement given to me personally and in confidence of a character too delicate to mention here as to the personal treatment they severally received from the Indians during captivity.

This has been one of the roughest trips I ever made and am suffering intensely with rheumatism. Expect to reach the Southern Ute Agency day after tomorrow.

WM. J. POLLOCK, *Inspector*

Adams sighed in deep disappointment and perplexity. Then he left the room, found Count Dönhoff and told him what he had just read.

They agreed that Adams had a duty to perform before the peace commission hearings could begin at Los Pinos. Within an hour, they had packed up and saddled their horses and had left Los Pinos bound for Denver and for Greeley, where Adams planned to visit the Meeker mansion at Plum and Monroe Streets.

CHAPTER XXIV Family Reunion

RALPH MEEKER, RECENTLY BACK IN NEW YORK after a year as
London correspondent for the *New York Herald,* was in his
Greenwich Village apartment on October 8 when Carmelita
Circovitch, his fiancée, brought him newspapers confirming the
White River massacre. Nine days later, after Secretary Schurz
made him a special agent of the Interior Department, he joined
Inspector Pollock in Denver. He met his mother, Josie and
Flora Ellen Price at Ouray's farm on the twenty-fourth.

It was a happy reunion. For a little while the three Meekers
put aside the tragic past. Even Flora Ellen was gay, and told
Josie that never in her whole life had she laid eyes on so
elegant a gentleman as Mr. Ralph Meeker. His year in London
had indeed done a lot for him. A veneer of fashionable poise
concealed his innate shyness and sensitivity. Arvilla was entranced with his slight British accent, his high-buttoned tweed
knicker suit, Ascot scarf and Eton cap. To complete the stylish
effect, he wore the ultra-ultra Plimsoll sport shoes. He showed
his mother his new false teeth and told her that he seldom
suffered from catarrh or gastritis any more, though, as she
could see, baldness threatened him again.

He put on a good front of calm reassurance. Actually, the
events since September 29 were as shattering to him as they
were to Arvilla, though in different terms. The death of his
father was not so much the shocking removal of a loved parent
(Ralph's filial devotion had gone to his mother). To him,
rather, Nathan Meeker was a landmark of his environment,
imperishable as a mountain or a great oak or a cathedral. The

sudden void had stunned him with a sense of the precariousness of life and he had sought security in the arms of Carmelita Circovitch. He was wildly in love with her by now and his greatest need was to marry her at once.

And yet he saw that marriage must be put out of mind for the present. He had four penniless female relatives on his hands and only one of them, Josie, was capable of self-support. He was greatly moved to receive from Horace Greeley's daughter, Gabrielle, a contribution to the family of two hundred and fifty dollars. Her accompanying letter compared Nathan Meeker to Jesus Christ and the Utes to the mob who had demanded His crucifixion. But Gabrielle's gift would not last long. Thereafter, more than half his earnings would have to be given to Arvilla, Rozene and Mary, indefinitely.

That was simple arithmetic. But something else was far more disturbing — his awareness that the strange fate which had arranged the massacre was plotting not merely to destroy the Colorado Utes. It would attempt to destroy the Meeker family as well. The awful poison of injustice, accumulating over the decades through the selfishness and thoughtlessness of mankind, was spilling over to infect innocent white people as well as innocent Indians.

One focus of infection, Ralph feared, was his neurotic and frustrated sister, Rozene. Her mind at thirty was displaying aberrations which suggested more strongly than ever that her brain had been permanently damaged when she had nearly drowned in the well at Hiram as a child. On the day after Nathan Meeker's murder was confirmed, Rozene wrote and published a letter in the *Denver Tribune* which was reprinted throughout the United States. Ralph read it in the *New York Herald:*

GREELEY, COLORADO
October 9, 1879

TO THE EDITOR OF THE TRIBUNE:
Had there been one half as much expedition and force put in operation from the time of my father's calling for troops

until the battle as there has been since the battle, this horrible massacre would never have occurred. The Government with its slow movements has let my father be murdered when it could have been prevented. My father wrote Governor Pitkin on September 10 that his and all the lives at the Agency were in peril and requested troops. After three weeks' delay, so small a detachment were sent as were overcome. Had the cowboys of Colorado been called on September 10 they would have gotten there in time to save the lives of the Agency and they would have made so clean a work of the red devils that it would have been hard to find one alive today.

The life of one common white man is worth more than the lives of all the Indians from the beginning of their creation until the present time. And yet such a man as my father with brains, intellect and power to move the thoughts of men — his life is now ignominiously put out by the hand of a savage foe, whose life or soul is not worthy of a dog. And no power in all the land to stay the deed! What a magnanimous Government we have to pamper a set of creatures whose existence should have been a thing of the past long ago! Oh, my father, could I but have died in your stead! My protector, my hope and joy!

Oh, the broken hearts of widows, daughters and sisters who today — this hour — mourn the loss of their dear martyred ones who were their support, love, life and their all, are now gone from their side forever, with only sorrow and desolation for their comforter through life!

Who can pay the price of this mighty woe? Truly the blood of the martyred ones cries out for vengeance and shall the voice of anguish be hushed?

ROSE MEEKER

As an ardent admirer of Carl Schurz and of Schurz's pioneer efforts to help the Indians, Ralph deplored this letter and its nation-wide circulation. And still he recognized that Rozene's views were not unusual in a political sense. They differed only in intensity from those expressed by Senator Teller and Governor Pitkin. What distressed Ralph was his idea of Rozene's motivation. He knew that she had not written the letter because she loved her father and yearned to avenge him. She had never cared for him and had criticized him harshly of late both for nearly drowning her as a child and for forcing her to run the boardinghouse in Greeley. He felt that what had moved her partly was her hatred and jealousy of Josie and Ralph; she was jumping at this chance to oppose their liberalism before a vast audience. He believed that she was moved also by her desperate desire for acclaim and attention — which she felt that she deserved much more than Arvilla's other children, who had always seemed to have the world at their feet. Ralph suspected that half the time Rozene imagined that she herself had endured the massacre and captivity instead of Josie. Finally, Ralph saw in Rozene's phrase "Shall the voice of anguish be hushed?" a scheme to set Arvilla, and everyone else in Greeley, against Josie and Ralph, who she knew would continue to defend Indians.

As Ralph expected, Rozene's letter was exploited by Governor Pitkin as the incontestable argument for drastic and immediate military action against all the Utes by combined Army and volunteer State forces. On his westward journey from New York to the Uncompahgre, Ralph followed the hot newspaper debate on this issue between the Governor and Secretary Schurz. On October 23, the papers quoted Pitkin as having wired Schurz in part:

INFORMATION FROM SOUTHWESTERN COLORADO SATISFIES ME THAT MOST OF CHIEF OURAY'S WARRIORS WERE IN THE THORNBURGH FIGHT. THEY WHIPPED THORNBURGH'S COMMAND AND NOW COLONEL MERRITT HAS BEEN HALTED AT WHITE RIVER AT YOUR REQUEST. IF YOUR POLICY OF MILITARY INACTIVITY CONTINUES, OUR FRONTIER SETTLEMENTS ARE LIABLE TO BECOME THE SCENES OF MORE MASSACRES.

With a snort of disgust, Ralph turned to Schurz's wired reply — and began to smile long before he came to the end of it. The tyro Pitkin, he thought, would have done better not to try to match wits with the wiliest politician of his era:

GOVERNOR FREDERICK W. PITKIN

DENVER, COLORADO

YOUR DISPATCH IS RECEIVED. I ENTRUSTED WITH THE IM-
PORTANT DUTY OF SPECIAL AGENT TO THE UTES, GENERAL
CHARLES ADAMS, A CITIZEN OF COLORADO WHO, A MONTH
AGO, WAS REPRESENTED TO ME BY YOURSELF AS A GENTLEMAN
OF ABILITY AND ENERGY AND INTIMATELY ACQUAINTED WITH
THE UTES AND EMINENTLY QUALIFIED TO DEAL WITH THEM
IN AN EMERGENCY.

HE IS WITH THEM NOW AND HIS LAST REPORT OF OCTOBER
18 WAS: "NONE OF OURAY'S UNCOMPAHGRE UTES OR IGNACIO'S
SOUTHERN UTES AND ONLY A PART OF THE WHITE RIVER UTES
HAVE BEEN ENGAGED IN THE TROUBLES. ALL RUMORS OF
DEPREDATIONS OFF THE UTE RESERVATION ARE UNTRUE EX-
CEPT THE DRIVING OFF OF HORSES FROM BEAR RIVER AND
THIS OCCURRED BEFORE OURAY'S ORDER TO CEASE FIGHTING
WAS RECEIVED."

GENERAL ADAMS REPORTS THIS AFTER HAVING TRAVERSED
SOUTHWESTERN COLORADO, WHICH IS THE SOURCE OF YOUR
INFORMATION. HE ALSO STATES: "THE CAPTIVE WOMEN AND
CHILDREN WHOM I HAVE ASSURANCES ARE SAFE WILL BE DE-
LIVERED. TROOPS SHOULD NOT PROCEED SOUTH FROM WHITE
RIVER AS I BELIEVE THAT YOUR CONDITIONS TO SECURE PEACE
WILL BE COMPLIED WITH."

THIS REPORT OF A RESPONSIBLE MAN WHO HAS YOUR CON-
FIDENCE AS WELL AS MINE AND WHO SPEAKS FROM PERSONAL
OBSERVATION IS CERTAINLY ENTITLED TO CREDIT. THE LIBERA-
TION OF THE CAPTIVE WOMEN AND CHILDREN IS THE FIRST
THING TO BE ACCOMPLISHED. GENERAL ADAMS EXPECTS TO
BRING THEM IN — IF NOT INTERFERED WITH — IN A FEW
DAYS. HE WILL THEN REPORT ON THE SURRENDER OF THE
GUILTY INDIANS. MEANWHILE, THE MILITARY PREPARATIONS
HAVE NOT BEEN RELAXED, SO THAT FAILURE OF THE EFFORTS
MENTIONED MAY BE FOLLOWED BY ENERGETIC ACTION.

WE ARE ENDEAVORING TO PREVENT A GENERAL WAR WITH

THE WHOLE UTE TRIBE, WHICH WOULD BE A BETTER WAY TO
PROTECT YOUR BORDER SETTLEMENTS THAN BY A GENERAL
ATTACK UPON THE INDIANS BY ARMED CITIZENS AS YOUR
DISPATCH SEEMS TO SUGGEST.

CARL SCHURZ

AT OURAY'S FARM, Inspector Pollock took the testimony of the
late captives in private and separately. But Ralph gathered
from their pointed remarks to him that they had escaped anything approaching outrage. He was very glad, for he had considered the terrible effect, on Josie in particular, if the nation's
millions began reconstructing sexual experience in detail to
satisfy their prurience — to say nothing of what Rozene would
make of this ultimate in incendiary material.

Captain Cline escorted them all by stage on the twenty-sixth
to Lake City where Ralph spent $25.40 of Interior Department
funds to buy gloves, stockings and shoes for the women and
clothes for Mrs. Price's two children. They rested a day in
Alamosa at Judge Hayt's home and continued to Denver on
October 30 by the morning narrow-gauge train. At every depot
— Fort Garland, Walsenburg, Pueblo, Colorado Springs, Denver — they found huge crowds waiting for them. The crowds
were kind and quiet, but Ralph perceived that they had come
principally out of curiosity as to just what these poor ladies had
actually endured while passing twenty-three days and nights in
the lodges of polygamous and immoral savages.

All the while, Ralph took notes for a book about the captives'
experiences which he would write and Josie would sign, and for
lectures which Josie might give to help the family budget until
Congress voted them some compensation and released Nathan
Meeker's unpaid back salary. As he heard the ladies talk, he
observed how the human spirit, even in the most abnormal
circumstances, clings with all its strength to its normal reactions.
Josie, for instance, betrayed subtly that she had not been too

upset in the wilds to enjoy being Queen Captive. Though Flora Ellen was younger and more voluptuously endowed, Josie implied (with a small giggle) that the Ute male had regarded her as the more attractive. She had been put on a pedestal by being assigned to cook. Flora Ellen had been the flunky; she had cleaned up, built fires and carried water. Similarly, Ralph found Arvilla recalling clearly her resentment over Persune's way of kneeling for Josie to mount whereas Douglas had tossed Arvilla on her horse like a sack of potatoes. At one of Arvilla's waspish comments, Ralph's mouth fell wide open. Wasn't she hinting that Persune must have got some kind of reward for being nice to Josie?

From the Denver depot, W. F. Sperry drove the celebrities in his own carriage to his Alvord House at Larimer and 18th streets. Arvilla went to bed at once, where she was plied with hot tea and toast before falling asleep. The impassive Flora Ellen and Josie, most appealing in her blanket gown and big cavalry hat with purple tassel, stayed with Ralph in the crowded lobby for hours talking to friends, having photos made and repeating often, as if by rote, the phrase, "No, the Indians never attempted or offered personal violence. But we fared badly in other respects."

Everyone took particular interest in Arvilla's much-traveled *Pilgrim's Progress,* poring over its gaudy illustrations of Madame Wanton, Prudence and Innocence and staring romantically at the pressed cranesbill from Arvilla's Agency flower bed which she had pasted on the title page, its leaf brown but its pink flower still in full color.[1] At one point, Josie sent Ralph to the Champa Street office of Dr. Avery, the lady physician, to make check-up appointments for herself and Flora Ellen. When Ralph asked if Arvilla wanted an appointment too, Josie looked at him, vaguely startled, and said Arvilla didn't need to be examined.

And next afternoon, their train pulled very slowly into Greeley depot to avoid injuring the thronging thousands. The train stopped and Ralph pushed Arvilla to the vestibule. Max Clark was there to help her down, and the Henry Wests and the A. E. Gipsons and David Boyd and all the other original settlers of Union Colony and members of the Farmers' Club. Ralph saw Mary Meeker and Win Fullerton smiling at him, and Rozene, her almost-pretty face pinched and hungry for need of affection but bright with excitement.

As Arvilla limped down the car step she gazed west up Locust Street past the *Greeley Tribune* office and to the public square designed by Nathan, and on past the fine homes of the now-thriving city — every foot of which derived from the imagination, courage and faith of her wonderful husband. And then of course she had to weep, realizing at last in unbearable completeness the tragedy of Nathan Meeker's death just when everything he had struggled to attain was almost within his reach.

She wrote later:

> As I stepped from the cars I was astonished to see the crowd. Nearly all the people of Greeley were at the depot and their pleasant but sad faces and earnest looks showed the deep interest they had in our escape. As our carriage turned up Monroe Street, behold a sheet of white canvas stretched across the street, under which we rode, having printed the words in large capital letters, "Mother, Welcome Home!"

Max Clark's carriage took them all up Walnut to Monroe and southward, dropping Flora Ellen Price and her children off at the home of one of many friends who had asked to take Flora Ellen in. And then they came to the big square Plum Street house, more than ever the community showplace with its nine-year-old trees and shrubbery. Arvilla limped into the first bright parlor and on to the second. Here, at least, nothing had changed in the past sixteen turbulent months. Here were the Founder's tall cherry desk and Arvilla's marble sideboard and the Italian vase shaped like a hand and the Trumbull Phalanx mementoes and the framed letters from Henry Clay and Ralph Waldo Emerson. Arvilla's faded sampler, dated 1827, still hung in the kitchen. Arvilla sank gratefully into her old rocker, feeling almost peaceful and secure. She was thinking that here, perhaps, the widow of Nathan Meeker might find sanctuary, living out the rest of her days shielded by those adobe walls from further contact with the unhappy outside world.

The front door bell clanged. Ralph answered it and came to her with an opened telegram. Arvilla read the place mark — DEL NORTE, COLORADO — and the signature: CHARLES ADAMS, MEMBER, UTE PEACE COMMISSION. He stated that he would arrive at the Meeker home on Wednesday, November 4, with a Government stenographer to take her final testimony on the late White River troubles.

The outside world intruded still.

CHAPTER XXV **Visit to Plum Street**

THE DEPOTS OF THE NARROW GAUGE were jammed again on November 2 and 3 as Adams and Dönhoff rode to Denver with a long night's rest at Adams's home in the cottonwoods near Manitou. But the depot crowds at Pueblo and Colorado Springs were not subdued now, as they had been when the women had passed through. Instead the people cheered boisterously when Adams appeared on the car vestibule and shot pistols and threw confetti while the bands of beer-inspired volunteer firemen played on.

In three short weeks, the General's status had changed from that of an obscure postal inspector to a national hero whose deeds were discussed endlessly by most Americans from Rutherford B. Hayes on down. Every red-blooded boy across the land strutted about with his broomstick Winchester giving orders in a German accent to vicious savages cowed by his towering physique and moral grandeur. Every romantic American girl dreamed that she was the luminous Josie Meeker, imperiously asking her fiendish tormentors to shoot her, and laughing in their hideously painted faces when they confessed that they dared not.

With placid grace, Adams allowed himself to be engulfed in the tidal wave of acclaim. Through it all, he practiced his habit of seeing life, himself included, with half-amused, half-pitying detachment. He knew very well that his period of glory would be brief. In a few weeks he would be forgotten and his place in the hearts of his countrymen taken by someone jumping off the Brooklyn Bridge.

But today was today and he accepted the fact that he was at
the moment the most popular man in the United States. What
he said and what he did to prevent a general Indian uprising
would bear on most of the political issues of the decade — transfer, the novel notion of a just Indian policy, Carl Schurz and
reform, the renomination of President Hayes and how far a
new state could go in opposing Federal authority. Schurz had
foreseen Adams's popularity in daring to name a pro-Ute Peace
Commission — Chief Ouray, General Adams, and General
Hatch. The last-named didn't love the Utes exactly, but he was
a fighter for minority rights as a founder in '66 of the pioneer
Negro regiment, the Ninth Cavalry. Adams's popularity prevented Senator Teller from organizing a howl in Congress
against this loading of the dice to favor "red murderers" against
"white settlers and miners," who were gathering at the Reservation border already to take over Ouray's superb kingdom.

On the morning of November 4, Adams stepped from the
Denver-Cheyenne train at Greeley to find out what sort of
"personal treatment" the late captives had received to upset
Inspector Pollock so. He said good-by to Count Dönhoff, his
good companion of many adventures, who was continuing to
Cheyenne, and set out morosely on foot up the slight grade
toward the Meeker home half a mile away, and toward the home
near it where Flora Ellen Price was staying. He had a court
stenographer with him but he discouraged conversation, being
absorbed in the problem of how to ask Methodist gentlewomen
about matters deemed inappropriate even between many hus-
bands and wives.

The problem had burdened his mind for days. His experience of women was limited but he believed that all of them
regarded forced sexual relations as the ultimate disaster with
psychological, social, medical and religious consequences too
horrible to contemplate. His view was sustained by Victorian
literature, the heroines of which always preferred to kill themselves before violation could occur or soon after.

He decided to question Flora Ellen first, on the theory that a teen-age farm girl with two children might have less delicate sensibilities than a city-bred virgin like Josie. But, having found Flora Ellen at home and willing to talk, he had trouble coming to the point. The trouble was increased when Flora Ellen mentioned that a Greeley man had just proposed marriage to her and she had accepted. She added that she was sick of notoriety and would leave soon with her husband-to-be for far-off Ellensburg, Washington, where she had relatives.

Adams marked time, asking Flora Ellen again to name Utes whom she thought might have killed the Agency men. He was testing her to see what kind of witness she would make if by some miracle Carl Schurz should cause a revolution in American jurisprudence and bring the Ute suspects to trial as individuals before an impartial jury, which was their right under the Constitution. Flora Ellen stated that Jane's husband, Pauvitz, killed Meeker. When he asked her to describe Pauvitz, she shook her wide shoulders and said blandly, "Now, Mr. Adams! How could I describe an Indian? You know they all look alike and have no whiskers and nothing but mean looks." The General had to smile, thinking of what a good defense lawyer would do with that remark.

At last, he took the plunge. "Did that Uncompahgre Ute who captured you, that Ahutupuwit — did he treat you well?"

She said calmly, "Not very."

"Did he beat you, or anything of that kind."

"No, Mr. Adams."

"And Johnson — did he treat you well?"

"Tolerably well. But I guess he wouldn't 've if it hadn't been for Susan."

"Is Jane one of his squaws?"

"No, Mr. Adams. Jane is Pauvitz's squaw. And she leads him a chase, I would say."

"Did any of the Utes treat you badly, or strike you?"

Flora Ellen looked thoughtful. She was wearing a red calico

dress and Adams noted, as men at the Agency had noted, the feeble attempt of any dress to hold in all of Flora Ellen. She said, "Well, none of them struck me."

"What did they do?"

"I do not like to say. You know them and can guess."

Adams felt that the ice had been broken. He relaxed and spoke gently, "Mrs. Price. This is an official investigation, and I cannot guess at things. It is your duty to tell me what happened in order that we may know the extent of the crime and try to find out who the guilty parties are."

"It will not be made public in the papers, will it?"

"Certainly not through the Ute Peace Commission which I am representing."

"I would not want — my fiancé to know. Men are funny about some things."

"Your privacy is my first consideration."

Her voice did not tremble. Her expression was serious but not tragic. "Well, this Uncompahgre Ute and Johnson outraged me."

"Johnson! Susan's husband?"

"Yes, sir! Johnson!"

"Did any others outrage your person?"

"And the Uncompahgre Ute. Those two were all."

"Was it by force?"

Flora Ellen said sharply, "Of course!"

"What did the Uncompahgre Ute give you?"

"He gave me Mr. Post's watch the night we rode out from the Agency."

"Was that before or after he had outraged you?"

"That was before."

There was a lull. Adams wanted to ask what her feelings had been at the time of outrage but she gave him no lead. He said, "Did any of the Utes treat you kindly?"

"Yes, sir. Mrs. Johnson treated me very kindly — that is Susan. She wept over my troubles and said she was sorry for what had happened at the Agency. And she did not want them to kill at the Agency. But they would do it."

"Did she know what Johnson had done to you?"

"No, Mr. Adams. If she had, she would probably have killed me."

"Did Johnson threaten you with death?"

"Yes, sir."

"Unless you yielded?"

"Yes, sir."

"How many days was that before Count Dönhoff and I came?"

"The very same day. It was just before you arrived. He came down there in the willows by the stream."

The General had a quick picture of the lovely Plateau Creek setting as he had first seen it bathed in sunlight. "Was Mrs. Meeker down there with you?"

"No, she was up in Johnson's lodge sleeping. She came down a few minutes after."

"Were the outraging and threatening to kill at the same time?"

"Yes, sir."

The General stepped over to his stenographer and read the last few lines. With rising concern he visualized their content in newspaper headlines and he could almost see Colorado's militiamen mobilizing with frenzied fury to invade the Western Slope and to kill every Ute man, woman and child on the Reservation. And he could see the Utes, forced to combine at last in self-defense, raiding and murdering in the unprotected mining camps of the Gunnison and San Juan areas.

He began to wonder if this testimony could be withheld even from Congress for the present. He asked Flora Ellen, "Did you tell anybody else besides Mrs. Meeker about this outraging?"

"I told Josie Meeker and Mr. Pollock."

He gestured to the stenographer to close his notes and began putting on his overcoat. "Is there anything further, Mrs. Price?"

For the first time, Flora Ellen's voice had a strident note. "I only want to have those Utes taken and killed," she said. "And I want to have the privilege of killing Johnson and that Uncompahgr*ee* Ute myself!"

Five minutes later, Adams and his stenographer sat down with Josie Meeker in the Meeker front parlor where coal glowed in the grate. She seemed as composed as Flora Ellen but came close to tears talking of curly-haired Frank Dresser, who had always hated to be alone, and of his lonely death in the old Danforth coal mine after twenty-one hours of suffering. Josie thought that he must have returned to the Agency after dark on September 29 to get his brother Harry's coat and savings of four hundred dollars. She reasoned that the Utes had wounded him next day as he had tried to reach the Milk Creek troops and he had bled to death in the mine.

Then Adams led off, "How long did Persune keep you, Miss Meeker?"

"All the time, sir."

"Has he a squaw?"

"Yes, sir. *Two* squaws. And two children."

"Did he treat you well when you were with him?"

Her large blue eyes looked first at him and then widely around the parlor and she pursed her lips a little. For a plain girl, he thought, Josie had an effect of beauty. She said, "I do not know, Mr. Adams. Of course we were insulted."

"What do you mean by 'insult'? What did it consist of?"

"Of outrageous treatment at night."

"Am I to understand that he outraged you several times at night?"

"Yes, sir."

"Forced you against your will?"

"Yes, sir."

"Did he threaten to kill you if you did not comply?"

Josie's blue eyes turned cloudy with sudden distress. Her soft voice was low. "He did not threaten to kill — Persune did not. On one occasion, I asked him if he wanted to kill me. He said, 'Yes.' I said, 'Get up then and shoot me and let me alone.' He turned over and did not say anything more that night."

Adams calculated. Josie had been Persune's captive for twenty-three nights and he was away for one week. That left sixteen nights which she had spent with him. He asked, "When did Persune do it first?"

"The first night, Monday, September 29. Of course, they were drunk. We dared not refuse them to any great extent. A good many times I pushed him off me and made a fuss and raised a difficulty."

"Was it done while his own squaws were in the tent?"

"Yes, Mr. Adams."

"And they knew about it?"

"Yes, sir."

"Did any other men do the same thing to you?"

"Oh, no, sir. Persune took me as his squaw and of course the rest dared not come around."

Adams nodded his understanding at Josie's acceptance of Ute customs. He recalled doing the same thing when he had lived with Ouray at Los Pinos. He asked, "Have you told this to anybody besides your mother?"

"I told Mr. Pollock, and Dr. Avery in Denver."

"Alida Avery?"

"Yes — the lady physician. She will not tell, and naturally we don't want the papers to get hold of it. But Indians delight in such talk and it was generally discussed around camp and a good many white settlers call in now and then and they will spread it if they can."

"Do you think Ouray knows it?"

"They have probably told him."

"Did they seem to think it was very wrong?"

Adams was astonished to see Josie's lips curve into something like a smile. "No, sir. They thought it was a pretty good thing to have a white squaw. Persune's squaws asked me not to make a fuss about it — that it was pretty good. And Jane said, 'Well, I cannot help it if Persune wants to take you and protect you. He will give you enough to eat and you will not starve. If he wants to protect you, I cannot help it.' I told Jane that I did not think much of Persune's protection."

"Did Douglas ever offer you any insult?"

"Not to me. But he did on one occasion to Mother. I think that made trouble. His squaws were jealous of her and did not want her there."

"Was that why your mother was turned over to Johnson?"

"No, sir. Douglas could not stay with her because he and Jack were busy on Roan Plateau watching the soldiers. Only Johnson and a few others went to Plateau Creek with us away from Douglas's big Grand River camp. Douglas said if the soldiers advanced they were going to kill them and they thought they could. They were preparing to hold their ground. They didn't dare go south beyond our camp because Ouray sent word to them not to come further into the Uncompahgre country."

"Was Persune the only man guilty of outraging you?"

"Yes, sir."

For several minutes Adams sat in silence musing over the contrast between the calm way Josie spoke of her experience and the hysterical way he would have expected her to speak. He wondered what Victorian novelists would make of such a matter-of-fact attitude toward the presumed fate worse than death. But her case was special. Her normal reactions must have been anaesthetized somewhat by the ghastly shock of the massacre, as soldiers often felt nothing when their legs were shot off.

And the horror of being violated many times by a red man may have been softened by her understanding of and sympathy for her Ute friends. Perhaps her feelings were quite different from what they would have been if she had been thrown to the ground and her clothes torn off by some drunken white man in a Greeley back alley. In terms of Ute society nothing very terrible had happened. Adams noted that Persune's squaws had taken a lively interest in what Persune was doing to Josie and had told her that she should be pleased to have him do it.

To them his behavior was in a spirit of innocence and carried no taint of prurience or perversion. They wanted Josie to realize — and it seemed to Adams that she had tried to realize — that she had received a high honor, the bestowal of which bound Persune to very serious responsibilities. By making Josie his squaw, he pledged himself to defend her person to the death thereafter.

At last Adams said, "Thank you, Miss Meeker. Could I talk to your mother now?"

Mrs. Meeker entered the parlor insubstantial as a moth. She greeted Adams and sat down apathetically before him. But her concern was acute as he described his visit to the graves of the massacre victims who had been buried by Colonel Merritt's soldiers where they fell. Her relief was great when he explained that the bodies were preserved well. The body of her husband could be disinterred and moved to Greeley whenever she was ready to receive it. He proceeded then to the questioning. Like the others, Mrs. Meeker admitted that she had seen no killings but believed that Pauvitz or Antelope had killed Meeker. Adams asked, "As to the outrages, what of them?"

She displayed no alarm, answering the blunt query with the toneless ease of one discussing the weather for want of a better subject. "It was made known to me that if I did not submit I would be killed. And after I gave up nothing was said about it. Douglas I had connection with once and no more."

"He forced you to submit."

"Yes, sir. His squaw was gone that night."

"Where was his squaw?"

"She was with his son. Douglas called her his 'old squaw.' His young squaw was in the tent and whether she knew of it I do not know. The Ute men talked about things until midnight. After they went away, Douglas came to my bed."

"Was he drunk then?"

"No, sir."

"Had you been notified that you would have to submit?"

"He himself had not but his children said I had to be Ute squaw that night and used indecent language. I expect Douglas wanted everything ready for him. I was made to understand that I was to submit when he came. He made up my bed and told me where to sleep and as soon as the men went away he came there. One great advantage in it was that he was protection for me from the other Indians. More than a dozen asked me to sit down in their tents and I said I was Douglas's squaw and that kept them from me."

"When you went with Johnson that last week, was he kind?"

A flicker of interest crossed Mrs. Meeker's pale face. "Oh, yes! Johnson would say, 'Come, mother. You sit in Johnson's tent. Johnson will take good care of you.' As for dear Susan — why, Mr. Adams, you should have seen Susan and Mrs. Price together! You would never have known Flora Ellen was a captive. The two of them would talk and laugh all day!"

"How did Johnson get Mrs. Price away from those who had her first?"

Mrs. Meeker was just like any gossipy woman now.

"That was an interesting thing. He simply took her away. He didn't have to ask permission. Johnson is a pretty rich Indian. He and Ouray — his brother-in-law, you know — the two of them work together in the horse business. Uriah Curtis told me they are the best pair of horse traders in the mountains. But I meant to tell you about Josephine. When she was captured, Douglas took a notion to take her from Persune, who isn't a chief or anything — not even a captain. Josephine did not know but what they would have a duel. Well, sir, Persune didn't budge an inch and pretty soon Douglas put up his gun and backed off."

IN EARLY EVENING, General Adams returned to Denver, called at once on Governor Pitkin at his home and prepared a telegram to Secretary Schurz while the Governor read the women's Greeley testimony. When Pitkin had finished reading, Adams proceeded without preamble to ask his cooperation in suppressing the contents for the present. He said that he recognized its great propaganda value to Pitkin politically. The Governor could make very effective use of it to incriminate Ouray's Uncompahgre Utes as well as the White River bands, because Mrs. Price charged the Uncompahgre, Ahutupuwit, with outrage. And soon thereafter he could force extinguishment of title to their Reservation and offer most of the Western Slope to the impatient hordes of homesteaders and miners waiting at the Ute border. By this achievement, he could gain a strong claim to Henry Teller's Senate seat in 1882.

Adams declared that no sensible politician would put up with the headaches and picayune salary of the Governorship unless he expected to become a United States Senator in time. But, he said, Pitkin was not primarily a politician. He was a gentleman first. As such, he could not, Senate seat or no Senate seat, make political hay out of the release of news which would cause infinite embarrassment and still more anguish to three destitute and sorrowing women. Besides, release of the shocking news would wreck all efforts to bring the handful of guilty Utes to punishment and to solve the Ute crisis peacefully. And the terrible disclosure that outrage had been committed even on the body of Mrs. Meeker, a distinguished old lady sixty-four years old, was sure to cause a protracted and bloody war which would destroy not only all the Utes but hundreds of whites.

When Adams finished, the tall and fragile Governor asked a single question: "If I cooperate, will the Secretary of the Interior cooperate in turn with me?"

The General took from his pocket a telegram which he had received the day before from Carl Schurz. He read one sentence: "I leave to your judgment to inform Governor Pitkin confidentially that a settlement of the Ute question in accordance with interests of the people of Colorado is earnestly intended."

Pitkin smiled his approval. The two men shook hands as the Governor agreed cordially to accept equal responsibility with Adams and Schurz for the temporary suppression of an official United States government document.

It was almost midnight when Adams left Pitkin's home and filed a telegram at Western Union:

DENVER, COLORADO
NOVEMBER 4, 1879

HONORABLE CARL SCHURZ
SECRETARY, WASHINGTON, D. C.

THE EXAMINATION UNDER OATH OF THE LATE CAPTIVES DIS-CLOSES SUCH BRUTAL AND BARBAROUS TREATMENT OF THEM IN WHICH CHIEFS DOUGLAS AND JOHNSON ARE IMPLICATED AND WHICH HAS BEEN UNKNOWN AND UNEXPECTED TO ME AS I ALSO BELIEVE TO OURAY THAT I FEAR NOW WITH LIVING WIT-NESSES AGAINST THEM THAT PERHAPS THEY WILL NOT OBEY OURAY'S ORDERS AND TROOPS WILL PROBABLY HAVE TO BE USED AGAINST THEM. STILL IN ORDER TO CARRY OUT OUR AR-RANGEMENT I SHALL GO BACK TO LOS PINOS AS IF NOTHING FURTHER HAD TRANSPIRED. SHALL NOTIFY OURAY AND LOOK THE SITUATION OVER. THE CAVALRY AT FORT GARLAND SHOULD MOVE TO INDIAN CREEK EITHER VIA SAGUACHE OR LAKE CITY WHERE THEY CAN BE STOPPED IF NECESSARY AFTER CONSUL-TATION WITH OURAY: BUT I NOW CONSIDER IT MORE PROB-ABLE THAT THEY WILL HAVE TO BE USED WHILE, BEFORE THIS GREELEY VISIT, I FELT OTHERWISE. I HAVE HEARD FROM GEN-ERAL HATCH, AND ANYTHING TO ME TOMORROW WILL BE FORWARDED TO ME AT LOS PINOS FROM HERE.

CHARLES ADAMS
SPECIAL AGENT

He returned to his room at the Alvord House and did some packing for the long trip back to Los Pinos Agency. There, a

week hence, the three-man Ute Peace Commission would begin
to take testimony from all Utes who would talk about the White
River affair. He went to bed soon but sleep came slowly. He
made himself deeply unhappy by revisiting in his mind the
breathlessly beautiful vales and ridges, the soaring peaks and
heavenly streams of the Ute country where he had known such
joy while hunting with Ouray, Sowerwick and the rest. He did
not see how these men could stand to exist anywhere else on
earth. And yet somewhere else was where they and their wives
and children and grandchildren were going to have to live in
the near future.

He was depressed still in the morning and his sad spirit sank
lower as he read the last lines of a corroborative telegram from
Secretary Schurz:

> I NEED SCARCELY IMPRESS UPON YOU THE GREAT IMPOR-
> TANCE TO THE COUNTRY ON THE SUCCESS OF YOUR MISSION.
> YOUR COURAGE AND JUDGMENT HAVE SO FAR WON SUCH AP-
> PLAUSE THROUGHOUT THE COUNTRY THAT A FAILURE OF
> PEACEABLE SETTLEMENT NOW WOULD BE A GREAT DISAP-
> POINTMENT AS WELL AS DISASTER. YOU MUST NOT FAIL. I
> EXPRESS MY OPINION FRANKLY. DO THE SAME.
>
> C. SCHURZ, SECRETARY

"The success of your mission." That was the phrase Adams
hated. Just before boarding the Alamosa train, he wired Schurz
glumly:

> YOUR DISPATCH RECEIVED. ALL RIGHT. WILL DO THE BEST
> I CAN AND STILL HOPE TO BE SUCCESSFUL. MY OWN LIFE IS
> NOTHING IF WAR CAN BE AVERTED FROM COLORADO.

"I hope to be successful." And what was he hoping to be
successful about? To rob his friends of all they possessed while
claiming to them and to the world that such robbery was the
very best thing that could happen.

The cloudy day fitted his dark mood. As the train entered

Castle Rock he glanced west out the car window to look at the jagged contour of Devil's Head. But a descending cloud almost obscured it. The cloud, Charles Adams thought, was like the curtain which was descending on Chief Ouray and the Ute Nation.

CHAPTER XXVI

Knothole Commission

AMONG THE COUNTLESS commissions which have struggled with snarls in American history, the Ute Peace Commission of 1879 was unique. The hearings — boring, futile and confused — occurred at the tumbledown Los Pinos Agency one hundred miles from the new telegraph office at Lake City. The Commission's council room and guardroom were improvised in a smelly stable of cottonwood logs. A single potbellied stove warmed the rooms in spots, and the most solemn deliberations were apt to be interrupted by the hysterical scramblings of a hayloft of chipmunks. Fifty yards away, teetering at an angle, was the official privy with most of the shingles missing. On its door, George Sherman had posted an inviting notice: WATCH OUT FOR SNAKES!

The Commission's three members — General Hatch, Adams and Ouray — faced worse dangers than snakes in their privy. Ouray expected assassination because he was Ute chief as well as Commission member and would have to compel surrender of whatever Indians might be finally charged with crime. The Commission's further duty was to convince three fourths of the Colorado Utes that the best thing for them was to consolidate the White River bands with the Uintah Utes in Utah and to settle the Uncompahgre Utes on farm plots along the Uncompahgre and Gunnison Rivers. The splendid reward for this virtual liquidation of their ten-million-acre Reservation would be the government's prompt payment of some one hundred and forty thousand dollars owed them under old treaties, plus the still-unpaid ten thousand dollars which they had been promised for Uncompahgre Park.

The commissioners were almost defenseless if some Utes should start a brawl in protest against being liquidated. When the Peace Commission sat first, on November 12, only twenty-five white men were there at Los Pinos. Hatch had an escort of fourteen soldiers. Lieutenant Gustavus Valois of the Ninth Cavalry was recorder and George Sherman was clerk. Adams picked Uncle Lafe Head, now Lieutenant Governor of Colorado, as interpreter, but Head's pepperish *señora* refused to approve such a perilous junket and Hatch hired a Santa Fe man, John Townsend, instead. Four reporters covered the hearings, including W. F. Saunders of the *Denver Tribune* and the fulminating pundit, Dave Day, editor of the new Ouray weekly, the *Solid Muldoon*. Agent Wilson Stanley and Joe Brady completed the white roster.

Adams had arranged an Indian police of fifty under Sapovanero, Shavano and, of all people, Piah, who had been an eminently respectable Uncompahgre ever since his alleged murder of Old Man Elliott and Joe McLane in '78. Lieutenant Valois's minutes showed that the Commission sat forty-one times between November 12, 1879, and January 7, 1880, but all three commissioners were present at only twenty meetings and testimony was taken at fifteen. Ouray was often too ill to attend. He rode to some of the meetings from his farm in his Germantown carriage and had to be helped to his place in the shabby council room.

General Adams bore with patience the weeks of a tedium accentuated by the withered melancholy of the dying year. He found some diversion in minor incidents. During the first meeting, Louis McLane arrived all the way from far-off Cheyenne Wells to demand that the Commission hang Piah at once for killing his brother Joe in '78 out on the Colorado Plains. Hatch remarked that Piah's alleged sins were not on the agenda, thank God. Then Piah's Indian police surrounded McLane, just as the Ouray stage pulled up. It continued south with an unexpected fare.

From the start, Adams feuded with Agent Stanley, an Illinois farmer and "Indian expert" of four months' standing who resented not being on the Commission, and expressed it by trying to influence Ouray against the other two commissioners. Stanley accepted from Ouray Lieutenant Silas Wolf's watch, which the runner Cojoe had picked up at Milk Creek (it was Wolf's 1878 West Point graduation present from his mother). Ouray gave him also the twenty-six dollars in bills and the four dollars in silver which Arvilla Meeker had given to Douglas. Adams told Stanley to stop meddling in Commission business. Thereupon, Stanley went on a long drunk which Reporter Saunders, desperate for news, wrote up in detail for the *Denver Tribune*. When Stanley read the piece, he ordered Saunders to leave Los Pinos. But before Saunders could pack, Secretary Schurz wired Stanley to retire to his Illinois farm.

The relations of the commissioners with the Los Pinos press corps were not cordial, partly because of the news-killing policy of closed hearings and partly because the Commission had no funds to set up bar service. Dave Day of the *Solid Muldoon* expressed the general bitterness:

> This standing for hours in two feet of snow outside the council room with one ear over a knothole is too much for the constitution. *P. S.* The supply of liquid refreshment is failing and want is staring us in the face.

Day's December 25 story read:

DAISY DEAN'S CHRISTMAS REPORT
Christmas morning!
Nothing of a startling nature is happening.
Neither Utes nor eggnogs are in sight. No elixir of life closer than Ouray's house.
Life's a Burden!
Discharge me or send relief!
Ouray honored us with a call and, after a confidential buzz

with General Hatch, came over to the reporters' quarters, which was originally a hen house, and made himself quite agreeable. Ouray and his illustrious colleague, General Hatch, seem to take pride in referring to the d——d reporters and to blame them equally with the Mormons for the stubbornness of the Indians.

                                                              DAY

The closed meetings were held usually in the mornings. Ouray translated Ute into Spanish and Interpreter Townsend translated Ouray's Spanish into English. Twenty Utes gave testimony, including half a dozen who just wanted to hear themselves talk. Nobody pretended to tell the truth about the massacre or its aftermath. Johnson said that he had done only what his wife Susan had told him to do. Douglas said he had been busy taking care of his boy Freddie who had shot himself in the foot. But he had kindly accepted custody of Mrs. Meeker when he had found her "wandering around loose." Douglas, Johnson, Sowerwick and Yanko collaborated in concocting an elaborate fairy tale about Johnson's late brother Jata — the one Frank Dresser shot. Jata, they said, had rushed about killing Meeker and practically everyone else, including the freighters, Carl Goldstein and Julius Moore. But plausible reports of the Milk Creek affair were given by Jack, Colorow and Joe Brady. After hearing them, the three commissioners agreed that the shooting there began by chance and no Ute could be blamed for the death of Major Thornburgh or any of his soldiers.

Adams got some pleasure from knowing that each passing day made war less likely as deep snow closed the Western Slope passes. What he could not bear was the pitiful disintegration of his friend Ouray, paralleling the break-up of the Ute Nation. With infinite sadness, Adams watched the twilight of a great career which had begun in the Year of Shooting Stars only forty-six years ago. Adams recalled how Ouray had mastered the fetishes of three civilizations, achieved unexcelled physical prowess and matched wits with the finest white minds — per-

ceptive Kit Carson, scholarly John Evans, slick Edward Mc-
Cook, saintly Felix Brunot, brilliant Carl Schurz, driving Henry
Teller, cultured Frederick Pitkin. Though his vast Reservation blocked the westering path of fifty million whites, he had
resisted for twenty years the most powerful pressures of expansion ever seen on earth.

Now Ouray's splendid body was crumbling with nephritis
just as the autonomy of his people was crumbling. One day he
confessed to Adams that the root of the Ute tragedy could not
be placed on any such simple thing as the insatiable greed of
land-hungry whites helped by their political servants, Teller
and Pitkin. He had warned his Utes long ago what would happen to them — what happened to all human beings who closed
their eyes to change and clung foolishly to ways of life made
invalid and impractical by the shifting tides of the world's life
force. They had ignored his plan to adjust their hunting economy to fit that of the whites and now they would be forced to
adjust it on white terms. All Ouray could do with his last bit
of strength was to try to soften the terms.

The hearings creaked on toward a dull and frustrated climax
which was caused by Adams's decision to produce the women's
testimony, including the suppressed passages. Ouray reacted
by informing Adams that their friendship was over and by attending sessions thereafter in full Ute buckskin and beads instead of his usual frock coat. Also, he sent a message to Secretary
Schurz stating that he had lost faith in the Commission and asking permission to bring a Ute delegation to Washington to settle
all problems.

From the women's testimony, General Hatch and Adams drew
up a list of twelve Utes who were to surrender to the Commission for trial for unspecified crimes before an unspecified court
at an unspecified time and place. Ouray voted against the list
on the grounds that you couldn't believe what women said,
particularly a teen-aged woman like Flora Ellen who thought all
Indians "looked alike with no whiskers and nothing but mean

looks." But Ouray was outvoted and the list stood. The twelve suspects — and their approximate sins — were:

CHIEF DOUGLAS: Mrs. Meeker claimed that Douglas "had connection" with her once by force. Even Ouray favored trying Douglas for something.

JOHNSON: Flora Ellen said that Johnson outraged her once in the willows near Plateau Creek on October 21.

PERSUNE: Josie said that Persune outraged her often, starting September 29 (by implication at least once a night during sixteen nights).

AHUTUPUWIT (an Uncompahgre): Flora Ellen said that a very small Ute outraged her once on September 29. Colorow testified that the very small Ute's name was Ahutupuwit.

ANTELOPE: All three women thought that maybe Antelope killed Nathan Meeker, or perhaps he killed Wilmer Eskridge, or both.

PAUVITZ: All three women thought that maybe Pauvitz killed Nathan Meeker, provided, of course, Antelope didn't kill him. At the Grand Mesa camp near Plateau Creek Johnson told Mrs. Meeker that he wouldn't put his lodge near the lodge of Pauvitz and Jane because he thought Pauvitz might have killed Nathan Meeker.

EBENEZER: Flora Ellen thought that probably Ebenezer killed Wilmer Eskridge, provided, of course, Antelope didn't kill him.

TIM JOHNSON: Flora Ellen said that the teen-aged Tim Johnson boasted to her that he had killed William Post.

JOHNNY (Douglas's son-in-law): Flora Ellen said that Johnny was at the Agency on the afternoon of September 29.

SERIO: Josie said that Serio was there that afternoon.

CREEPS: Mrs. Meeker almost forgot to mention seeing Creeps there that afternoon.

THOMAS (a Uintah): All three women thought that Thomas was there that afternoon. Hatch and Adams opined that if he was there he was probably promoting something for the Mormons.

The climax of the hearings came at noon on December 6 as a cold wind swirled snowflakes about the dejected Agency buildings. Jack, Colorow, Shavano, Sapovanero and ten other Utes arrived from Ouray's farm and shambled into the council room where General Hatch and Charles Adams sat in uneasy silence. Ouray sat apart from them, his brown face bloated from Bright's disease and every breath an effort. Irritably, almost shame-facedly, Hatch read the names on the accused list and demanded that the twelve men surrender.

Ouray asked, "How do we know that these Indians did any-thing wrong? We can't rely on what those women said."

Hatch retorted, "What else can we depend on? We've heard the testimony of twenty Utes and not one of them told the truth."

A short flurry of general talk followed. Then Adams rose and embarked on a long speech. He spoke sadly but with kindness, like a Dutch uncle, recalling his years at the two Ute Agencies and his friendships with Ouray and Sowerwick, and his efforts to help the Utes achieve what no Indians had ever achieved — white man's status. Carefully he summarized the White River disaster, his rescue mission, his messages to Carl Schurz, his trip to halt Colonel Merritt and what he had done since to see that the Utes got the benefit of every doubt. Then his manner changed. Anger came into his voice and his German accent be-came pronounced. "We don't want," he said, "to punish Jack or Colorow or any of the Indians at Milk Creek. That was a fair fight. But the cowards who killed their white friends at the Agency and outraged the women who had been good to them — these men we want and will have. I'll say no more. I am done." He strode from the room quickly.

General Hatch stood up. He looked tired and vexed. "For the last time," he said, "will you deliver up these twelve?"

A chair scraped — Colorow's. Very deliberately the huge-stomached old biscuit-eater, known to every ranch housewife from one end of Colorado to the other, lit his long pipe. Each Ute in the council room including Ouray drew his knife and laid it on his knee. From upstairs came the sound of a brief chipmunk riot. Hatch stared fascinated as Colorow's pipe moved from Ute to Ute and returned to its owner, who puffed dramatically. Suddenly, Colorow grasped his knife and twirled it to the floor where the point stuck quivering.

A weak grin spread over Hatch's pale face. The Utes, he was thinking, had not crossed their knives. Colorow had not smashed his pipe. The knife in the floor was a gesture of conciliation.

Ouray was speaking, "We cannot deliver up these twelve men unless they are to be tried in Washington. They could not get a fair trial in Colorado. And we will need time to bring them in."

Hatch pondered a moment and gave his approval. As the chiefs began to walk out, he sat down to compose a telegram for Secretary Schurz.

The days of waiting to hear from Schurz were the dreariest of all. The Los Pinos press corps disbanded. Dave Day ended his long drought in the cozy confines of a Ouray saloon. Interpreter Townsend was discharged. General Hatch and Lieutenant Valois gave their cabin a warm muslin lining in case they had to stay on at Los Pinos for weeks while Jack and Colorow were out gathering the twelve suspects for Ouray. Charles Adams dreamed of his wife Margaret and of her cooking at Manitou. He packed his things, including a beautiful Navajo blanket which Chipeta had presented to him.

On December 11, a wire came from Schurz reporting that President Hayes and his cabinet had just approved holding the trial of the twelve Utes outside of Colorado. Next day, further instructions arrived:

DECEMBER 9, 1879
WASHINGTON, D. C.

GENERAL HATCH
UTE PEACE COMMISSION
LOS PINOS AGENCY, VIA LAKE CITY, COLO.

RECEIVE THE SURRENDER OF THE INDIANS DESIGNATED BY YOUR COMMISSION WITH THE UNDERSTANDING THAT THEY

WILL BE GUARANTEED A FAIR TRIAL. OURAY WILL BE RECEIVED
HERE WITH FOUR OR FIVE UNCOMPAHGRE UTES, THREE SOUTH-
ERN UTES AND THREE WHITE RIVER UTES. TAKE GOOD CARE
THAT GOOD AND INFLUENTIAL MEN BE SELECTED, ESPECIALLY
FROM THE WHITE RIVER UTES. IT WILL PROBABLY BE DESIR-
ABLE TO HAVE JACK HERE. TAKE POSSESSION OF THE PRISONERS
WITH A MILITARY GUARD AND CONVEY THEM IN THE FIRST
PLACE TO FORT LEAVENWORTH.

CARL SCHURZ, SECRETARY

ONE WEEK LATER Charles Adams, massive and benign, attended
a reception in his honor given by the citizens of Manitou at the
residence of their leading druggist, Dr. Isaac Davis. To the
Gazette reporter, the General "looked the picture of health."
He had had three days of rest and good food at home after a
rough trip from Los Pinos and he had regained some of the
forty pounds he had lost during his epic travels in the wilderness with Count Dönhoff. His spirits were improved, too. It
seemed to him that public opinion against the Utes was sub-
siding. He even heard it said here and there that Douglas and
Johnson deserved some credit for treating their women captives
well.

The big reception was cheering. Adams was modest in his
slightly pompous way during the address of the Reverend
Westervelt, who eulogized him for his wisdom and tact in res-
cuing the captives and averting war. The applause was deafen-
ing when two babies, a boy and a girl, were trundled in by their
proud parents and named Charles Adams Davis and Margaret
Adams Davis. Then came the high point of the evening — the
rendition of a poem composed by a Manitou lady, "F. C. S.,"
who was too shy to recite her creation herself. She entrusted the
task to a visiting Mr. Hooke of Evanston, Indiana, where he was
well known for the sonorous presentation of heroic verse. Mr.
Hooke proceeded with gusto and suppressed emotion:

IMPROMPTU LINES

The tocsin sounded fierce and wild
Throughout the breadth of land,
And blood ran chilled as father, child,
Thought of that Indian band

Who with their hands yet wet in gore
Drop't every aim but brute,
And now defenceless women tore
From home and love—the Ute!

"To the rescue!" cried each heart,
From West to East and back,
While vale and hill and busy mart
Forgot all but *"the rack."*

"Give, give us aid!" — O! Who will go?
Within those jaws of hell!
And bring the loved ones from the foe —
Untutored savage fell!

He must have courage, wisdom, tact,
Be fearless, bold and brave:
With trust in God's strong arm no lack,
From Indian's grasp to save.

"He's found!" cried Schurz at Washington,
"He's bold, he's brave and true!"
"He'll go, he'll rescue — save — 'tis done!"
He was found at Manitou!

Let history's record mark this page,
And romance deck with gold,
That strife was quelled, by wisdom sage,
Forgetting deeds of old.

Now welcome back, our hero home;
Deep in our hearts enshrine;
He's fought the faith of *"peace* to come" —
Good will to all mankind.

Next afternoon Adams read with pleasure the *Gazette's* glowing report of the Manitou reception. But two items in the *Denver Tribune* filled him with dismay.

The first item alluded to "The Star List" of twelve Utes accused at Los Pinos and hinted that Douglas and Persune had been charged by the women with unmentionable acts but that their testimony had been suppressed to protect the Schurz crowd. Adams wondered if Reporter Saunders was coming out at last with things he had eavesdropped through Dave Day's council room knothole.

The second *Tribune* item was a paean of praise for a fanatically anti-Ute, anti-Schurz and anti-Adams lecture which Rozene Meeker gave on December 13 in Washington, D. C.

CHAPTER XXVII Arvilla's Letter

ROZENE'S LECTURES (she called herself "Rose" professionally) were part of the heart-rending battle within the Meeker family which began when the late captives arrived back in Greeley. On one side were the gentle forces of reason and compassion — Ralph, Josie and Mary Meeker and Mary's fiancé, Win Fullerton. Against them was the much stronger force — the bitter, nihilistic personality of Rozene. The objective was conquest of the weak mind and body of Arvilla Meeker, but the issue surpassed family lines. Its outcome would determine once and forever the stark fate of Chief Ouray and the Ute Nation.

The fight revolved around the state of family finances. The Meekers were penniless again. Ralph and Josie pinned their faith for relief on Secretary Schurz, who was promising Josie a stenographer's job in the Interior Department and was arranging payment of her Agency salary from June through September, 1879. Schurz assured Ralph also, through his private secretary, Bob Mitchell, that the women would receive in time modest annuities to be paid out of Ute tribal funds.

It was easy for Rozene to demolish such a sentimental stand. She told her mother that Ralph and Josie were truckling to Schurz for their own selfish ends. Meanwhile, they were wrecking Arvilla's health and breaking her heart by inferring that the Utes had been driven to their awful crimes by the viciousness of her beloved husband, Nathan Cook Meeker. Rozene urged Arvilla not to be deterred by Josie's alleged delicate sensibilities. She ought to tell the world exactly what kind of relations she and Josie and Flora Ellen were forced to have with Douglas,

Persune and Johnson. Then, Rozene argued, the enraged Colorado populace would rise and exterminate the Utes and the American people would demand that Congress award the ravished women the greater part of Ute tribal funds of more than a million dollars.

Poor Arvilla loved all her children deeply. She strove to keep an open mind but she had to admit that Rozene had a case. Why should the sick and aging widow of one of the very greatest men in the West be forced to live on the charity of her children? She began to agree with Rozene that Josie and Mary showed no regard for her needs when they spent their time collecting money and clothes for Flora Ellen, who was secretly engaged already — and her late husband hardly cold in his White River grave. As Rozene pointed out, more practical people were capitalizing on her reticence. Mrs. Dresser, for instance, was seeking help from Senator Teller to get huge compensation for the death of her boys, Harry and Frank. Mrs. Dresser! A well-to-do woman with an able husband and three grown children!

The Ralph *vs* Rozene conflict came to a head in mid-November. While Josie was in the middle of her modest lecture tour of Greeley, Denver, Leadville and Cheyenne, Rozene announced triumphantly her own six-month lecture series, to be managed by William Arlington, the well-known promoter. Arlington himself reported for the *Denver Tribune* Rozene's first Greeley lecture, describing her as a "bright, interesting brunette endowed with many of the womanly graces." The lecture was temperate but Ralph knew that Rozene would use heavier guns when she talked away from home. At one point she said:

> I believe that the Utes should not be allowed to interfere with white men's rights — men who work, found schools and manufactures and help in civilization in general; and my views are very much the same as those of Governor Pitkin, the miners and other people of Colorado. In this respect I am more radical than some members of my family. My letter criti-

cizing the Government for allowing my father to be killed, and which was first published in the *Denver Tribune,* has been more widely copied I believe than perhaps anything which has been written on the subject of the massacre and by that letter I stand today.

Washington news stories about the lecture caused pain in the Interior Department. Since Rozene did not make it clear (then or later) which of Nathan Meeker's daughters had been the heroine of the captivity, Indian Commissioner Hayt confused her with Josie and wired complaint of her remarks to Ralph who wired back: YOUR REPORT THAT JOSEPHINE'S SPEECH ABUSED GOVERNMENT ENTIRELY UNTRUE. IT IS ROSE MEEKER WHO CRITI-CIZES SEVERELY. He wrote also a signed *Greeley Tribune* editorial disputing Rozene's charges that Schurz had been dilatory:

> The Indian Department and Mr. Schurz asked the War Department for troops on the very day that Mr. Meeker's request came announcing danger. Even the messengers in the Department say that Assistant Secretary Bell, in Mr. Schurz's absence, was in great alarm and said he should spare no effort to save the Agency people. Mr. Schurz was prompt in sending General Adams to the front and his action shows he has heart and sympathy.

On Thanksgiving Day, the Meeker family got into a sad squabble about the Utes which caused Ralph and Josie to decide that the Plum and Monroe Street home was too small for them and for Rozene too. After dinner, Ralph telegraphed Bob Mitchell at Washington to rent a room for Josie in Mrs. Goodall's boardinghouse and to expect her for work in Schurz's office in ten days. Ralph sent a second wire to his old friend, Dan Frohman, the big theater man, accepting his standing offer to put Ralph in as his road company manager at the fine salary of seventy-five dollars a week. Before this current family money crisis, Ralph had preferred to be a newspaperman and work for less.

In sending the wires, Ralph realized that he was about to leave Colorado and the shattering unhappiness of recent weeks.

That made him think with great yearning of his own pleasant life, and of his own Carmelita back in Greenwich Village. As his father and mother had always done before him, he was moved to express his surging emotion in verse. He wrote for Carmelita:

A Thanksgiving Song

Thanksgiving for you, dear, is sweet thanksgiving
For what you were in all the past to me,
For what you are, a joy that's sweetness living,
For what you are to me.

Thanksgiving for your eyes, the kind, the splendid,
Dear eyes whose light the whole wide world would miss,
Your voice, in which all melodies are blended,
Thanksgiving for your kiss.

After Ralph and Josie had left Greeley, Rozene's lectures became much more virulent and she extended her opinions by giving frequent interviews and by sending letters to editors. Her *Denver Tribune* letter of December 17 indicated that she had rewritten some of Ralph's Sioux fraud articles of 1875–1876 for her own use:

Now, we Colorado people are getting somewhat tired of this farce, and we invite the miners, the "cow-boys" and all other good people to see to it that these Indians never leave Colorado soil alive, by simply putting a rope necktie around the neck of each, which is to fit close and snug, thereby relieving these murderers and their friends at Washington of all further anxiety.

Secretary Schurz, etc., form a corrupt ring more powerful than the Army, Congress or even the President. It has captured the Eastern press and pulpit, thence distilling vicious poison through the minds of the people. This Indian Ring favors the Indians because of the thousands of dollars they wring out of them daily. The time has come when Colorado must protect itself against Indians as well as the Indian Bureau. The latter for cruelty, dishonesty and failure has never been equalled since sin took its abode with man.

ROSE MEEKER

Ralph read that *Denver Tribune* letter in the New York exchanges and struggled for hours trying to write an explanation of it to Bob Mitchell in Schurz's office. Soon after, he came across the same *Denver Tribune* broad hint of outrage and cover-up to protect Schurz that had dismayed Charles Adams at Manitou. Meanwhile, letters from his mother showed that Rozene was rapidly winning Arvilla over to her point of view. At Christmas time, Arvilla wrote Ralph suggesting that she would gain nothing for herself unless she exposed Schurz's suppression of the truth and announced publicly what the Utes had done to their captives, so that they would get the punishment they deserved.

Her letter continued:

I expected General Adams would bring in this important evidence against the guilty Indians. As I understand it, it was suppressed by the Interior Department to shield the Indians. I for one wanted nothing suppressed that would help clear these guilty fiends. You have yourself said things in their behalf that you ought not to have said, seeing they killed your father and did violence to your mother and sister. People in Denver and in Greeley were so horrified and taken aback by your remarks that they nearly lost all sympathy for us. . . . We have $10 left of the $35 you gave me before you went away. I will get at the cost of living as soon as I can. I shall keep an account of everything. Still gaining slowly. Your faithful mother,

MRS. N. C. MEEKER

Rozene's final victory over Ralph and Josie came on December 31, 1879, when the *Colorado Chieftain* of Pueblo published a letter in response to the newspaper's direct query. It read:

GREELEY, COLORADO
Dec. 30, 1879.

TO THE EDITOR OF THE *Colorado Chieftain*:
DEAR SIR:
I arise from a sick-bed to state a few facts which you and the people of Colorado demand. We three captives of the Utes — Mrs. Price, myself and daughter — were all interviewed sepa-

rately, being put under oath by the officers of the government
to tell the whole truth of our treatment by the Indians, and
if they outraged our persons, and each one of us gave in our
testimony an answer in the affirmative against the Indians.

I gave in my testimony for the use of the Government to do
with it just as they should see fit. There was nothing said about
its being suppressed on either side. I just simply gave my testimony to the Government officers innocently supposing that
they knew their duty and would do it. I also thought I had
done all that belonged to me to do by telling these officers
the sickening and most humiliating misfortune that can befall
a woman, and if they and the Interior Department have not
done their duty by the people of Colorado, it is they who are
to blame, and not me.

On arriving home in Greeley, I have found myself completely broken down in mind and body, and have had a long
spell of severe sickness from which I am just recovering.

Yours truly,

MRS. N. C. MEEKER

For all its mild tone and colorless presentation, Arvilla's letter
rocked the nation. The worst suspicions of Coloradans were
now confirmed. The letter gave the people of the state the signal
to go ahead in righteousness and do what they had been itching
to do for a long time. The Utes Must Go! In addition to a flood
of editorials demanding removal, there were these other reactions:

At Greeley, Rozene Meeker signed a contract for a long series
of additional lectures in Methodist and Presbyterian churches
throughout the Middle West.

At Los Pinos, General Hatch, expecting to receive at any moment the twelve accused Utes for trial outside of Colorado,
learned that most of them had suddenly disappeared.

At Washington, Henry M. Teller saw his chance and began
work on his Senate castigation of Secretary Schurz, entitled, "A
Solution to the Indian Problem in One Easy Lesson."

CHAPTER XXVIII Sunset

THE FIRST SECTION of the Ute delegation — Ouray, Shavano, Jack, Sowerwick and five others — reached Washington on January 11, 1880, after changing trains at Pueblo where a hoodlum mob tossed coal at the Santa Fe car windows and chanted "Hang the red devils!" Otto Mears was with the Utes, and William H. Berry, the new Los Pinos Agent. At the Washington depot, nobody tossed any coal, though a few people glowered. A ripple of cheers greeted the dimpling Chipeta in her beautiful doeskin dress. The Washington press already had decided to make a heroine of Chipeta, implying that she was the power behind Ouray's throne and telling a pretty tale that Ouray had refused to come East until President Hayes invited "Queen" Chipeta too.

The well-guarded guests were installed in the Tremont House. The owner, F. P. Hill, had a floor reserved for them at a dollar-fifty per day per Ute, including meals, and with a fireplace in each room. Magnanimously, Hill threw in free use of the bathroom. Charles Adams joined them soon and so did the four-man Southern Ute group headed by Chief Ignacio and his young lieutenant, Buckskin Charlie. Once more those old Washington hands, Ouray, Sowerwick and Jack, endured the trite routine of marveling with white men over their wonderful accomplishments. They went to the United States Mint and sat boredly holding a million dollars in fifty-dollar bills while ecstatic Treasury officials looked on. Somehow the different groups on Ute escort duty got their schedules crossed. The listless Indians were carted off four times to George Washington's

Mount Vernon, where Ouray, thinking of another great American, Governor Pitkin, caused a stir by asking: "Did George Washington ever want to be a Senator?"

Ouray spent some time with doctors, who told him that he had better get done whatever he wanted to do. And he talked at length with Secretary Schurz. Between them they worked up an agreement for Senate and tribal ratification.

The agreement proposed moving the White River Utes to the southern part of the Uintah Reservation in Utah; moving the Southern Utes thirty miles west from their lands below Pagosa Springs, and cutting their acreage by a third; and putting the Uncompahgre Utes on agricultural lands around the Grand River-Gunnison River junction, if enough land could be found there.

This was one of the most remarkable documents in the whole history of American Indian policy. It reflected a decade of revolutionary thinking by Carl Schurz on how to start merging the ways of the red man with those of the white. It represented the similar conclusions of Ouray, whose mind was as acute as Schurz's on general matters and much more acute on Ute psychology.[1] The terms of the agreement were designed to destroy the anachronistic tribal setup, because each of the proposed three new Ute Reservations would be owned by the bands concerned instead of by the whole tribe. Even band ownership of a Reservation need not be permanent, because any Ute could be allotted in his own name a homestead-sized farm within his reservation and the band could sell the unallotted surplus of reservation land, the proceeds to be added to the government's principal fund for that band. The provision for individual allotments was called "lands in severalty," a plan which had been tried before, but never on such a scale.

Most of the Ute delegation approved the Schurz-Ouray agreement, including the payment of annuities to ten relatives of the white men killed at the Agency. But Congress would not consider ratifying it until at least some of the twelve accused Utes surrendered themselves for trial. Therefore, early in February, General Adams, Sowerwick and Jack journeyed all the way back to Los Pinos and picked up Douglas, the Uintah Ute Thomas and the boy Tim Johnson.

This event caused a new crisis in Washington, since the Department of Justice had no rules for handling this kind of Indian prisoner, vaguely indicted by God knew whom. In desperation, Secretary Schurz got a War Department verbal okay to dump the three alleged criminals at Fort Leavenworth Military Prison near Kansas City. He wired Adams at Alamosa about it, whereupon the Uintah Ute Thomas flew the coop, saying he'd go to Washington for trial but nowhere else. The teen-aged Tim Johnson wept so piteously that Adams, Jack and Sowerwick couldn't stand leaving him at Leavenworth. They made him an official member of the Ute delegation and brought him on back to the Hotel Tremont.

So poor old Douglas of the wispy whiskers said he might as well be the goat, and he permitted Adams to leave him at Leavenworth, thereby causing this War Department exchange:

POST OF FORT LEAVENWORTH, KS.
February 26, 1880

ASSISTANT ADJUTANT GENERAL
DEPARTMENT OF THE MISSOURI

SIR:

I respectfully report that Indian Chief Douglas was turned over to and received by the guard at this post last evening by General Adams of the Interior Department, without any papers or information of any kind. I shall cause quarters in the guard house and necessary supplies to be furnished him until orders are received in the case.

Very respectfully,
Your obdt. servant,
(*Sgd*) C. H. SMITH
Colonel 19th Infantry, Comdg. Post

The Colonel got his orders the same day from General Pope — not very informative, but better than nothing:

HEADQUARTERS, DEPARTMENT OF THE MISSOURI
COMMANDING OFFICER
FORT LEAVENWORTH, KAS.

SIR:

Your report of the turning over of Chief Douglas to your
guard is received. The Department Commander directs that
you cause him to be held under such restraint as may be necessary to prevent his escape, but accompanied by no more harsh-
ness or discomfort than is necessary for that purpose.

Very respectfully,
Your obedient servant,
E. N. PLATT
Asst. Adjt. General

While Schurz and Ouray quietly did their work of drawing
up an agreement, the House Committee on Indian Affairs held
twenty-two farcical hearings between January 15 and March 22
which disclosed nothing new about the White River troubles
and allowed some garrulous whites to make campaign speeches
(Governor Pitkin), deny charges of corruption (ex-Indian Commissioner Edward A. Hayt), make dubious damage claims
against the Utes (James B. Thompson and William Byers), or
just keep the tongue wagging aimlessly (Henry C. Olney of
the *Lake City World*). Captain Payne and Lieutenant Cherry
described the Milk Creek battle, and Josie Meeker was helpful
and charming. After the twelve white witnesses had talked
enough to fill 182½ pages of type, Ouray, Jack, Sowerwick and
Henry Jim had their say, requiring only 22½ pages.

The Washington hearings, like those at Los Pinos, were
closed and were very lean pickings for the Washington newsmen
in the corridor. They passed the time by contriving items to
build up public interest in "Queen" Chipeta, who would be
one of the last to testify. They implied that Ouray's plump wife
knew far more than he about the massacre and captivity and
they hinted that time might show that she, and not General
Adams, had braved the ire of the savages and rescued the
women. They suggested further that extraordinary revelations

might be made on the morning of March 19 when "Queen" Chipeta took the stand, tastefully arrayed in a "seal-skin sacque, silk dress and fashionable hat."

The Washington papers sold briskly that afternoon and most readers turned first to read Chipeta's testimony, which was released to the reporters by the House Committee:

THE CHAIRMAN: Madame Chipeta, could you tell us how far from the Agency where Mr. Meeker was Agent were you at the time the massacre took place?

CHIPETA (demurely): I do not know the exact time when the massacre occurred and do not know where I was.

CHAIRMAN: Please state all you know about the difficulty between the Utes and the whites, the battle and the massacre?

CHIPETA: I know nothing about it.

CHAIRMAN: Were you at home when the Meeker women came there? If so, who brought them there, and what was their condition?

CHIPETA: They seemed to be all right.

CHAIRMAN: What reasons did the Indians give for committing this massacre at the Agency?

CHIPETA: I do not know.

CHAIRMAN: Did they say that Mr. Meeker was a bad man?

CHIPETA: I heard some say that he was a bad man.

CHAIRMAN: In what respect?

CHIPETA: They said he talked bad.

CHAIRMAN: Did they say that he did anything bad?

CHIPETA: Some of them claimed that he was always writing Washington.

CHAIRMAN: Is that why they killed him?

CHIPETA: I do not know. I know nothing personally about it except what I have heard talked among the women.

CHAIRMAN: Tell us what you heard on that subject — all you heard?

CHIPETA (dimpling): I already have.

CHAIRMAN (with a sigh): Next witness.

On April 2, 1880, as Chief Ouray, "Queen" Chipeta and their delegation journeyed back to Los Pinos, Senator Teller de-

livered before the Senate his furious assault on Carl Schurz
which he had been preparing since January.[2]

The formidable speech demonstrated Teller's infinite ca-
pacity for taking pains — which, as usual, put the Senate to
sleep in an hour or so. Teller revised history to show that the
Utes had never held the Colorado Rockies, that it was bad for
them to be anywhere in Colorado now, that they had killed ever
so many Colorado taxpayers whereas no taxpayer had ever killed
a Ute, and that he liked Indians and knew what was best for
them far better than any sentimental Eastern Secretary of the
Interior. Besides, the Grand River was full of placer gold.

Then he really went gunning for Schurz. He blamed him for
the Nez Percé and Ponca removal tragedies, for the Indian killing of white settlers in Kansas, for the pathetic trek of Northern
Cheyennes, for Major Thornburgh's death, Nathan Meeker's
murder and the rape of the captives. He accused him of three
years of cover-up to protect the Indian Bureau from its own
stupidity and corruption.

He pressed on with a scathing denunciation of Schurz's whole
theory that the red man could be treated as an individual by
"lands in severalty." With loving care he developed the old
fantasy about inconvenient minorities which has woven its er-
ratic and depressing way through most of history. The American Indian, Teller believed, was hopeless in the foreseeable
future and could not be treated as a human being with his
rights guaranteed by the Constitution. Being useless as well as
hopeless, the red man ought to be quarantined in tribal units
on land as incapable of development as himself. And then someday, later on, if he survived his barren environment, the Government might do something for him. "This Ute bill," Teller
concluded, "is preposterous. It is an insane effort."

Though the Teller speech helped to drive both Schurz and
President Hayes from public life, it failed to destroy Schurz's
severalty policy or to hamper his conduct of the Interior Department during his remaining months as Secretary. The Ute

agreement passed both houses of Congress, partly because Schurz spoke in its favor, and nobody ever fell asleep when Schurz was speaking. During one Joint Committee meeting, this exchange occurred:

SECRETARY SCHURZ: Senator Teller tells me that it would not be satisfactory to him unless every Ute left Colorado.

SENATOR TELLER: I did not say exactly that. I said this agreement was just as much a perpetuation of an Indian reservation as the old arrangement.

SCHURZ: It is certainly not the perpetuation of an Indian reservation in anything like the old sense. It is not any more so than the settlement of so many whites there would be. I may say that, if there are any people in Colorado who prefer an Indian war to a peaceable settlement, this agreement will, of course, be unsatisfactory to them.

MR. AINSLEE: The removal of these people from Colorado — is it satisfactory to the people of Utah and New Mexico?

SCHURZ: A vote of the people of these Territories would probably favor having no Indians there. But the Indians must live somewhere. In justice to them we cannot always be governed by the wishes of people who do not want any Indians in their neighborhood. Indians have rights just as well as other men.

During the Ute debate, Schurz induced General Sherman to move six hundred soldiers under General R. S. Mackenzie from Fort Garland to the Uncompahgre. The cantonment was established in late May midway between Ouray's farm and Los Pinos Agency, a nine-mile stretch lined with Ute tepees.

Schurz didn't ask for troops for fear of the Indians. His problem was to block the path of thousands of settlers, miners, bartenders, gamblers, railroad surveyors, confidence men, male and female floaters and land speculators from all over the United States whose wagons and buggies, pack trains and covered wagons, wheelbarrows and farm machinery choked the San Juan and Gunnison roads for miles up to the Reservation boundary. The troops arrived in the nick of time. When Congress passed the Ute bill in June, the would-be trespassers had reached the proportions of an invading army, being convinced by Teller and Pitkin that the Reservation would be open to settlement at the instant of the bill's passage. Thereafter, the soldiers had their hands full patrolling the border day and night to catch trespassers trying to slip through to examine the land.

In mid-July, Schurz's five-man Ute Commission to seek Ute ratification of the bill reached Los Pinos Agency. Its make-up had the picturesque Schurz stamp — full of dynamite and yet politically sound. Otto Mears was a member, which, Schurz knew, would please Pitkin, Mears's protégè. Counterbalancing Mears was J. J. Russell of the Interior Department. Member Three was John B. Bowman, a Teller man with Colorado mining interests.

The rest was the dynamite. Schurz's Commission chairman was the notorious Indian lover, George W. Manypenny, former Indian commissioner and rabidly anti-Army author of the sensational exposé of white injustice, *Our Indian Wards*. The fifth member was Alfred B. Meacham, editor of the Indian rights magazine, *Council Fire*.

The Commission's work proceeded smoothly at first. Though deathly ill, Ouray accepted the awful task of trying to explain to his people why they were being pushed off the earth, why their nation had to die, why it was inevitable and why the Ute bill was the best they could hope for. Then he vested his authority in Sapovanero while a total of 111 Uncompahgres touched the pen of the clerk who inscribed their names. In August, Manypenny, Mears, Bowman and Russell crossed the San Juans by wagon to Ignacio, new site of the Southern Ute Agency, and recorded 254 Southern Ute names. Back at Los Pinos, in September, they worked three weeks more until the grand total of Ute adult males approving the bill came to 581, which was more than three quarters of the total adult male population.[3]

From then on, the Commission's affairs became wildly hectic. Schurz was slow in forwarding the seventy-five thousand dollars in coin, the current annuity payment due the Utes at the time of ratifying the agreement. The Commission clerk, Will Stickney, died of a strange fever. His replacement, John R. French, lost his only pair of pants in a Denver hotel fire.

At Los Pinos, Piah strode up to Alfred Meacham daily, demanding his annuity money while threatening the Commissioner with a buggy whip. Meacham and Will Berry, the Los Pinos Agent, became the most hated men in Colorado for delaying the removal, keeping swindlers away from the Utes and telling reporters that many whites were more savage than Indians. Every right-thinking Coloradan hoped that Meacham would fall down a hole or otherwise vanish from the scene. For a time, this seemed likely when a drunken freighter, A. D. Jackson, killed Shavano's son on Son of a Bitch Hill east of Los Pinos, and was killed in turn by a Ute posse. Next day, Meacham and Berry found themselves indicted as accomplices in murder. They went to Denver to await trial but Judge Hallett refused to keep them in jail and the case kept getting postponed until it died of old age.

Such friction developed between Chairman Manypenny and Commissioner Mears that the Chairman retired disgusted to Columbus, Ohio. Mears and Bowman had a way of disappearing for weeks on mysterious business while Schurz kept the telegraph wires hot trying to locate his Commission. Clerk John French burdened Schurz with interminable letters of protest. One nine-page epistle complained in part:

> During my four months with the Commission I have never detected an act or a word by Mr. Mears or Mr. Bowman that evinced the slightest interest in their job with the Commission or the Indian problem. They care as little for the welfare of the Indians as they do for the barking coyotes. Their only interest is in certain Colorado speculations they have at hand and they are using the Commission in hopes of pushing them. If the success of the Ute agreement will forward their speculations, they are for it. If not, they are just as satisfied if it is defeated. They think there are valuable mineral lands on the Reservation. They intend to use membership on the Commis-

sion to enable them to snatch these ahead of others. They
have had agents on the Reservation and its boundaries all
summer, who are still there.

For all its troubles, the Ute Commission achieved its objec-
tives before 1880 ended, having secured Ute ratification of
Senate Bill 1509 and finally paying the Utes their current annuity. Chairman Manypenny laid out the new Southern Ute
Reservation for Ignacio's people. Most of the White River Utes
were accepting rations at the Uintah Ute Reservation. Arrangements were made for the Uncompahgre Utes to subsist in the
neighborhood of Ouray's farm pending their removal in 1881
to agricultural lands around the Grand River-Gunnison River
junction, "if enough land could be found there."

Having chaperoned Ouray's bereaved people during the first
months of their new existence, the weary commissioners were all
back in their homes in time to enjoy the sugarplums at Christmas.
Next June, 1881, a reduced Commission of Otto Mears, J. J.
Russell and Judge Thomas McMorris went Reservation hunting from Los Pinos with Ouray's chiefs, Sapovanero and Guero.
They discovered that the Gunnison-Grand area was deficient in
farm lands and they chose instead to put the new Uncompahgre
Reservation on a Utah tract extending along Green River for
twenty-five miles beyond its junction with White River and
some distance also up Duchesne River. Mears had more than
$100,000 to spend, and by August he had an army of con-
tractors rushing east from Salt Lake City with materials for
the new Uncompahgre Agency.

On August 29–31, Agent Will Berry sold the buildings of
Los Pinos Agency to the thousands of whites thronging to grab
the old Reservation. On September 1, General Mackenzie began
moving, on their 350-mile journey to Utah, the vast agglomera-
tion of 1458 Ute men, women and children, their 8000 ponies,
their 10,000 sheep and goats, their travois and tepees and pack
trains of food and cooking equipment. By September 3, many

of them were beyond the Uncompahgre-Gunnison junction but some hung back, so Mackenzie threatened to seize their guns and livestock.

The General had arranged his cavalry, infantry, artillery and signalmen on the mesa above the river, stretching north for miles. As his seizure order went out, he observed suddenly through his glasses the huge-stomached Colorow and fifty well-armed Utes in war paint galloping toward him in a brave, mad last attack. Mackenzie shouted a dozen rapid orders. Seconds later, the mesa tops flamed into what seemed like the blazing activity of the whole United States Army. Cannon boomed. Signal flags waved. Rifles pinged. Soldiers shouted. Cavalry by the hundreds plunged down in the valley.

Mackenzie saw Colorow rein up with his battalion and gaze about him in bewilderment at the overwhelming fireworks display. Then his big shaggy head sank to his breast. With a hopeless gesture, he turned his pony and rode slowly and sadly northward.

CHIEF OURAY clung to life with magnificent obstinacy through that sad summer of 1880, determined not to succumb to Bright's disease until the Ute agreement was ratified and he could pass into history along with the Nation of his forefathers. When the Commissioners left Los Pinos on August 4 to gather Southern Ute names, Ouray grew fearful that Chief Ignacio and Buckskin Charlie might oppose the agreement. On August 15, as he approached the terminal stage of his disease, he ordered Sapovanero to lift him on a horse and he set out for Ignacio, one hundred and thirty miles away by trail. With him were Chipeta, a white doctor, Chipeta's half-brother, John McCook, and a few friends.

Their route was not the twelve-day wagon route taken by the Commissioners. Instead, it passed through the granite heart of the San Juan Mountains, that supreme pyramid of the North

American continent. From Los Pinos at sixty-four hundred
feet they toiled out of the green valley and into the spruce up-
lands along the line of splendid peaks. And then they traversed
that bleak, broken, high country where their ponies slid and
tumbled and fought their way through countless ravines and
gulches, across windy ridges and alpine meadows bright with
wildflowers at altitudes above twelve thousand feet. How Ouray
could have survived three days and nights of such travel is a
mystery. Perhaps he drew strength and peace from these last
hours in the wild grandeur of his beloved mountains, as most
dying men find peace within the womblike confines of a familiar
bedroom.

He did not complain. He did not, apparently, talk at all.
What his thoughts were on that last incredible pilgrimage cannot be known. But his mind was still the same spacious instrument which began its development in the tolerant byways of
Taos. It was the same mind which grew with the remarkable
economic, social and political growth of the Colorado Utes during the first half of the nineteenth century. It was the mind
which became razor-sharp after the Civil War, when Ouray put
aside personal pleasures to try to avert the disastrous collision
between two races whose differences might have been composed
if his councils had been heeded.

The disaster came and, in the struggle over Nathan Meeker,
Ouray watched the white man win once again. The nature of
the triumph was not new. It was a peculiarly complete demonstration of what had happened hundreds of times before, since
the conquest of the Aztecs by Cortes. The white man always
won, not because of innate superiority but because the pressures
of his environment caused him to be better equipped for this
kind of battle.

The triumph over the Utes was an old story, but with the
difference that it brought an end to many injustices. Ouray
knew that the year 1880 marked a turning point. Because of
his own efforts and those of men like Carl Schurz and Charles

Adams, white Americans could continue their shameful ways no longer. Neither could they ignore their immense debt to the American Indian. The old rattle-headed scorn would wane. Henceforth, they would be more just — and more grateful to the red man for revealing to them the most fruitful empire on earth, for tempering their restless materialism and their self-centered illusion that the planet revolved for their benefit, for teaching them humility in the presence of nature and for passing on unique skills for its enjoyment and use.

When the anxious little party reached Ignacio on August 18, Ouray's stout heart was beating still and his indomitable mind was clear. All the rest of him was wreckage and seepage, racked with pain and almost inoperative. He slept for two days, and was present on August 20 at the first full Ute Commission council with Ignacio's protesting bands. On the twenty-first and twenty-second he talked to Southern Ute leaders and was told that they would follow his wishes and would ratify soon, after a show of further resistance. On August 23, Ouray tried valiantly to attend the day's council. He could not be moved from his tent. He thanked his white doctor for his services, dismissed him and called in the medicine men. They began their howling incantations at once.

He died next day, August 24, 1880, at 11 A.M., aged about forty-seven. His friends wrapped his body in a blanket and placed it with a few dead ponies under a huge rock at the head of a secret arroyo near Ignacio. Thus ended the life — and the times — of a great Indian who had done his gallant best for his people and for all men.

Postscript

THE STUNNING EVENTS of September 29, 1879, seemed to cast a blight on the lives of those concerned, like a lingering disease. The Meekers had it worst of all. Mary Meeker and Win Fullerton married in 1881, and had a daughter whom they named Josie. Two years later Mary died in childbirth. Her daughter died in '89. Rozene married an English mining man, Edward S. Skewes, who left her soon. She began to take drugs and to feed her mother skim milk and bread without butter to save money for them. Arvilla's health had improved after Nathan Meeker's body was moved from White River to Linn Grove Cemetery in Greeley, but it declined again under Rozene's treatment. In time, Ralph persuaded Arvilla to leave Rozene and live in White Plains, New York, with him and with Carmelita, whom he married in 1885. Carmelita died of cancer in 1904, Arvilla of senility in 1905.

Ralph was with Dan Frohman briefly and spent the rest of his life as an able metropolitan journalist. In 1921 he returned to Colorado and made his first visit to the lovely little cow town of Meeker three miles upriver from the Powell Park Agency site. He died of pneumonia in Greeley that December. Rozene never made up with him and she grew queerer year by year. She raised turkeys and ducks, chickens and pigs, guinea hens and peacocks inside and outside her Greeley home at 229 13th Street. In 1931, she entered Greeley Hospital where she complained of the food, service and accommodations until she died in 1935, aged eighty-six.

In Washington, during the summer of 1882, Josie Meeker was

promoted from "copyist" to assistant private secretary to the new Interior Department Secretary, Henry M. Teller, at seventeen dollars a week. By now, she was receiving her five-hundred-dollar annuity which boosted her total weekly income to twenty-seven dollars. That was ample for a modest young lady of twenty-five. She sent five dollars a week to Arvilla, and spent two dollars more on the colored children in her Lincoln Mission Sunday school class. She had enough left to dress well and pay her keep at Mrs. Goodall's boardinghouse, from which she was nearly evicted one night for being caught on the front porch in the arms of a beau. Newspapers still speculated about whether she had been in love with Persune and about whether she had contracted syphilis, or consumption, or both, during captivity, but her news value faded as her health bloomed.

Josie enjoyed corresponding with old White River friends like Eugene Taylor and Joe Collom, and she was delighted when Arvilla sent her a missive from Flora Ellen Price who was, apparently, still unwed:

> ELLENSBURG, WASHINGTON,
> *Sept. 15, 1880*
>
> MY DEAR MRS. MEEKER:
> I will take the present opportunity of droping you A few lines to let you know where I am and how I am getting along I was greated with A warm return among my folkes I can't express how glad we were to see each other how nice it is to have a father and mother to talk to they are very kind to me and the children May and Johney thinks they is no body like gramma the children growes real niceley & Johney talkes everything he can run A conversation almost as well as May could when you last seen her. do you know how mutch we get from the goverment I haven't been situated so I could here does Josephine talk of coming home. how I should love to see you all I have one of thoes flowers I picked from your garden the last time I was there it pressed bautifull & I shall keep it for the rembrence of that after noon.
>
> How is your health? Are you getting well? I've got some of my podia splt. & will you send to Denver and get me two

bottels & express it to me carfuley packed. So not to get broken and I will send you the money in the next letter. Will you give me Carver's adress, as my Father has composed A piece of porty on our troubels and it so trew I want it published in A Greeley paper.

Won't write mutch this time. My foalkes sendes there kindness regards, from your kind and loving friend. A kiss to you goody. Pleas write as soon as conveanent. As my medison is almost given out & we can't get it out here.

Yours very trewley,

F. E. PRICE

adress to PO adress MRS. F. E. PRICE, ELLENSBURG, PO, YAKIMA COUNTY, WASHINGTON.

On December 21, 1882, the weather in the capital turned damp and depressing. Josie woke feeling tired and did not go to work. She spent Christmas in bed and her fever passed when Ralph arrived for a visit. But she was very weak. The two doctors sent to her by Secretary Teller were worried. On December 29, they told Ralph that she had pneumonia. Next morning, at 9:30 A.M., Josie clutched Ralph's hand in panic and said that she seemed to be going blind. As she tried desperately to talk on, her voice failed, though her lips moved still. Then she fell asleep. She died an hour later still clutching Ralph's hand.

More than one hundred and fifty people, including Henry Teller and Josie's colored Sunday School class, were present at her Washington service. The ever-faithful Ralph, himself ill with grief, escorted the body of his best-loved sister back to Greeley, where the whole town attended the funeral at the First Methodist Church. She was buried with her parents in the family plot at Linn Grove Cemetery.

ONE OF THE GREAT EVENTS of early-day Omaha, Nebraska, was the Knights Templar funeral of Major Thomas Tipton Thornburgh at Masonic Hall on October 22, 1879. Most of the thirty thousand people of the town filed past the handsome Major's catafalque to see him in full regimentals. At the ceremony, a huge crowd pressed around Lida Thornburgh, the two children, General George Crook and the brass of Fort Omaha. Hundreds followed the cortege along Capitol Avenue and Sixteenth Street to Prospect Hill Cemetery. The sobs were loud when a small casket was placed on top of the Major's in the single grave. It contained the body of Lida's Centennial baby, George Washington Thornburgh, exhumed from the cemetery at Fort Steele. After the Episcopal service, the Major was given the usual three volleys. Lida dried her tears and that was that.

The Major's pretty widow did not remarry. She passed the long lonely years in Washington and in Oakland, Maryland, to be near her friends, the George Crooks. A later diversion was amusing the progeny of her daughter, Olivia, and her son-in-law, Dan Casement. One week end she took her teen-age granddaughter, Mary Casement, and Mary's friend, Madeleine Connell from Colorado Springs, to see Irene and Vernon Castle in New York. The girls informed Lida that the spot for overnight these days was the Hotel Algonquin on West Forty-Fourth Street. Lida liked the place, and enjoyed her oysters and a cold glass of Pouilly during dinner in the Rose Room. Then came the main course, served on big plates engraved with the profile of an Algonquin Indian. Lida stared at the face on her plate, and stood up. To the Rose Room in general she announced: "I will not patronize a hotel that glorifies Indians. Come, girls." Ten minutes later, they checked out of the Algonquin and were in a cab bound for the Martha Washington. Lida died in 1930 at Dan Casement's famous Hereford cattle establishment, Juanita Farm, in Manhattan, Kansas.

Twelve rank-and-file heroes at Milk Creek received Medals of Honor or Certificates of Merit soon, but it was not until the 1890s that Captain Payne, Captain Dodge and Major Thornburgh (posthumously) were cited by Congress for gallantry. Payne's poor health got poorer after Milk Creek. He retired from active service in '86 and served in Washington on the Pension Board until his death in 1895. He was buried with his fox-hunting ancestors at Warrenton, Virginia. Poor Lieutenant Sam Cherry was the victim of sad mischance. In May, 1881, four men robbed a combination saloon and bawdyhouse called the Hog Ranch near Cherry's post, Fort Niobrara, Nebraska. Sam led a detachment after the robbers. One of his men, Private Thomas Locke, had been drunk for two weeks and developed delirium tremens. He began shooting at all the soldiers in sight. Only Cherry was killed.

Lieutenant James Paddock, who led the Milk Creek wagon guard, got two bad wounds in the battle and carried two bullets in his body for the rest of his life. Old Captain Joe Lawson, perhaps the ablest Indian fighter in the White River Expedition, failed rapidly and died in '81. Lieutenant Silas Wolf rose to lieutenant colonel before retiring in 1910. Captain Francis Dodge left field duty to become an Army paymaster; by 1904 he hit the top — Paymaster General. Scout Joe Rankin spent the 1880s basking in the glow of local fame as Carbon County's Paul Revere and furthering the prestige of the Scottish Rites Masons. When Benjamin Harrison became President he named Joe as United States Marshal for Wyoming.

General Charles Adams was rewarded for his heroism at Plateau Creek when President Hayes sent him to Bolivia for two years as United States Minister. He returned to be head Post Office Inspector for Colorado until President Cleveland removed him in '85 for "offensive partisanship." Thereafter, he had business in Manitou Springs, with a few days off in 1894 to command a brigade of deputy sheriffs who tried unsuccessfully to take Bull Hill at Cripple Creek from a force of striking miners. On Sunday, August 19, 1895, Adams dined alone rather sumptuously at Tortoni's in Denver and retired early to his room at the Gumry Hotel on Larimer Street. Soon after midnight, the hotel's steam boiler blew up. The whole rear of the bulding was

demolished. More than twenty people died in this worst accident in Denver history. Adams's body was not found in the
wreckage until three days later. He was fifty years old.

As CHIEF COLOROW and the last Uncompahgre Utes departed for
Utah in September, 1881, settlers, miners and speculators
moved in, although Congress did not declare the Ute Reservation to be public land until June 28, 1882. The Uncompahgre
and Gunnison Valleys, up to the Gunnison-Grand juncture,
filled up much faster than White River Valley, partly because
White River was smaller and partly because General Palmer's
Denver and Rio Grande Railway in 1882 was rushed over Marshall Pass and down the Gunnison to Grand Junction, which
had grown to nearly one thousand residents. When the Army
pulled out of White River in the fall of 1883, the town of
Meeker spread over the campsite. The development of Grand
River Valley upstream from Grand Junction was slow until
the Denver and Rio Grande and Colorado Midland Railroads
managed to get over the Continental Divide from the Leadville
mining district in 1887–1888.

Most of the men on the Ute Peace Commission's "star list" of
twelve accused Utes vanished forever after 1880. The sacrificial
goat, Chief Douglas, waited patiently in his Fort Leavenworth
cell for the War Department or the Justice Department or the
Interior Department — or somebody — to try him for something, somewhere, sometime. Of course everyone ducked the
issue, knowing the government's case was feeble and fearing
to raise juridical problems about the legal status of Indians
which might backfire politically. At length, on February 9,
1881, the Assistant Adjutant General of General Pope's Department of Missouri instructed the Prison Commander at Fort
Leavenworth to . . .

> . . . turn Chief Douglas over to Lt. Keefe, 19th Infantry, who
> is directed to convey him to Fort Garland, Colorado, and turn

him over to the Commanding Officer of that post, who will send him to the Agency at Los Pinos. It is the wish of the War Department that this transfer be made as quietly as possible as fears are entertained for Douglas' life if his identity were known; and you are desired to take every precaution to prevent any knowledge of the movement from getting abroad.

The Assistant Adjutant General had his tongue in his cheek when he counseled secrecy "to protect Douglas." The secrecy was to protect War Department and other government officials, who otherwise might have been asked by some nosey Indian Rights person why they had held a man in prison for three hundred and forty-eight days and then had freed him without ever taking the trouble to explain, or even to decide, why they had held him in the first place. It was not surprising that, after his release, Douglas developed a dangerous persecution complex and drank much more than before. In 1885, while returning to Uintah Reservation from a drinking spree in Meeker town, he became threatening and was shot to death by a member of his own band.

Ouray's old rival of the 1860s, Kaneache, was struck by lightning near Ignacio shortly after Ouray's death. War Chief Shavano was killed in '86 by a friend after advising the wrong medicine for the friend's sick child. Piah committed suicide in '88. Jane died in 1908 on Uintah Reservation, still stoutly anti-white and owner of two fine farms.

Chief Jack, the most intelligent of the White River Utes, refused to go to Uintah Reservation, preferring to become a teamster on the Rawlins-Fort Washakie road. On April 29, 1882, the Fort Washakie commander, Major J. W. Mason, sent Lieutenant George Morgan, Sergeant Casey and five privates to a nearby Indian village to arrest Jack for questioning about a horse theft. Jack declined to surrender and was wounded in the arm as he ducked into a tepee. When the soldiers pulled down the tepee, Jack ran to another, "well filled with bales of robes and raw hides by which he was well protected from our bullets" (Mor-

gan's report). During attempts by the soldiers to pull down this
second tepee, Jack fired his carbine and killed Sergeant Casey.
Major Mason arrived then and, in his own words, "upon learning the condition of affairs, I caused a shell from a mountain
howitzer to be fired into the tepee in which Ute Jack was, killing him."

In the long record of white foolishness where Indians were
concerned, nothing seemed to surpass in absurdity what is still
called "Colorow's War." Because the White River country
gained white population slowly, many displaced Colorado Utes
continued to hunt in its vast empty spaces from their Utah
reservations. Among them were the huge and surly Colorow,
and his small band of eight or ten lodges which Chipeta had
joined with her new husband, Com-mo-gu-uech. Colorow —
who, you recall, wasn't a Ute at all but a Comanche — hadn't
changed a bit. Some settlers found him amusing and colorful,
but some didn't — especially ranch wives who were annoyed or
frightened by his old habit of shambling into their kitchens to
demand biscuits.

In August of 1887, two members of Colorow's band were
alleged to have stolen two horses near Rangely on lower White
River and to have sold them in Meeker. Garfield County had
just been created and its officers were politically self-conscious
and anxious to show their mettle. The new Garfield County
Grand Jury indicted the alleged horse thieves and sent the new
sheriff, Jim Kendall, and a posse of seventy-two deputy sheriffs
up White River from Meeker to remove them from Colorow's
band. At a point on the river just short of present Buford, the
posse entered Colorow's camp. A hot argument followed. A gun
was fired and Colorow's forty or fifty Ute men, women and
children retreated up Beaver Creek northward to the White
River-Milk Creek divide below Sleepy Cat Peak.

In this incident, Sheriff Kendall and his posse conceived a
scheme to make themselves heroic in the Ned Buntline tradition of Buffalo Bill fiction. Here was their chance to scare the

redskins out of Colorado for good, to demonstrate the cowboys' superior fighting skill over General Crook's regulars, and to guarantee re-election for Sheriff Kendall. Some posse men galloped to Meeker to proclaim that Colorow and his band (they didn't say that it contained only a dozen or so adult males) were coming to murder them all. The rest of the posse trailed Colorow on his route along the divide to Milk Creek and his Morapos Creek camp near Williams Fork.

The proclamation in Meeker caused a snowballing of panic which reached incredible proportions. Most — but not all — Garfield County ranchers stampeded to Meeker with their families and prepared to stave off the reported swarm of savages. In a sensational move to thwart Colorow's twelve-man army, Governor Alva Adams called out seven brigades of the Colorado National Guard and commandeered all available cars of the Denver and Rio Grande to rush them to the Gypsum railhead from whence they could fight their way through Colorow's lines to lift the siege of Meeker.

The seven brigades of a thousand guardsmen lifted the siege on August 22, 1887, by which time many people realized that the "Colorow War" was a fake. Meanwhile, some of Kendall's posse came upon Chipeta and other squaws picking berries near Yellowjacket Pass. The white men pointed at this and that squaw with indecent gestures, as though choosing partners in a parlor house. Chipeta grabbed a gun and dispersed them. The squaws complained to Colorow, and he started his band hurrying out of Colorado. This act led Sheriff Kendall to ask that a hundred guardsmen rush down White River from Meeker to corral the Utes as Kendall drove them to the river at the mouth of Wolf Creek. It just wouldn't do for Colorow's band to be allowed to leave the state voluntarily.

The guardsmen failed to intercept the band, which went on west down White River through Rangely. Meanwhile, the guardsmen and Kendall's posse began a competition as to which would stop the Utes and force them to fight. The two groups did waylay them on August 25 at the big White River bend two miles from the Utah line (Colorow thought that they were actually safe in Utah). During the muddled three-hour skirmish in the White River willows, some one hundred Utes from Utah joined Colorow to help him evacuate his women and children. Three white men and eight or more Utes were killed. When the contestants ran out of bullets, the "battle" ended. Colorow's band rode on home — voluntarily. The guardsmen and Kendall's posse returned to Meeker, almost as mad at each other as they had been at the Utes.

The "Colorow War" cost Colorado taxpayers $80,314.72, which was a lot of money to spend on a fake. It solved nothing. The Utes kept on hunting for years on Colorado public lands above White River. Chief Colorow himself died in his camp at the mouth of White River on December 11, 1888. Quite a few ranch wives expressed regret that the old biscuit-beggar would frighten them no more.

AFTER OURAY'S DEATH, Chipeta shed every vestige of white ways which her husband had taught her. She gave away her forks and spoons, her lace curtains, her chairs and beds, and most of the five thousand dollars in one-hundred-dollar bills which Otto Mears had paid her for Ouray's Uncompahgre farm improvements. She reverted largely to Ute customs, summering in a wickiup far up Bitter Creek in Utah sixty miles northwest of Grand Junction with her sheep and goats, and wintering downstream in a small cabin near Dragon, Utah. She saw Buckskin Charlie's family occasionally at Ignacio, took the baths at Glenwood Springs for rheumatism and visited Colorado Springs to appear in rodeos and festivals and to see her old friend, Mrs. Charles Adams.

All the while the myth of "Queen" Chipeta grew. Her imaginary feats as diplomat, sociologist, military strategist, Methodist convert and Plateau Creek heroine threatened to raise her in stardom on the Ute stage even above Ouray and Charles Adams, Nathan Meeker and Major Thornburgh. The map of Colorado became dotted with place names in her honor. Later on, she went blind, despite expert treatment paid for by Grand Junction friends. Blind or not, she kept on making beautiful cradle boards, executing the bead patterns with the beads of different colors distributed in bowls. Rope guides around her Bitter Creek cabin permitted her to do simple chores.

She died there at last on August 16, 1924, aged eighty-one, and was buried in careless Ute style in a nearby gulch where her exposed bones were found six months later. Through the initiative of Albert H. Kneale, the Ute Indian Agent, the Montrose Chapter of the D. A. R. bought part of Ouray's Uncompahgre farm and placed Chipeta's bones in a mausoleum among the harebells and hollyhocks on the property. Today, the site (four miles south of Montrose, Colorado), is owned by the State Historical Society which maintains a Ute Indian Museum of dioramas and exhibits. The site is called Chief Ouray Historical Monument, though Ouray's remains lie in the cemetery at Ignacio.

AND SO THE wondrous world and its people move on, sometimes unimaginably cruel, sometimes infinitely tender and kind. During the past seventy-five years, the Western Slope of Colorado has been subdivided into some twenty-five counties and one hundred and eighty extraordinarily engaging towns and villages. It boasts fourteen national forests, with twelve thousand miles of horseback trails and four thousand miles of offbeat roads quite apart from the regular highway system. It has seven fascinating national monuments and Mesa Verde National Park, home of the ancient Cliff Dwellers.

This heartbreakingly beautiful land of great peaks and generous valleys used barely to support 3500 Utes under their inefficient hunting economy. Now it maintains 250,000 people, in superlative comfort. The comfort derives from the profits of stock raising, of the fruit industry under Grand Mesa, of Rangely's oil, of Ignacio's gas, of old and new metals including uranium and molybdenum, of a vast tourist industry serving motorists, dudes, mountain climbers, health and culture seekers, pack trippers, intrepid jeepsters, skiers, trout fishermen and hunters for big and little game.

The world moves on, but with wise glances backward. The Ute civilization which died with Ouray produced human experience of very great value to all Americans.

May it rest in peace.

Notes

CHAPTER ONE: The Child of Enoch

1. Albert Brisbane was the father of the famous Hearst newspaperman, Arthur Brisbane.

2. Arvilla preserved the incorrect birth date to the end. Meeker's pink granite tombstone in Linn Grove Cemetery, Greeley, Colorado, has him born in 1814.

CHAPTER TWO: Utopia, Incorporated

1. J. Max Clark, an original Colonist and one of Meeker's few close friends, wrote in his book "Colonial Days" that the Founder invested $15,000 in Union Colony.

2. Time would show Meeker to be entirely right in preferring the Cache la Poudre tract for its agricultural possibilities. Today the Cache valley produces ten times more crops and livestock than El Paso County (Palmer's valley).

3. David Boyd, an original Colonist, wrote in 1890 that twenty years were spent completing the four ditches which Meeker planned to finish in a few months. Up to 1890, the four ditches cost $412,000.

4. Meeker's 1870 fence consisted of two smooth wires strung on huge wood posts to stand the strain of cattle leaning against them and scratching. Four years later, Joseph F. Glidden of Dekalb, Illinois, introduced his barbed wire which cut fencing costs to $100 a mile.

CHAPTER THREE: Ralph Meeker, Crime Buster

1. This *New York Herald* summary, dated January 3, 1877, and titled "The Indian Ring," was fourteen galleys long. The galleys can be read today among the Maude Meeker Gilliland papers, State Museum, Denver, Colorado.

2. Schurz helped make Hayes Governor by swinging to him the

German vote in Ohio. Schurz's rise to great power derived from the fact that 8,000,000 Germans became United States citizens between 1849 and 1880, and many of them supported Schurz.

CHAPTER FOUR: The Foundering Founder

1. Birth dates of the Meeker children were: Ralph Lovejoy — born at Trumbull Phalanx, near Warren, Ohio, Jan. 26, 1845; George Columbus — Trumbull Phalanx, Aug. 15, 1847 (died Apr. 26, 1870, near Greeley); Rozene Meeker — Munson, Ohio (near Cleveland), July 5, 1849; Mary Meeker — Hiram, Ohio, June 17, 1854; Josephine Meeker — Hiram, Ohio, Jan. 28, 1857.

Josie, aged thirteen, first saw Greeley's drab setting in the summer of 1870, but she hid her dismay in her first letter to a friend back in New York.

DEAR SCHOOLMATE:

Our town is on the railroad near Denver and the finest river you ever saw flows through a delightful green valley. Thousands of little gray antelope come down to the bank and drink of the clear water. Excursion parties go to the mountains almost every day where they fish, hunt and gather wild flowers among the granite rocks.

From
JOSIE

CHAPTER SIX: The Sky People

1. In skipping warily over the quicksands of archaeology, I have been guided by Al Look's entertaining book, *In My Back Yard* (The University of Denver Press, 1951).

2. From Frances Densmore's *Northern Ute Music* (Smithsonian Institution, Bureau of American Ethnology, Bulletin 75, 1922), I have taken these tongue-twisting Ute words: *Mutusukwigant* (supernatural medicine man); *avinkwop* (bear dance enclosure); *uintaugump* (at the edge of the pine). *Ankapagarits* combines the Ute words *anager* (red) and *pagarits* (lake), to make "red lake." Uncompahgre is the white man's version of this word.

3. In piecing together Ute history my major sources have been: "The Southern Ute of Colorado," by Marvin K. Opler, in the book *Acculturation in Seven American Indian Tribes*, edited by Ralph Linton (Appleton-Century Co., New York, 1940); Frank Gilbert Roe's *The Indian and the Horse* (University of Oklahoma Press,

Norman, 1955); R. M. Zingg's "The Ute Indians in Historical Relation to Proto-Azteco-Tanoan Culture" (*Colorado Magazine,* July 1938); Irving Howbert's *The Indians of the Pikes Peak Region* (The Knickerbocker Press, New York, 1914); and Ernest Ingersoll's *Knocking Around the Rockies* (Harper & Co., New York, 1899).

4. My Spanish Trail authorities are: *The Old Spanish Trail,* by LeRoy R. and Ann W. Hafen (Arthur H. Clark Co., Glendale, Calif., 1954), and *The Course of Empire,* by Bernard DeVoto (Houghton Mifflin Co., Boston, 1952).

CHAPTER SEVEN: Young Ute on the Make

1. The origin of Ouray's name was explained by Ouray himself to Agent James B. Thompson.

2. Ute parents regarded Catholicism with amused respect. Salvador created his own Noah legend for his boys. The Ark, he said, landed atop Devil's Head near Pikes Peak, and Noah left the animals with a shrewish old woman while he explored the Plains. The old woman beat the animals with her red willow broom and they ran off to the Western Slope.

3. By the terms of this treaty, the Utes agreed to allow white Americans passage through their lands, to return stolen property, to stop roving and to be self-supporting. Congress voted $18,000 to fulfill the treaty.

4. For Ute-Mormon data I am indebted to John Major Reese's "The Indian Problem in Utah, 1849–1868" (undated University of Utah Master of Science thesis), and to Paul Bailey's *Walkara — Hawk of the Mountains* (Westernlore Press, Los Angeles, 1954).

5. The lack of evidence that the Utes killed Bill Williams is noted in William Brandon's *The Men and the Mountain* (William Morrow & Co., New York, 1955).

CHAPTER EIGHT: Treaty Trouble

1. This Tabeguache Ute Treaty was dated October 7, 1863, and ratified by the U.S. Senate on March 12, 1864. It reserved for the Uncompahgre Utes (and the Muaches too, if they would leave the Cimarron) a circular region including and surrounding the Elk Mountains, with a circumference of 475 miles and an area of 5,785,000 acres. For a decade the band was to receive $20,000 worth of supplies annually and monthly rations.

2. The Reservation's southern boundary was the New Mexico

border. The west boundary was the Utah border. The east boundary was the 107th parallel of longitude which passed two miles west of the present town of Gunnison, Colorado. The north boundary was the present northern boundary of Rio Blanco County, Colorado. That made an enormous oblong, 110 miles from east to west, 220 miles from north to south. The tribe would receive $60,000 annually for annuities and rations (the Senate reduced the sum to $50,000). Two agencies would be built. The Southern Agency would serve the Uncompahgres, Muaches, Capotes and Weeminuches. In the north, a White River Agency would serve the Yampas, Grand Rivers and Uintahs. (There were no Uintah Utes living in Colorado, but Brigham Young had them included in this Treaty of 1868 to make it easier to move them out of Utah if the chance arose.) The Cimarron, Abiquiu and Middle Park Agencies were supposed to be discontinued as soon as the two Agencies on the big Colorado Reservation were built.

3. This 4,000,000-acre bite was 60-odd miles from north to south, 90-odd miles from east to west.

A thread of sadness ran all through Felix Brunot's relations with Ouray. As early as 1870, Brunot knew that Chipeta could not bear children and that Ouray longed to find his son by his first wife. This son had been captured by hostile Indians in 1863 while Ouray was hunting buffalo in the Republican River country near the Kansas-Colorado border. Brunot spent much time on his Western trips trying to find this boy, without success.

CHAPTER NINE: Man Bites Man

1. The Margaret Adams quotations are taken from her manuscript, "The True Story of the Packer Case," which was discovered for me by Miss Dorothy Smith, curator of the Pioneer Museum, Colorado Springs.

2. I will repeat here a hardy old Colorado fable. Judge Gerry, who presided at the first Packer trial in 1883, was a Georgia gentleman who became one of the most militant Democrats in Colorado. Because of his ardent political persuasion, his preamble to sentencing Packer to hang was reported to have been: "They was seven Democrats in Hinsdale County, and you ate five of them. Stand up, you voracious man-eatin' son of a bitch, and take yo' sentence."

CHAPTER TEN: Uneasy Chief

1. The Fort Pueblo Massacre has been described fully by Janet

LeCompte in the tenth *Brand Book* of the Denver Posse of the Westerners, 1954.

CHAPTER ELEVEN: South of Rawlins

1. Distances and altitudes along the Rawlins–White River Agency road were: Rawlins (alt. 6,755 ft.) to Continental Divide (alt. 7,100 ft.), 15 miles. Continental Divide–Sulphur Springs, Wyo. (6,900 ft.), 15 miles. Sulphur Springs–Little Snake River (6,243 ft.), 45 miles. Little Snake–Bear River divide (6,800 ft.), 18 miles. Bear River divide to junction of Fortification Creek and Little Bear Creek (6,480 ft.), 16 miles. Little Bear Creek to Peck's Store, Bear River (6,180 ft.), 12 miles. Peck's Store to Williams Fork divide (7,500 ft.), 7 miles. Williams Fork divide to Williams Fork at Deer Creek (6,236 ft.), 12 miles. Williams Fork–Milk Creek divide via Deer Creek (7,500 ft.), 16 miles. Milk Creek divide to edge of Ute Reservation on Milk Creek (6,400 ft.) 4 miles. Milk Creek–Yellowjacket Pass (7,400 ft.), 10 miles. Yellowjacket Pass to White River Agency (6,500 ft.), 15 miles. Total mileage, Rawlins–White River Agency, 185.

CHAPTER TWELVE: The Adventures of Captain Armstrong

1. Arthur Carhart, the Rocky Mountain conservationist, writes that Meeker's trout was a black-spotted cutthroat or "red-sides." East of the Continental Divide, these native cutthroats are of the green-back variety.

2. Quoted by J. Max Clark in *Colonial Days* (Smith-Brooks Co., Denver, 1902).

CHAPTER FOURTEEN: Road to Ruin

1. The "back White River trail" ran from today's Kremmling southward up the Blue River, crossed Gore Range near Sheep Mountain, ascended Sheephorn Creek southward, and down Piney Creek to the Colorado River at present State Bridge; on down the canyoned Colorado almost to Eagle River; and west up Deep Creek to Deep Lake and fifty other lovely little lakes in White River National Forest. From there, the trail continued west along the Colorado River–White River divide to the Old Squaw Camp on Piceance Creek.

2. The alleged murder of Joe McLane was one of hundreds of crimes charged to the Utes without any evidence at all. It was not until March 31, 1881, that a skeleton was found twenty miles northwest of Cheyenne Wells which Joe's brother, Louis McLane, claimed to be that of his brother.

3. Data in Letters Received, 1879, Interior Section, National Archives, show that Secretary Schurz approved the threshing machine purchase on June 28, the grist mill on May 24 and the plows on June 5.

CHAPTER FIFTEEN: Almost There

1. Mrs. Meeker's letter of August 3, 1879, to Ralph Meeker (in the Maude Meeker Gilliland Collection, State Museum, Denver) establishes that Meeker left White River for Denver about July 29.

2. According to the Fort Steele post returns for 1879, Thornburgh boarded the cars at Cheyenne on August 5. Meeker mentioned meeting him on the Union Pacific in an August letter to Commissioner Hayt.

3. This shabby requisition is in Letters Received, 1879, Interior Section, National Archives.

CHAPTER SIXTEEN: Help Wanted

1. The Jake Thornburgh material came to me from Jake's son, Judge John M. Thornburgh, and from his daughter, Miss Laura Thornburgh, of Knoxville, Tenn.

2. I received my impressions of Major Thornburgh from long talks and correspondence with his granddaughter, Mrs. Harold Furlong (Mary Casement) of Chardon, Ohio.

3. Tom and Bill's genealogy is an item in Major Thornburgh's scrapbook, which was given to the State Historical Society of Colorado in 1928 by his daughter, Mrs. Dan (Olivia) Casement.

4. The Nebraska junket had one light moment during a conference between Thornburgh and the Sioux allies of the Cheyennes, Red Cloud and Man Afraid of His Horses, at Camp Sheridan. Red Cloud belittled the Army Springfield rifles. The major grabbed one and went into his act of hitting half dollars. The Sioux were astonished and named him "The Chief Who Shoots the Stars."

5. Mrs. Harold Furlong owns this letter.

CHAPTER SEVENTEEN: Troopers South

1. Contents of the annuity wagons have been reconstructed from Meeker's requisition of January, 1879, in the National Archives, and from the claims affidavit made by Martin L. Brandt for James France in October, 1879 (a copy of this affidavit is in the University of Wyoming Library, Laramie).

2. Fort Fred Steele and Fort D. A. Russell 1879 Post Returns (Old Army Section, National Archives) show the composition of the White River Expedition.

3. J. Scott Payne came from a Warrenton, Virginia, fox-hunting family. In 1866, he joined the Fifth Cavalry and had to leave the Army for making too many stump speeches in praise of Jefferson Davis. He edited the *Daily Whig* in Knoxville briefly, got himself somewhat reconstructed, and returned to the Fifth Cavalry by special dispensation of President Grant.

CHAPTER EIGHTEEN: Death in the Morning

1. Mike Sweet was exiled to the sutler tent from the Little Snake area by George Baggs for carrying on with George's buxom wife Maggie. "Carrying on" is putting it mildly. A little later, Maggie sued George for half the value of his ranch (she couldn't sue for divorce because she and George had never been married). She was awarded a third of the ranch. She sold it and took her red-eyed lover, Mike, to California for a hectic honeymoon lasting until her money ran out. Then they separated and Maggie wound up running an apartment house in Galveston, Texas.

2. A good description of Milk Creek Valley is found in *Random Recollections* (Walker Publications, Kansas City, 1955), by Major Thornburgh's posthumous son-in-law, Dan Casement, the pioneer Colorado Hereford breeder. The name Milk Creek is explained variously. Wilson Rankin attributes it to the story that a freighter in 1872 dropped two cases of Gail Borden Eagle Brand condensed milk near the stream. Lt. C. A. H. McCauley reported in 1878 that the name derived from "the whitish water due to matter in solution acquired in its flow over Cretaceous deposits at its headwaters." The Valley's standing as a sportsman's paradise seems indisputable, though in 1955 the present author found complaint in two notes chalked on the blackboard of the old schoolhouse on the bench

above the creek. One hunter wrote: "There's too damn' many deer flies around here to suit me." The other wrote: "Christ but it's cold!"

3. It came out later that one of the Utes was Jack. The other was Yanko, an Uncompahgre who was up courting a White River girl.

CHAPTER TWENTY: Colonel Merritt Takes Over

1. The iron parts of the threshing machine were gathered up much later by Abe Fiske, a Hayden pioneer, and fitted into a new wood frame. The machine ran for many years before being set up as a historical relic on the Routt County Fair Grounds, Hayden.

2. Estimates of the number of Utes killed at Milk Creek vary from twenty-three to thirty-seven. Estimates vary also as to how many Utes fought there. Chief Jack testified that only fifty Utes were on the long ridge at the start. More came over Monday afternoon from White River. The maximum force, maybe 125, was present when the sage was fired. After Monday, the warriors came and went, dividing their time between Milk Creek and council camps south of White River.

3. Up to October 11, 1879, twenty-seven soldiers and civilians died and forty-four white men were wounded at White River and at Milk Creek.

CHAPTER TWENTY-ONE: Doom and Moonlight

1. The conversations in this book are taken from official and newspaper reports. Conversations in this chapter can be found in "White River Ute Commission Investigation, Los Pinos, Colorado, 1879," Forty-Sixth Congress, Second Session, House Executive Document 83.

CHAPTER TWENTY-TWO: "The Damned Dutch Secretary"

1. Charles Adams's own account of this little-known meeting is filed at the Pioneer Museum, Colorado Springs.

2. Schurz drew one good laugh though by remarking. "Some of you call me "Mr. Shers" and some of you call me "Mr. Shirts" but I suppose most of you call me 'that damned Dutch Secretary.'" Properly, the name is pronounced "Shoorts."

3. I learned about the mysterious Count Dönhoff from his charm-

ing daughter, Countess Marion Dönhoff, a well-known German magazine writer.

CHAPTER TWENTY-THREE: Ordeal on Grand Mesa

1. The route of the captive women followed trails marked on the 1877 drainage map of F. V. Hayden's Tenth Annual Report of the U.S. Geological and Geographical Survey of the Territories. The route: White River Agency south along Grand Hogback to east fork, Piceance Creek, 20 Miles; Old Squaw Camp to Camp Number Two on Rifle Creek, 19 miles; Rifle Creek to Camp Number Three at Grand River and Parachute Creek, 25 miles; Parachute Creek to Douglas's main Grand River-Roan Creek camp, 10 miles; Roan Creek to Plateau Creek via Wallace and Kimball Creeks (Escalante's trail in 1776), 20 miles. Total distance, 94 miles. From Plateau Creek to Ouray's farm was also 94 miles. From the farm to Denver and Greeley via Alamosa was 534 miles — for a grand total of 722 miles. Quite a trip for an old lady sixty-four years old with a bullet wound in her hip!

2. The oddest incident of Adams's whole adventure occurred on this return visit to Douglas's Grand River Camp, where he found two Mormons, Peter Dillman and Clinton McLean, who said that they had come from Uintah Ute Agency to rescue Josephine Meeker and were sorry to find that she had been rescued already. Adams disbelieved their story until they produced a letter in Josie's handwriting which had somehow reached Uintah Agent Critchlow. It read: *"Grand River (forty to fifty miles from White River Agency) October 10, 1879. To UINTAH AGENT: I send this by one of your Indians. If you get it, do all in your power to liberate us as soon as possible. I do not think they will let us go of their own accord. You will do me a great favor to inform Mary Meeker at Greeley, Colorado, that we are well and may get home some time. Yours, etc.* JOSEPHINE MEEKER, U.S. Indian Agent's Daughter."

CHAPTER TWENTY-FOUR: Family Reunion

1. This five-pound, 9-by-12-inch volume with its 60 colored engravings is displayed at the Meeker Memorial Museum, Greeley. Pasted opposite the flyleaf is this message in Ralph Meeker's clear hand:

To THOSE WHO MAY LIVE AFTER US —
    This is the *Pilgrim's Progress* that Mrs. Nathan C. Meeker saved

from the White River Agency when her husband and all the employees were massacred at 1 o'clock on September 29, 1879. Chief Douglas allowed her to go back for what she called her "Spirit Book." The buildings were on fire, but she got the book, and the Indians respected it enough so that they carried it through the wilderness for her during her captivity of twenty-three days.

She was accompanied by her daughter Josephine and Mrs. F. E. Price and her two children (girl and boy, the girl three years, the boy sixteen months). They were finally released through the efforts of General Charles Adams in the special service of the Interior Department, Carl Schurz, Secretary. The captives also owed their escape to the assistance of Chief Ouray, his wife, and his sister Susan, who was the wife of Chief Johnson who had charge of Mrs. Meeker in the last days of her captivity.

(Written by her son Ralph Meeker, Greeley, November 6, 1879.) N.B. The Indians took much interest in the book and they improved every opportunity to look at the pictures. As a "Spirit Book" they attached a mysterious value to it and preserved it for *you*, good friend, to read and admire. R.M.

CHAPTER TWENTY-EIGHT: Sunset

1. The agreement proposed the payment from White River Ute funds for twenty years of annuities totaling $3500 to relatives of the murdered Agency employees. These relatives were: Mrs. Arvilla D. Meeker, $500; Miss Josephine Meeker, $500; Mrs. Flora Ellen Price, $500; Mrs. Maggie Gordon (Teamster George Gordon's wife), $500; George Dresser (father of Frank and Harry Dresser), $200; Mrs. Sarah M. Post, $500; Mrs. Eaton (mother of George Eaton), $200; Arthur Thompson's parents, $200; Fred Shepard's father, $200; Wilmer Eskridge's parents, $200.

The agreement stipulated further that the Utes would receive $50,000 annually forever, plus $25,000 annually forever by terms of the "Brunot Treaty," plus $350,000 moving expenses, $140,000 in back annuities, and $10,000 still due them for Uncompahgre Park. The Southern Utes (Weeminuches, Muaches and Capotes) would accept a reduced acreage centered around a new Agency at Ignacio west of Pagosa Springs. The White River Utes would settle on the southern portion of the Uintah Ute Reservation in Utah. The Uncompahgre Utes would take agricultural lands around the Grand-Gunnison junction if enough land could be found there. If not, then on such lands as might be found in that vicinity or in Utah. The effect of the agreement would be to throw open nearly all of the Western Slope of Colorado to white settlers and miners, not as homesteads, but by pre-emption at $1.25 an acre, the proceeds to be earmarked for the Ute bands up to the amount which they would receive in trust.

In practical substance, it can be claimed that Schurz offered the Colorado Utes about $2,000,000 for their vast kingdom of 16,000,000 acres as defined by the Treaty of 1868. That came to 12½ cents an acre.

2. In spite of his Indian bias, Henry Moore Teller was perhaps the greatest political leader Colorado ever had. He served thirty years as Senator, three as Interior Secretary under President Arthur and was at various times the Senatorial nominee of every conceivable party from Republican to Populist. His Spartan formula for the good life was: "Don't drink, don't smoke, marry early, rise early, work hard, sleep well, eat moderately and spend the first hour of each day thinking."

3. Tradition has it that Otto Mears induced the Colorado Utes to ratify the Ute agreement by paying two dollars to each of fourteen hundred Utes. Later, the story continues, Mears was reimbursed and praised for his alleged act of bribery by Secretary of the Interior Kirkwood.

There are many considerations which suggest that it would have been impossible for Mears to have made such payments. Furthermore, in recent years the Washington law firm of Wilkinson, Boyden, Cragun & Barker did prolonged research on the Ute Commission while winning thirty-two million dollars in compensation for the Utes from the Government. John W. Cragun wrote me on November 23, 1954: "I have no recollection that Otto Mears made payments from his own pocket to individual Utes to persuade them to sign the agreement of 1880." On January 14, 1955, after my own week's fruitless search in Washington, I received this letter: "Dear Mr. Sprague: A thorough examination of the records of the Bureau of Indian Affairs and the Office of the Secretary of the Interior, now in the National Archives, has failed to reveal any information relative to the alleged payment of two dollars apiece to some fourteen hundred Ute Indians. Yours sincerely, Jane F. Smith, Chief, Interior Section, National Archives."

If the story is in fact a myth, it may derive from Mears's participation in the distribution of much official Ute money in 1880–1881. I hope it is a myth, because it clashes with Otto's lifelong record of fair dealing and integrity.

Bibliography

Government Documents

Annual Reports, War and Interior Departments, 1865–1900.

Annual Reports, Board of Indian Commissioners, 1870–1880.

Hayden, F. V., 7th, 8th, 9th and 10th Annual Reports, U.S. Geological Survey of the Territories (1875–78).

46th Congress, Second Session, House Executive Document No. 1, Part 5. "Report, Ute Commission of 1878."

46th Congress, Second Session, House Executive Document Number 83. "White River Ute Commission, Colorado, 1879."

46th Congress, House Miscellaneous Document No. 38. "Testimony in Relation to Ute Outbreak, Washington, January–March, 1880."

46th Congress, House Report No. 1401. "Agreement with Ute Indians of Colorado."

46th Congress, Senate Executive Document No. 31. "Correspondence Concerning the Ute Indians in Colorado."

46th Congress, Third Session, Senate Executive Document No. 31. "Report of the Ute Commission of 1880."

Letters Received, 1878–1879, Interior Department.

Post Returns, 1878–1879, Fort Fred Steele, Fort D. A. Russell, Fort Garland, Fort Lewis.

Lt. Burnett's report, " 'Colorow War' of 1887," to Adjutant General, Department of the Platte.

Books

(Ute History)

Alexander, Hartley Burr. *The World's Rim.* University of Nebraska Press, Lincoln, 1953.

Alter, J. Cecil. *James Bridger.* Shepard Book Co., Salt Lake City, 1925.

Dobie, J. Frank. *The Mustangs*. Little, Brown & Co., Boston, 1952.

Dodge, Colonel R. I. *Our Wild Indians*. A. D. Worthington & Co., Hartford, 1883.

Emmitt, Robert. *The Last War Trail*. University of Oklahoma Press, Norman, 1954.

Hafen, LeRoy R. and Ann W. *Old Spanish Trail*. Arthur H. Clark Co., Glendale, Calif., 1954.

Hollon, W. Eugene. *Beyond the Cross Timbers*. University of Oklahoma Press, Norman, 1955.

Linton, Ralph (Editor). *Acculturation in Seven American Indian Tribes*. Appleton-Century, New York, 1940.

Ormes, Robert. *Guide to the Colorado Mountains*. Sage Books, Denver, 1952.

Rockwell, Wilson. *New Frontier*. World Press, Denver, 1945. *The Utes: A Forgotten People*. Sage Books, Denver, 1956.

Roe, Frank Gilbert. *The Indian and the Horse*. University of Oklahoma Press, Norman, 1955.

Sabin, E. L. *Kit Carson Days*. Press of the Pioneers, New York, 1935.

Stegner, Wallace. *Beyond the Hundredth Meridian*. Houghton Mifflin, Boston, 1953.

Underhill, Ruth M. *Red Man's America*. University of Chicago Press, 1953.

Wallace, W. S. *Antoine Robidoux*. Glen Dawson, Los Angeles, 1953.

Waters, Frank. *The Colorado*. Rinehart & Co., New York, 1946.

(Army)

Bourke, J. G. *On the Border with Crook*. Charles Scribner's Sons, New York, 1892.

Catton, Bruce. *U. S. Grant and the American Military Tradition*. Little, Brown & Co., Boston. 1954.

Finerty, John F. *War-Path and Bivouac*. Donohue Brothers, Chicago, 1890.

Rodenbaugh, T. F., and Haskin, W. L. *The Army of the United States*. Maynard, Merrill & Co., New York, 1896.

Sandoz, Mari. *Cheyenne Autumn*. McGraw-Hill Book Co., New York, 1953.

Woodson, Carter G. (Editor). *Negro Policy of the United States Army*. Association for the Study of Negro Life and History, Washington, D.C., 1949.

(General)

Beebe, Lucius, and Clegg, Charles. *The American West*. Dutton & Co., New York, 1955.

Boyd, David. *Greeley and the Union Colony of Colorado*. Greeley Tribune Press, Greeley, Colorado, 1890.

Ellis, Elmer. *Henry Moore Teller*. Caxton Printers, Caldwell, Idaho, 1941.

Gantt, Paul. *The Case of Alfred Packer*. University of Denver Press, 1952.

Hall, Frank. *History of Colorado*. Blakely Printing Co., Chicago, 1891.

Krakel, Dean. *South Platte Country*. Powder River Publishers, Laramie, Wyoming, 1954.

Leckenby, Charles. *The Tread of Pioneers*. Steamboat Springs, Colorado, 1944.

Manypenny, George. *Our Indian Wards*. Robert Clarke & Co., Cincinnati, 1880.

Meeker, Josephine. *The Ute Massacre*. Old Franklin Publishing House, Philadelphia, 1879.

Meeker, Nathan. *The Adventures of Captain Armstrong*. New York, 1856. *Life in the West*. Samuel R. Wells, New York, 1868.

Rankin, M. Wilson. *Reminiscences of Frontier Days*. Smith-Brooks Co., Denver, 1935.

Schurz, Carl. *The Reminiscences of Carl Schurz*. McClure Co., New York, 1908.

Slattery, C. L. *Felix Reville Brunot*. Longmans, Green & Co., New York, 1901.

Magazine Articles

Burkey, E. R. "The Thornburgh Battle." *Colorado Magazine*, May, 1936.

Chamberlin, R. V. "Some Plant Names of the Ute Indians." *American Anthropologist*, Vol. XI, No. 1.

Clarke, A. K. "A Visit with Piah." *Colorado Magazine*, August, 1928.

Covington, J. W. "Federal Relations with the Colorado Utes." *Colorado Magazine*, October, 1951. "Ute Scalp Dance in Denver." *Colorado Magazine*, April, 1953.

Eitner, Walter. "Walt Whitman's Western Jaunt." *Empire Magazine, Denver Post,* September 18, 1955.

Hafen, LeRoy R. "Otto Mears, Pathfinder of the San Juan." *Colorado Magazine,* March, 1932.

Harrington, J. P. "The Phonetic System of the Ute Language." University of Colorado Studies, Vol. VIII, 1910.

Howbert, Irving. "A Bit of Indian History." *Frontier Magazine,* September, 1905.

Jeancon, J. A. "The Pagosa-Piedra Region." *Colorado Magazine,* November, 1923.

Kroeber, A. L. "Notes on the Ute Language." *American Anthropologist,* Vol. X, 1908.

LeCompte, Janet. "The Fort Pueblo Massacre." Denver Westerners' *Brand Book,* 1954.

Londoner, Wolfe. "Colorow, Renegade Chief, Dines Out." *Colorado Magazine,* May, 1931.

Nankivell, Major J. H. "Colorado's Last Indian War." *Colorado Magazine,* November, 1933.

Payne, Captain J. Scott. "The Campaign Against the Utes." *United Service Magazine,* January, 1880.

Pennock, Taylor. "Recollections of Taylor Pennock." *Annals of Wyoming,* July–October, 1929.

Reed, Verner Z. "The Ute Bear Dance." *American Anthropologist,* Vol. IX, 1896.

Richie, Eleanor. "General Mano Mocha of the Utes." *Colorado Magazine,* July, 1932.

Thomas, A. B. "Spanish Expeditions into Colorado." *Colorado Magazine,* November, 1924.

Thompson, Major J. B. "Chief Ouray and the Utes." *Colorado Magazine,* May, 1930.

Thorp, R. W. "Hunting Experiences of Dr. Carver." *Western Sportsman,* February–March, 1940.

Whittier, Florence. "The Grave of Chief Ouray." *Colorado Magazine,* November, 1924.

Wiegel, Mrs. C. W. "The Re-Burial of Chief Ouray." *Colorado Magazine,* October, 1928. "The Death of Ouray." *Colorado Magazine,* September, 1930.

Wilber, Ed P. "Reminiscences of the Meeker Country." *Colorado Magazine,* September, 1946.

Wyman, W. D. "The Uncompahgre Ute Goes West"; also "A

Preface to the Settlement of Grand Junction." Both in *Colorado Magazine,* January, 1933.

Zingg, R. M. "The Ute Indians in Historical Relation to Proto-Azteco-Tanoan Culture." *Colorado Magazine,* July, 1938.

Pamphlets, Manuscripts

Adams, Charles. "The Meeker Massacre." Pioneer Museum, Colorado Springs.

Adams, Mrs. Charles. "The True Story of the Packer Case"; "Life of an Indian Agent"; "A Breakfast to a Band of Ute Indians." Pioneer Museum, Colorado Springs.

Anonymous. "History of the Ninth Regiment, U.S. Cavalry." U.S. Cavalry School, Fort Riley, Kansas.

Dawson, T. F., and Skiff, J. V. "The Ute War." Denver Tribune Press, 1879.

Pitkin, F. W. "The Governor's Letter Press, 1879–83." State Archives, Denver.

Startzell, A. M. "Thornberg Massacre at Meeker." State Museum, Denver.

Thompson, James B. "Recollections." State Museum, Denver.

Wildhack, H. A. "Comments on the Ute War of 1887." Owned by his daughter, Mrs. Leona Clubine, of Meeker.

Newspaper Articles

Chipeta's Obituary. *Colorado Springs Gazette,* August 24, 1924.

Colorow's Obituary. *Denver Times,* December 12, 1888.

Foster, Jack. *See* Uncompahgre Cantonment.

Jane's Obituary. *Grand Junction Daily Sentinel,* July 4, 1908.

Lipsey, John. *See* Sand Creek Massacre.

Mears, Otto. On the Ute Commission of 1880. *Denver Tribune,* October 17, 1881.

Meeker Massacre. As described in the newspapers of 1879, collected by Mrs. Charles Adams and given by her to the Pioneer Museum, Colorado Springs.

Meeker, Ralph. Open letter defending the Utes. *Greeley Tribune,* November 3, 1879.

Meeker, Rozene. "The Indian War." *Denver Tribune* letter, October 9, 1879. "Pioneer View." *Denver Tribune* letter, December 10, 1879.

Sand Creek Massacre. "John Chivington, Hero or Hellion?"

John J. Lipsey in *Colorado Springs Week End,* August 10, 1956.
Uncompahgre Cantonment. Jack Foster in *Rocky Mountain News,*
June 27, 1954.
Women Captives — First Report. *Denver Tribune,* October 25,
1879. Their arrival in Denver. *Denver Tribune,* October 31, 1879.
Arvilla's letter. *Colorado Chieftain* (Pueblo), December 31, 1879.

Acknowledgments

In writing this book, my greatest debt is owed to Nathan Meeker's niece, Mrs. Maude Meeker Gilliland, who permitted me to be the first to examine a trunkful of Meeker's letters, diaries, poems, unpublished novels, articles and countless letters. This material now constitutes one of the most interesting historical deposits in the West, the Maude Meeker Gilliland Collection of the State Historical Society, Denver, Colorado.

I am deeply grateful also to Major Thornburgh's granddaughter, Mrs. Harold Furlong, for much new family history, and to the Major's nephew, Judge John M. Thornburgh, and his niece, Miss Laura Thornburgh. I was helped greatly by Martin Wenger, then Assistant Archivist, Colorado State Museum, Denver, and by Miss Dorothy Smith, curator of the Pioneer Museum, Colorado Springs. Countess Marion Dönhoff of Hamburg, Germany, gave me hitherto unknown material about her father, Count August Dönhoff. I was aided throughout by Richard G. Lyttle, publisher of the *Meeker Herald*. I spent a valuable hour in Denver hearing about Governor Pitkin and about Otto Mears from the Governor's son, Robert Pitkin.

I have been blessed beyond counting by librarians. I want to thank Miss Louise Kampf, Dr. Ellsworth Mason, Miss Laura Tait, Mrs. Virginia Samuelson and Mrs. Janine Seay of Coburn Library, Colorado College; Mrs. Margaret Reid, Mrs. Lora Light and Miss Edith Kearney, Colorado Springs Public Library; Mrs. Alys Freeze and Mrs. Opal Harber, Denver Public Library; Miss Frances Shea, Colorado State Museum Library; Colonel W. J. Morton, Librarian, United States Military Academy; Mrs. Jennie C. Phelps and Mrs. Harriet M. Rankin, Greeley Public Library; and Mrs. Rose Demorest, Carnegie Library, Pittsburgh.

In Washington at the National Archives I am indebted specially to Miss Jane Smith, Dr. Richard Wood, and Frank A. Caflisch. In Denver I had the expert help of Mrs. Dolores Renze, State Archivist, and of Maurice Frink and Mrs. Agnes Wright Spring, State Historical Society. I received material from Dean Krakel of the University of Wyoming Library, Laramie; from Miss Lola M. Homsher, Wyoming State Historical Department, Cheyenne; from Miss Cornelia Hanna and Mrs. Helen Larson, Meeker Memorial Museum, Greeley; and from Mrs. Clifford Sundin and Mrs. Ed F. Bennett, Carbon County Museum, Rawlins, Wyoming.

Kind colleagues have come to my rescue, including Denver's historian, Miss Caroline Bancroft, David Lavender of "Bent's Fort," Dr. Nolie Mumey, Miss Bernice Baumgarten, Ned Bradford, Carl Brandt, Henry Castor and Frank Waters. I wish to thank also Mrs. Leona Clubine and Mrs. W. D. Simms of Meeker; Waymon Johnson of the Powell Park Ranch, which was once the White River Agency; Mrs. N. L. Pickard, who lives near the Old Squaw Camp site; Ranger Glenn E. Rogers of Little Hills Experiment Station; Mr. and Mrs. Carl Wunderly of Buford, Colorado; Lewis Orvis, Ridgeway, Colorado; Miss M. Patterson, Linn Grove Cemetery, Greeley; Dr. Samuel Mohler, Ellensburg, Wash.; President Ernest L. Wilkinson of Brigham Young University; A. F. C. Greene of the Wyoming Game and Fish Commission; Fenimore Chatterton, one of Wyoming's pioneers; John Love of Colorado Springs, my guide on legal history; Major General Thomas D. Finley, who tried to keep me straight on military matters; and my patient typist, Mrs. Maxine Whitworth.

And so at the last, the basic acknowledgment. I give thanks and love to Edna Jane, my most perfect collaborator, bookwise and otherwise.

Index

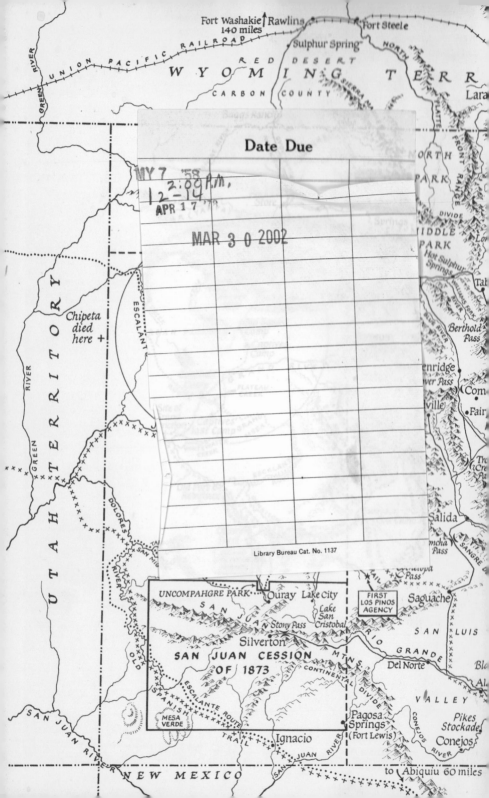